PR 6

13

23.

1?

14

DEATH
IN THE
DOLDRUMS

by the same author

Masters Next to God

They Sank the Red Dragon

The Fighting Tramps

The Grey Widow Maker

Blood and Bushido

SOS – Men Against the Sea

Salvo!

Attack and Sink

Dönitz and the Wolf Packs

Return of the Coffin Ships

Beware Raiders!

The Road to Russia

The Quiet Heroes

The Twilight of the U-boats

Beware the Grey Widow Maker

DEATH
IN THE
DOLDRUMS

U-Cruiser Actions Off West Africa

by

Bernard Edwards

Pen & Sword
MARITIME

First published in Great Britain in 2005 by
Pen & Sword Military
an imprint of
Pen & Sword Books Ltd
47 Church Street
Barnsley
South Yorkshire
S70 2AS

ISBN 1 84415 261 8

A CIP catalogue record for this book is
available from the British Library

Typeset in 11/13 Sabon by
Phoenix Typesetting, Auldgirth, Dumfriesshire

Printed and bound in England by
CPI UK.

Pen & Sword Books Ltd incorporates the Imprints of Pen & Sword
Aviation, Pen & Sword Maritime, Pen & Sword Military, Wharncliffe
Local History, Pen & Sword Select, Pen & Sword Military Classics and
Leo Cooper.

For a complete list of Pen & Sword titles please contact
PEN & SWORD BOOKS LIMITED
47 Church Street, Barnsley, South Yorkshire, S70 2AS, England
E-mail: enquiries@pen-and-sword.co.uk
Website: www.pen-and-sword.co.uk

For Noel Billy Williams, Radio Officer s/s Katanga

The western wave was all aflame,
The day was well nigh done!
Almost upon the western wave
Rested the broad, bright Sun;
When that strange shape drove suddenly
Betwixt us and the Sun.

Samuel Taylor Coleridge

Contents

Acknowledgements   viii

Chapter One   1
Chapter Two   9
Chapter Three   24
Chapter Four   39
Chapter Five   52
Chapter Six   65
Chapter Seven   76
Chapter Eight   89
Chapter Nine   105
Chapter Ten   119
Chapter Eleven   134
Chapter Twelve   148
Chapter Thirteen   165
Chapter Fourteen   180

Bibliography   194
Index   196

Acknowledgements

The author wishes to thank the following for their help in the research for this book:

Willem Hage, Albert Kelder, Sirri Lawson, Bernard de Neuman, David Silbey, Ken Williams, and National Archives & Records Administration, Washington, the National Archives, Kew, www.uboat.net, www.armed-guard.com, *Sea Breezes* magazine.

Chapter One

The sun climbed out of the eastern horizon with the dramatic suddenness peculiar to the equatorial latitudes, turning a cloudless sky quickly from pale grey to azure blue. Porpoises sliced lazily through the glassy-calm sea, welcoming a new day that promised to be hot and sultry. Ashore, behind the white-sand beaches of Liberia, the last wisps of early morning mist lifted, to be replaced by the blue smoke of native cooking fires.

Although the Great European War was in its fourth bloody year, the sound of its guns had not yet reached these remote shores. In the spring of 1918 the Gulf of Guinea, where once the slave traders sailed yardarm to yardarm seeking the 'black gold' for the plantations of the Americas, presented a tranquil picture. This was about to change.

Far out to sea, the water suddenly boiled, and with a loud roar as her main ballast tanks were blown, the long, grey shape of the German U-cruiser *U-154* broke the surface, sending shoals of silver flying fish skittering in all directions. The submarine's conning tower hatch clanged open while the water was still streaming from her casings and men came tumbling out to man her bridge. Hard on their heels others jumped down onto the casings and closed up on the long-barrelled guns, swinging them menacingly towards the shore.

Nearing the end of a month-long sweep of West African waters which had yielded nothing more than a few distant glimpses of enemy merchant ships, usually stern-on and going hull-down at a speed she could not hope to match, *U-154* seemed condemned to return home without a sinking to her name. But before she finally quit the Gulf of Guinea her commander, *Korvettenkapitän* Hermann Gercke, was determined to leave his mark on this distant outpost of American influence.

As the U-boat, her diesels throbbing, steered for the white-painted lighthouse visible on the summit of Cape Mesurado, Gercke examined the shoreline through his powerful binoculars, swinging round to scan the untidy cluster of houses on the south bank of the Mesurado River forming the town of Monrovia, capital of Liberia, and traditional homeland of freed slaves. To the north of the town two tall lattice masts reached for the sky, marking the American-operated wireless station. This was one target that could not run away from Gercke's guns.

At five miles off the shore, with the leadsman in the chains calling '20 fathoms and shelving', Gercke swung *U-154* around parallel to the beach and gave the order for the submarine's two 150-mm deck guns to open fire on the wireless masts.

The combined recoil of the two powerful guns threw the U-boat over on her beam ends, their thunderous roar deafening those in the conning tower. As she slowly returned to the upright, a cloud of acrid black smoke drifted astern low down on the sea as the gunners, working to a disciplined routine, swabbed out and reloaded.

The 1,500-ton German U-cruisers, of which *U-154* was one, were five times as big as the conventional U-boat of the day, and had started life as a commercial venture born out of the necessity of war. Right from the outbreak of hostilities in 1914, the Royal Navy had thrown a blockade around German waters that grew tighter with every month that passed. Almost completely cut off from her overseas trade, by January 1915 Germany was already running short of food. Bread was strictly rationed, butter, meat and other staples were increasingly hard to come by. In a country engaged in a world war and surrounded by her enemies on land and sea, this was not surprising. However, the situation had worsened dramatically when the harvest failed, and was followed by severe winter. The morale of the civilian population deteriorated to the point of revolution. And more worrying for the Kaiser's government was the desperate shortage of copper, zinc, tin and nickel; the essential metals of war. Even scouring the country for pots and pans, anything that could be melted down, failed to stem the shortage, and unless a solution was found soon

German guns on the Western Front might fall silent.

Largely due to the reluctance of the German Navy's surface ships to put to sea, the British blockade remained virtually unbroken. On the other hand, the U-boats were enjoying unprecedented success in the North Sea and western Atlantic. The Allies had not yet adopted the convoy system and their slow-moving merchant ships, sailing alone and unarmed, were easy prey for the U-boats whose great advantage was their ability to hide beneath the waves. The situation being what it was, it was not surprising that the German High Command decided to put this advantage to good use in breaking the blockade.

In late 1915, in great secrecy in the Baltic port of Flensburg, the keel was laid of the first of six commercial 'submarine freighters'. These were to be large, double-hulled vessels of nearly 2,000 tons displacement submerged. They would have a speed of 12.4 knots on the surface and 5.3 knots under water, with an endurance of 13,000 miles at 5.5 knots. Unarmed, their envisaged role was purely and simply as blockade runners, carrying cargo – 1,000 tons or more at a time – across the Atlantic. It was expected they would sail mainly on the surface, using their ability to submerge and travel underwater only when required to avoid British naval ships.

The first U-freighter, patriotically named *Deutschland*, launched on 28 March 1916, and crewed by merchant seamen under the command of *Kapitän* Paul König, sailed from Kiel on 23 June. In her holds she carried a cargo of chemicals, dyes and precious stones to the value of £150,000. Much to the relief of *Kapitän* König and his crew, their sixteen-day Atlantic crossing was uneventful and almost entirely on the surface. The *Deutschland* was forced to submerge only when passing between the Orkney and Shetland Islands to avoid British naval patrols.

On the night of 8 July, American pilots cruising off Cape Henry, at the entrance to Chesapeake Bay, saw blue flares burning out at sea, the recognized signal for a ship requiring a pilot. They went to investigate, expecting an inbound freighter for Baltimore, but were astonished when the low outline of a huge submarine emerged from the darkness. The *Deutschland* had arrived.

America not yet being in the war and, on the whole, not unsympathetic to the German cause, the *Deutschland* was turned round in a few days and re-crossed the Atlantic fully loaded with zinc, silver, copper, nickel and rubber; a cargo worth a king's ransom in beleaguered Germany. The submarine freighter's maiden voyage was a resounding success, fully justifying her designer's faith in the concept. Not unexpectedly, the British Government was not at all pleased. A diplomatic protest was lodged with America, demanding that the *Deutschland,* as a potential warship, be denied access to all her ports. The United States Government did not agree, pointing out that the submarine was not armed, and must be regarded as a merchant ship carrying a legitimate cargo.

The *Deutschland*'s sister-submarine *Bremen*, however, did not enjoy such good fortune. She sailed from Kiel in early September and disappeared without trace en route to America. Her loss, however, did not deter *Deutschland* from repeating her success, sailing from Bremen in the autumn to New London, Connecticut and returning with another priceless cargo of metals and rubber. Then, when it showed such promise, the U-freighter enterprise was brought to a sudden end. The *Deutschland* disappeared from sight, and nothing more was heard of her, except for an unconfirmed report that she had been sighted acting as a supply ship for a German cruiser operating as a commerce raider.

Up until this time, with the U-boats under orders to adhere to the Prize Regulations, by which it was forbidden to sink unarmed merchantmen without warning, their campaign against Allied shipping had achieved significant success, but not enough to seriously affect the enemy's supply routes. Meanwhile, following another poor harvest, by the spring of 1917 the British blockade had come very near to bringing Germany to her knees. At this juncture, Admiral von Tirpitz, desperate for a change in the fortunes of the Imperial Navy, proposed unrestricted submarine warfare against Allied ships. In other words, it was to be 'sink on sight'. No warning, no challenge; the torpedo, fired from a submerged U-boat, came first. The effect was immediate and catastrophic, for hitherto the war at sea, certainly with regard to the Imperial German Navy and Allied merchantmen, had been conducted on a gentlemanly basis. In the first three months of 1917, over 1,000 Allied ships were sunk with often heavy loss of life. And there was worse to come. In April of that year, as the U-boats' campaign of terror gathered way, a staggering total of 894,000 tons of British, Allied and neutral shipping was sent to the bottom. However, when he gave his infamous order, von Tirpitz had failed to take into account the effect it would have on the other side of the Atlantic. The indiscriminate slaughter at sea proved to be the final atrocity needed to draw the United States of America into the war on the side of the Allies.

This long overdue development rendered the *Deutschland,* and her sisters now nearing completion, redundant. North America was their only source of cargo, and to venture back across the Atlantic as commercial ships would inevitably lead to their capture or destruction. The alternative was to arm them and use them to attack shipping in American waters. And this they had the range and endurance to do.

The U-freighters – of which by now seven had been built – were taken over by the Navy, fitted with two 150-mm and two 85-mm guns and six exterior torpedo tubes, and then commissioned as the U-cruisers *U-151* to *U-157*. This armament, more suited to a light cruiser than a submarine, proved to be over ambitious. The 150-mm guns, in particular, were of too heavy a calibre, and their recoil when a broadside was fired was so violent that it threatened to capsize the narrow-beamed submarines. The exterior torpedo tubes were also something of a liability, being incapable of being re-loaded at sea after firing. The only real advantage the U-cruisers had over the conventional U-boats was their huge cruising range, which gave them the ability to penetrate waters far beyond the reach of their smaller sisters, i.e. North American coastal waters.

On her first war patrol, lasting three months, the *Deutschland*, now *U-155* and under the command of *Fregattenkapitän* Meusel, sank nineteen ships totalling 53,000 tons. She was followed by *Korvettenkapitän* von Nostitz und Janckendorff's *U-151*, which spent a month off the US coast laying mines. These mines were responsible for sinking four ocean-going ships and cutting two transatlantic cables. Von Nostitz also sank twenty-three small merchantmen by gunfire.

*   *   *

5

Hermann Gercke's leisurely bombardment of the wireless station at Monrovia was brought to a sudden end when a lookout reported smoke on the horizon. This was followed by the appearance of the masts and funnel of a ship with suspiciously British lines. Having been warned that enemy armed merchant cruisers patrolled these waters, Gercke immediately ceased fire on his target ashore and dived, remaining submerged while he watched the ship pass by to the south.

Blissfully unaware that he was being watched by an enemy submarine, Captain Yardley of the British & African Steam Navigation Company's steamer *Burutu*, continued on his voyage. Far from being an armed merchant cruiser, as Gercke had feared, the 3,902-ton *Burutu* was only a run-of-the-mill West African trader, completely unarmed and weighed down by a full cargo of palm kernels and timber from Nigerian ports consigned to Liverpool. In order to save fuel, always a consideration for a merchant ship's master, in war and in peace, Captain Yardley was sailing at an economical 8 knots, his ship's leisurely wake hardly disturbing the surface of the sea.

Having examined the *Burutu* closely through his periscope and satisfied himself that she was indeed a harmless, unarmed merchantman, Gercke took *U-154* closer inshore, and then surfaced. The submarine was invisible against the backdrop of the coast, and Gercke was now able to proceed at full speed and pull ahead of the *Burutu*. The chase was long and painstaking, but finally, late that afternoon, Gercke was in position to attack. Unfortunately for him, the *Burutu*'s lookouts were on the alert, and Yardley saw the torpedo coming. He threw the helm hard over and the German missile passed harmlessly down the British ship's port side.

Frustrated, Gercke surfaced and opened fire with his heavy guns from a range of 3,000 yards. The *Burutu* had nothing to hit back with, and Yardley, unwilling to contemplate surrender, took the only action open to him. Altering course to put the U-boat right astern, he gave a double ring full ahead on the engine room telegraph.

The *Burutu*'s engineers were made aware of the urgency of the order by voice pipe, and soon, with extra firemen hurling coal into her roaring furnaces as if their lives depended on it – and indeed they did – the British steamer surged ahead. Designed for a top sea speed of 10 knots, the *Burutu* responded valiantly. With thick black smoke pouring from her tall funnel and her rust-scarred hull vibrating angrily to the beat of her powerful, 525 nhp, engine, she quickly worked up to 12 knots.

U-154 was unable to match this speed, but Gercke gave chase, lobbing shells after the fleeing ship with his forward guns. The gallant little *Burutu* was hit twice by the heavy shells. Two of her men were killed, and she was holed below the waterline, but Yardley pressed ahead, soon opening the range to 7,000 yards. Gercke's shells began to fall short, and he soon suffered the humiliation of seeing the unarmed British ship, listing heavily, pull out of sight under the cover of the on-coming night. Yardley brought his ship safely into Freetown thirty-six hours later.

Next day, *U-154*, with her commander still furious at Yardley's *Burutu* for ruining his attack on the wireless station at Monrovia, and then having the audacity to escape his guns, joined up with her sister U-cruiser *U-153*, also returning empty-handed. The two submarines set course to the north in company to seek out enemy ships . On the 25th they were patrolling off the Canary Islands, when they came across the British Q-ship *Bombala*. The combined fire power of the two submarines overwhelmed the *Bombala*, and she was sent to the bottom.

Following their success, the U-cruisers separated, *U-153* heading directly for home, while Gercke took *U-154* further out into the Atlantic before turning north, determined to add to his meagre score. On 11 May, he reached a position 300 miles due west of the Straits of Gibraltar, and was idling on the surface hoping to fall in with ships sailing between the Mediterranean and America. Unknown to him, although the horizon appeared empty, he was not alone.

As a result of the sinking of the *Bombala*, the British submarine *E-35* had sailed from Gibraltar to investigate, and it was by lucky coincidence that in the early afternoon of the 11th, she was to the west of Cape St Vincent when *U-154* was passing on the northern leg of her patrol. *E-35*'s lookouts sighted an object to port at a distance of about three miles, but the U-boat's conning tower being low on the water, this could not be identified. The likelihood was that it was nothing more than a Spanish fisherman casting her lines in deep water, but *E-35*'s commander decided to investigate. He went to periscope depth, and shortly after 16.00 was astonished to find a large German U-boat in his sights. Gercke continued on his unhurried way, oblivious to the danger.

E-35 altered course to cut the U-cruiser off and went deeper. She returned to periscope depth twenty minutes later to find herself right astern of the German boat at 1,800 yards. This time *U-154*'s lookouts were more alert. When *E-35* fired her first torpedo, its track was seen, and Gercke altered course in good time to avoid it.

The chase was on, and by 18.25, as the sun was going down, the British submarine had overtaken *U-154*. Still at periscope depth, she waited until the enemy approached and then fired both bow tubes. It was classic shot, one torpedo striking *U-154* forward and the other aft of the conning tower.

When the smoke cleared, all that remained of the U-cruiser was a patch of oil and scraps of wreckage, to which a few survivors were clinging.

And so ended the German Imperial Navy's one and only attempt to terrorize shipping in the Gulf of Guinea. In spite of an abundance of passing traffic, the two U-cruisers involved, *U-153* and *U-154*, sank no Allied merchant ships. Elsewhere, particularly in American coastal waters, the U-cruisers, in the relatively short time they were operational, were a significant weapon, sinking 174 ships totalling 361,000 tons gross. Only one of their number, Gercke's *U-154*, was lost. Ironically, the ship Gercke had attacked off Monrovia, the gallant little *Burutu*, met an inglorious end only five months later, on 3 October 1918, when she was sunk in a collision in the approaches to the Bristol Channel while on passage from West Africa to Liverpool.

Chapter Two

Just after six o'clock on the evening of 11 February 1942, two sinister-looking grey shapes slipped out of the old French naval base of Lorient and headed into the gathering dusk of the Bay of Biscay. Twenty-four years after Hermann Gercke's *U-154* met her end, the U-cruisers were returning to the Gulf of Guinea.

At 76 metres long and displacing nearly 1,600 tons submerged, the new U-cruisers, Type IX's as they were designated – and *Seekuhs* (Sea Cows) as they were quickly nicknamed – unlike their predecessors of the First World War, were purpose-built to take the war to the enemy. Armed with twenty-two torpedoes, one 105-mm deck gun and four 20-mm and one 37-mm anti-aircraft guns, they had a top speed of 18.3 knots on the surface and a cruising range of 13,850 miles at 10 knots.

When America entered the war in December 1941, Admiral Dönitz had more than fifty Type IX's operational. Given their long-range capability, they were the ideal weapon to carry the war across the Atlantic, and six of their number were sent westwards without delay. The Americans, bystanders in this war for more than two years, had still not fully woken up to the awesome destructive power of the submarine, and continued to nurture a false sense of invulnerability. In coastal waters, merchant ships were sailing independently and without escort, totally oblivious to the danger that threatened. At night, silhouetted against the shore lights, which in many cases had not even been dimmed, they presented the battle-hardened U-boat commanders with targets they could not miss. At first, the losses were put down to mines laid offshore by the enemy, and many ships were lost and many men died before the true cause of the needless slaughter was realized. Only then did the United States Navy heed the advice the Royal

Navy had been pressing on them for some time, and organize convoys for their coastal shipping.

Following the unprecedented success of the Type IXs in American waters, Dönitz turned his attention to waters off the west coast of Africa, where many merchant ships, mainly British were said to be sailing unescorted. He decided to send two of his U-cruisers south to investigate. *U-68* and *U-505*, fully fuelled and provisioned for a long voyage, sailed from Lorient under the cover of darkness on 11 February.

U-68, a Type IX C built at Bremen in early 1941, was the lead boat for the expedition, and was in the experienced hands of *Korvettenkapitän* Karl-Friedrich Merten, Iron Cross First Class. Although *U-68* was thirty-seven year old Merton's first U-boat command, he was a regular Navy officer, having served in the surface ships from 1928 until joining Karl Dönitz's band of elite in the spring of 1941. Already, in his capable hands, *U-68* had sent four British merchantmen, totalling 23,697 tons, to the bottom.

In company with *U-68* was the Hamburg-built *U-505*, commanded by thirty-three year old *Kapitänleutnant* Axel-Olaf Loewe. Both *U-505* and her commander were new to the sea war, Loewe having commissioned *U-505* in August 1941, after which they had spent five months together with the 4th Training Flotilla in the Baltic. They had yet to open their score against Allied shipping.

February 1942 was proving to be a black month for Britain and her new American ally. For them the war in the Far East was going unbelievably badly. The supposedly impregnable fortress of Singapore had surrendered, leaving the whole of the Malayan peninsular in Japanese hands, whose advance units were already moving deep into Burma. The Pacific islands had been overrun, and Australia and New Zealand were under threat of invasion. In the Mediterranean, convoys attempting to get through to Malta, although heavily escorted, were being decimated by attack from the air, and it might soon be necessary for the British to take a leaf out of the Kaiser's book and use submarines to supply the besieged island. Nearer to home, on the broad reaches of the North Atlantic, the vital supply convoys were losing nearly half a million tons a month to Dönitz's torpedoes. And on that very night, as the two U-cruisers began their voyage south, British prestige was about to be dealt another blow. The German battlecruisers *Scharnhorst* and *Gneisenau,* accompanied by the light cruiser *Prinz Eugen* and a flotilla of E-boats, had left the Biscay port of Brest, where they had been sheltering since the previous spring, and were about to make an audacious dash up the English Channel. Next day, 12 February, they forced their way through the Dover Strait, contemptuous of the efforts of the Royal Navy and the RAF to intercept and sink them.

The U-cruisers were two hours out of Lorient, still on the surface, and heading south-west at full speed, anxious to run clear of Biscay and the ever present threat from patrolling aircraft of RAF Coastal Command. It was a dark, moonless night, with a light northerly breeze blowing and the notorious bay in an unusually benign mood. As if to urge them on their way, the thunder of gunfire was heard and the sky astern was lit by flares. Lorient was again under attack by RAF bombers, something that had become a nightly ritual while they were in the port. In their pens, protected by a roof of reinforced concrete sixteen feet thick, the U-boats had been safe, but the crash of the bombs and the resulting devastation in the streets imposed an intolerable strain on the morale of men already under great stress.

From his vantage point in *U-68*'s conning tower, Karl Merten could see the wake of Axel Loewe's boat a mile or so to starboard, keeping station on him, the throaty roar of her 4,400 hp diesels clearly audible on the night air. It was a comforting sound that would soon be lost as the two boats went their separate ways. Their sailing orders instructed them to make a broad sweep out into the Atlantic, to a point some 1,000 miles due west of Gibraltar, before turning south. The orders also stressed that they would be acting completely independent of each other.

In the Gulf of Guinea, little had changed since *U-153* and *U-154* had made their fruitless sortie twenty-four years earlier. The production of palm kernels and palm oil, used extensively in the manufacture of soaps and margarine, had increased substantially, and there was a growing demand for cocoa and ground-nuts, bringing a measure of prosperity to Nigeria and the Gold Coast. This had led to an increase in the number of ships on the coast, most of them British, but so far neither these ships nor their cargoes had warranted much attention. The primary target for Merten and Loewe would be the deep-laden ships from India and the Far East who, after their long haul north from the Cape of Good Hope, made their landfall on the coast of Liberia, before going on to Freetown to join a convoy. There were many of them, and the rewards for the U-cruisers promised to be great.

The raiders enjoyed an untroubled run south in good weather, spending most of their time on the surface, only twice being forced to dive when menaced by patrolling Sunderlands of Coastal Command off Cape Finisterre. They reached the latitude of the Straits of Gibraltar on the 20th, by which time *U-505*, plagued by an oil leak, was beginning to lag behind. On that day, far to the south, the British ship *Helenus* set sail from Cape Town on her long passage home.

Owned by the prestigious Alfred Holt & Co., known worldwide as the Blue Funnel Line on account of the colour of its tall, blue-painted funnels, the 7,336-ton *Helenus* was no stranger to war. Built on the Clyde in 1913, she had served in the 1914–18 war as an auxiliary troop carrier, and as such had often found herself under attack. In December 1917, she was torpedoed in the English Channel and severely damaged, but was eventually towed into port and repaired. Six months later, she was narrowly missed by another German torpedo in the North Sea, and in August 1918 she came under attack by gunfire from *U-90* in the North Atlantic, but fought back and escaped. Not surprisingly, the *Helenus* became known as a lucky ship.

Twenty-four years on, the *Helenus*'s reputation still held good. On her current voyage she had narrowly escaped from Penang before the invading Japanese hordes came racing across the Malayan peninsular, but she was no longer the smart cargo liner she had once been. Her distinctive blue funnel was anonymous under a coat of drab Admiralty Grey, her similarly painted hull was streaked with rust, and her triple-expansion steam engine wheezed and rattled as it strove to propel her at an economical speed – for war or no war, in British merchant ships economy was still paramount.

Commanded by Captain Philip Savery, she was manned by

British officers and Chinese ratings, and carried two DEMS gunners and ten passengers, a total complement of ninety-one. In her holds were stowed 1,350 tons of copper ingots, 2,000 tons of rubber, 1,500 tons of tea and 1,000 tons of sisal; a cargo priceless in terms of the needs of Britain at war.

As a result of the rapid westward advance of the Japanese, the hitherto untroubled Indian Ocean had suddenly become a very dangerous place. Soon after sailing, Savery received a radio message from the Admiralty warning him that at least fifteen Japanese submarines were moving in from the Pacific. The 5,300-mile passage to the Cape had become a race to keep ahead of them. In the event of trouble, the *Helenus* was well armed with a 4-inch anti-submarine, a 12-pounder, two Hotchkiss and two Lewis .303 machine guns, and two rocket launchers. However, the main threat was likely to come from below the waves, against which she had no defence.

It was a long haul down the Indian Ocean, but with the gentle north-east monsoon blowing it was blue skies and calm seas all the way. Savery took the precaution of zigzagging by day and steering a straight course at night, all the time with extra lookouts posted and the *Helenus*'s ageing engine running with an urgent beat. The enemy failed to put in an appearance, and making good a speed of 11.5 knots, Savery let go his anchor in the shadow of Table Mountain on the18th, in company with a dozen or so other merchantmen. Table Bay had not seen so much shipping since the heydays before the Suez Canal opened in 1869.

Bunkers and stores were taken in Cape Town, giving time for a brief run ashore for the lucky ones, and as the sun came up on the 20th, the *Helenus* cleared the harbour breakwaters again and lifted to the long Cape rollers as she turned north for the passage up the western side of Africa. She was again sailing alone, for these were considered by the Admiralty to be safe waters. Savery's orders were to stay well clear of the land and shape a course for Freetown, where the *Helenus* would probably join a convoy for the final and most dangerous leg of her voyage. This was to be confirmed by radio on the passage north.

Meanwhile, Merten and Loewe had joined forces again, and on the afternoon of the 24th, while to the west of the Canary Islands, they sighted the smoke of a convoy. The weather was fine, with a light north-easterly breeze, slight sea and good visibility. The two U-cruisers approached the convoy on the surface, and were soon in sight of half a dozen steamers making their way south at about 15 knots. There was no sign of escorting warships, and Merten and Loewe assumed they would be able to carry out a stealthy attack in their own time, and without interference. Merten raced to get ahead of the convoy, while Loewe approached from astern, but as they manoeuvred into position, a previously empty sky suddenly became full of British Sunderlands. Loewe reported between four and six of the great four-engined flying boats circling over the convoy.

The U-cruisers were forced to break off their attack and dive, but later surfaced and followed the convoy at a respectful distance. They hoped to close in on the enemy ships after dark, when the air cover had gone, but by the time night came the ships had pulled ahead out of sight. They decided to abandon the chase. Now it became clear that the need to conserve fuel was paramount, particularly for *U-505*, which was still troubled by an oil leak. Both boats slowed down to an economical speed of 6 knots. By the time they reached the Cape Verde Islands on the 28th, Loewe had lost nearly 10 tons of his precious diesel, and was obliged to reduce speed even further. *U-68* again drew ahead. On the night of 2 March Merten was off Freetown and ready to begin operations.

The port of Freetown, capital of Sierra Leone, opened up in 1787 as a base for freed slaves, possesses a large natural harbour with deep water and good shelter. In times of peace, it was rare for the harbour to hold more than one or two ships at a time, mainly West African traders. That all changed when, from the summer of 1940 onwards, the eastern Mediterranean and the Suez Canal were closed to Allied shipping. A steady steam of ships on the long haul around the Cape transformed what was once a sleepy backwater into the focal point of the West African coast. Convoys were assembled here, ships sailing independently called for bunkers and fresh water, and as the war progressed it was not unusual for fifty to a hundred ships to be anchored in the harbour. Freetown bustled and prospered, but the port, and the many ships using it, were under constant threat.

Wartime Freetown had the disadvantage of being only thirty miles from Sierra Leone's border with French Guinea, which was under Vichy control. Further north again was Senegal, and the port of Dakar, where Vichy French warships, including the battleship *Richelieu*, were holed up. The *Richelieu* had been damaged in the abortive attack on the port by British and Free French ships in 1940, but it was still unclear whether or not she was fit to put to sea. The threat to passing Allied ships and the Freetown convoys from the Vichy French Navy was assumed to be very real, and was proved to be so in June of the following year, when the *Criton* was lost.

The *Criton* was a 4,564-ton French steamer caught and boarded by the armed merchant cruiser HMS *Cilicia* when attempting to sail to Europe. She was taken into Freetown with the intention of putting her before a Prize Court, but the local Admiralty representative decided he was unable to deal with the case, and ordered her home.

The steamer's French crew, who had already sabotaged her engines, proved highly uncooperative. In the end, it became necessary to put the *Criton* under the British flag and look elsewhere for a crew. At that time, there were a number of British seamen, survivors from ships sunk in the area, who were awaiting a passage home. A call went out for volunteers, which was enthusiastically answered. With Captain Gerald Dobeson in command, the *Criton* moved to Pepel and loaded 6,000 tons of iron ore. She sailed from Freetown with Convoy SL 78, on 19 June 1941, bound for Belfast.

SL 78 was a slow convoy composed of a motley collection of British and Allied ships escorted by the armed merchant cruiser HMS *Esperance Bay*. The convoy's designated speed was 6 knots, a speed Captain Dobeson was confident he could match, but he was then not fully aware of the real extent of the damage to the *Criton*'s engines inflicted by her French crew. When the convoy speed was increased to 7 knots, Dobeson found his ship falling further and further behind, with his engineers powerless to coax even one more revolution from their machinery. By early

15

afternoon on the 20th, the *Criton* had become such a liability to the convoy that she was ordered to return to Freetown.

When she turned back, the *Criton* was only 160 miles west-north-west of Freetown, and it should not have been difficult for her to make port. However, the ex-French ship had no navigational aids, other than a magnetic compass of dubious accuracy and a radio direction finder which had been interfered with. Dobeson was therefore largely navigating by dead reckoning – 'by guess and by God', in other words.

At 09.30 on the 21st Dobeson, still without a definite fix, estimated he was approaching the buoyed channel of the entrance to Freetown harbour. He was not surprised, therefore, to see two warships closing on him. They were small vessels, possibly sloops, and were not flying ensigns, but Dobeson assumed they must be British. He was consequently surprised when both ships hoisted the two-letter International Code signal SN, an unmistakeably hostile challenge:

You should stop immediately. Do not scuttle. Do not lower boats. Do not use the wireless. If you disobey I shall open fire on you.

Dobeson at once realized that he was being challenged by enemy ships – they were in fact two ex-Air France fast rescue ships, manned by the French Navy and heavily armed. As they came nearer, they hoisted their French ensigns and opened fire on the *Criton* with what appeared to be 12-pounder guns. As the *Criton* was unarmed, except for six light machine guns thrown aboard in Freetown before sailing, Dobeson took the only course open to him, putting his stern to his attackers and ordering the wireless room to send out a QQQ (*I am being attacked by an unidentified enemy ship*) message.

With a top speed of only 6 knots, Dobeson could not hope to run away from the enemy, but he did hope to delay proceedings until an aircraft came out from Freetown in answer to his QQQ, which had been acknowledged. He succeeded in holding the French ships at bay for over two hours, but by 12.00, no help having arrived, he was forced to abandon ship as ordered. This was done while under heavy fire from the French, who seemed determined to sink their ship even before the British had left it.

In spite of the efforts of the French, Dobeson and his crew abandoned ship without injury. They were taken on board *Air France IV* and landed at Conakry, the French Guinea port sixty-five miles north of Freetown, where they were taken into custody by the local police, interrogated, and thrown into a barbed wire enclosure outside the port. There they languished, in the most primitive of conditions, until moved inland to a prisoner of war camp three months later.

Not content with sinking the *Criton* – their claim to which was at least arguable – in the winter of 1941 the Vichy French turned their attentions elsewhere in Africa. In early November, the Royal Navy seized five French-registered merchant ships off Cape Town, and in reprisal the Vichy French Government ordered the French submarines *Le Glorieux* and *Le Hèros* to attack Allied shipping off South Africa. The *Le Glorieux* chased one ship on 15th, but she got away. Two days later, however, the *Le Hèros*, commanded by Lieutenant Commander Lemaire, succeeded in sinking the Norwegian steamer *Thode Fagelund*.

The 5,757-ton *Thode Fagelund,* one of Wilhelm Wilhelmsen's crack Far East traders, under the command of Captain This Jorgensen, was on passage from Chittagong and Madras to a British port via Cape Town with a cargo of scrap iron, jute and tea. In the early hours of the morning of 17 November 1941, she was sixty miles east of East London, when she was torpedoed without warning by the *Le Hèros*. She was hit in her No.5 hold, and sank by the stern within a few minutes. All thirty-five crew got away in four lifeboats, and were later picked up by other ships. The unfortunate *Thode Fagelund* had the distinction of being the Vichy French Navy's only conquest in African waters.

At 12.00 on 27 February 1942, while Captain Gerald Dobeson and his men still languished in their camp, the *Helenus* was some 800 miles south of Cape Palmas and steaming north at 10.5 knots. It was doldrum weather, with hardly a breath of wind to disturb the placid sea, and the equatorial sun at its zenith in a cloudless blue sky. The mercury in the thermometer on the bridge was nudging 90°F; hot enough to melt the pitch in the seams of the

17

wooden decks and send rivulets of sweat running down the backs of Captain Savery and his officers as they took their noon sights.

It was even hotter in the wireless room abaft the bridge, where the *Helenus*'s Third Radio Officer, stripped down to a pair of shorts, struggled to beat the boredom of the watch with a well-thumbed Leslie Charteris novel. The air waves were silent, except for the occasional burst of static, and it had been that way since sailing from Cape Town. In wartime ships used their transmitter at their peril.

Another chapter of *The Saint* was digested then, at 13.22, the radio officer suddenly became aware that the silence had been broken by the chatter of distant Morse. He put down his book and adjusted his headphones. It was a jumble of letters and numbers; a coded message he could not make head nor tail of. Then, out of the confusion came the *Helenus*'s signal letters, loud and clear. This was a message addressed to his ship. He scribbled it down and ran for the bridge.

Captain Savery, who had been expecting a signal from the Admiralty advising him whether or not he would be required to join a convoy at Freetown, took the message form below to his cabin, where the code books were kept in the safe. Half an hour later, he still had not decoded the message. It appeared to be in a code not contained in his books. Later he was to learn that the code was only issued to ships capable of speeds of 15 knots and over. At best, the *Helenus* could manage 11.5 knots, and Savery had registered her at that maximum speed with the Admiralty in Cape Town. Someone, somewhere, had blundered.

Next day, Savery received the same message, and in the same undecipherable code. The *Helenus* was now less than three days steaming from Freetown, and in desperation Savery broke radio silence to ask for orders to be sent in the correct code. He received no reply to his signal, and decided to head straight for Freetown, rather than make a landfall off Cape Palmas. The decision was to cost him his ship.

There was a total eclipse of the moon on the night of 2–3 March, and taking advantage of the complete darkness, Merten slipped past Freetown unseen, and followed the coastline into the Gulf of Guinea. His destination was Cape Palmas, 240 miles south-east of Monrovia, and southernmost point of the western bulge of Africa. Cape Palmas, a rocky peninsular topped by a lighthouse, was the favoured landfall of ships coming from the Cape, and here Merten proposed to lie in wait for his victims. As it turned out, his first encounter with the enemy was to come much sooner than expected.

At 12.00 on 3 March, *U-68* was in a position seventy miles due west of Monrovia, and making her way south-eastwards on the surface at a leisurely speed of 6 knots. The weather was fine and clear, with light airs blowing, and as he was in relatively safe waters, Merten had allowed off-duty men to come on deck to escape the stifling temperatures in the boat. With washing draped along the jumping wire and a dozen men stripped to the waist sunning themselves on the casings, *U-68* had a holiday air about her. But Merten had not dropped his guard. Three lookouts were posted in the conning tower, scanning around the horizon with powerful Zeiss binoculars. It was one of these men who first saw the smudge of smoke on the horizon dead ahead. Merten immediately cleared the decks and prepared to dive.

Aboard the *Helenus,* steaming north for Freetown and unknowingly towards the submerged *U-68,* it was a typical lazy tropical afternoon. Lunch was over, and the off-duty watch keepers had retired to catch up on lost sleep. The only sound to disturb the peace was the measured thump of the gleaming pistons of the triple-expansion steam engine as it drove the loaded ship effortlessly through the water. An air of somnolence hung overall.

There was activity on the bridge, where Captain Savery, concerned at their increasing vulnerability as they neared the coast, had ordered a change of zigzag pattern. At precisely 14.23, the quartermaster put the helm over to alter onto the first leg of the zigzag, and in doing so, swung directly into the path of Karl Merten's first torpedo. Savery describes what happened then:

The first torpedo struck us evidently in between No.1 and No.2 bulkheads on the starboard side, because No.1 hatch was blown wide open and there was cargo all over the deck. No.2 double bottom tank was wide open to the sea and there

19

was thick grey smoke coming out of the double bottom air pipes. The second torpedo struck us between No.3 deep tank and the stokehold. I got the blast from the second torpedo but did not feel any blast from the first one. There was a terrific explosion, the second one being louder, and columns of water were shot up on the starboard side, running all over the bridge and fore deck. The man at the wheel jumped away, but the 2nd Mate, who was nearby, immediately took over. I did not see any flames from the explosion but there was a strong smell of cordite. The engineer in charge immediately stopped the engines and a second later water started pouring in through the stokehold door. The watertight doors were closed at the time. I realized in a very few seconds that there was no hope of saving the ship.

It was now a race against time to abandon the ship before she went down and, with ninety-one people on board, this was no easy operation. Fortunately, the weather was in their favour, the sea calm, with only a slight swell running, and the *Helenus*, despite having much of her starboard side blown open, appeared to be sinking in an upright position. This was probably due to the weight of the copper ingots in the bottom of her holds. When Savery reached the boat deck, however, he discovered that both lifeboats on the starboard side had been so damaged by the explosions that they were unusable. Furthermore, the six wooden life rafts, stowed three either side of the ship, had all been blown overboard, and one of the remaining lifeboats was damaged.

A quick muster revealed that five men were missing, four Chinese and a British deck boy. By this time the *Helenus* was dipping sharply by the bow, and a search for the missing was out of the question. Savery assumed they must have been killed in the blast, and ordered all the survivors into the two undamaged lifeboats, which were lowered without further delay. This was a timely move, for no sooner had the boats cleared the ship than she went under with a rush, her stern rearing high in the air. Only by digging their oars deep did the survivors avoid being sucked into the maelstrom the *Helenus* left behind her as she went to her grave 200 fathoms deep.

When his ship had gone, Philip Savery scanned the empty ocean around him with a sinking heart. His boat contained forty-nine people crammed shoulder to shoulder while the other, slightly smaller, boat, under the command of the Chief Officer, was equally crowded with thirty-seven. When the ship was hit, the blast had brought down her wireless aerials, but working feverishly, the radio officers had rigged a jury aerial and transmitted an SOS before they were forced to abandon the wireless room. Freetown had acknowledged receipt, and Savery hoped that help was on the way, but the reality was that the Royal Navy was very thin on the water, almost non-existent, in this area, and they might be adrift for many days. Fortunately, the sea was calm, and there was little likelihood of gales in these waters, but the sun, blazing down out of a cloudless sky, would make life very uncomfortable in the crowded boats.

For some time the survivors busied themselves with collecting extra rations from the life rafts that were drifting nearby. In the course of this, they came across the two damaged lifeboats, one of which was drifting bottom-up, the other waterlogged. They made an effort to right the overturned boat, without success, but the other boat, floating on its buoyancy tanks, seemed salvageable, if the holes in its hull could be patched. While they were working on this boat, Merten brought *U-68* to the surface and circled around them. Anticipating interrogation, and fearing he might be taken prisoner, Philip Savery stripped off his epaulettes and prepared to play a game of bluff. Fortunately for him, the need did not arise. While on the surface, and about to approach the *Helenus*'s lifeboats, Merten caught sight of another possible victim. He dived and moved off to investigate.

What Merten had seen was the British steamer *Beaconsfield* which had, quite inadvertently, stumbled upon the scene of the drama recently enacted. Some confusion followed. When she caught sight of the *Helenus*'s lifeboats, drifting close together, the *Beaconsfield* mistook them for a U-boat on the surface. She immediately went to action stations, and manned her guns. And as she was doing so, Merten fired a torpedo across her bows. For the *Beaconsfield*'s master this was proof enough that his ship was in immediate danger. He reversed course and made off, zigzagging at full speed.

21

Captain Savery was puzzled by the *Beaconsfield*'s behaviour, and he later reported to the Admiralty:

I was sure the *Beaconsfield* had seen us and after discussing the situation with the 1st Officer I decided to stay where we were thinking she would return to pick us up later. The 1st Officer had finished patching the 3rd boat now and I transferred 15 of my crew into the 3rd boat. We picked up a SSS message sent out by the *Beaconsfield*, giving our position. I decided that we had better stay where we were for the night and next morning, if nobody came along we could start sailing for Freetown. At 1800 however the *Beaconsfield* hove in sight again, she was still zigzagging at top speed. She made a signal to us asking if there was still a submarine in the vicinity, if there was she wanted us to lower our sails. I was not sure if the submarine was still around so I took my sails down in case. Immediately I did so the *Beaconsfield* shot off again zigzagging at full speed. I decided the only thing to do was to tie our 3 boats together and wait and see what the morning would bring forth. We put the damaged boat in the middle and made ourselves fast. The 15 men in the damaged boat had to bail all the time to keep themselves afloat.

The moon was due to rise between 2230 and 2300 and it was a dark night. We decided to curl up in the blankets and wait for daylight, but at about 2015 we heard the sound of an engine. At first we thought it might be another submarine, the engines kept coming closer and then fading away, then we realized it was a plane. At first it was too far away to see any flares we might have put up. We waited until about 2100 when the plane which had been circling around began to get closer to us. When she was about 5 or 6 miles away we put up flares. She saw them and came over to us and dropped a couple of markers, circled us three times and put her search-light on us and went off.

The Sunderland, which had been out to search for the *Helenus*'s survivors after their SOS had been picked up by Freetown, found the *Beaconsfield* which was some ten miles away, and brought her back to the boats. The big flying boat then stood by, assisting with flares, while the rescue operation was carried out. By this time the moon was up, and Savery was able to bring his boats alongside the *Beaconsfield* without difficulty. By 22.45, all eighty-six survivors were safely on board the rescue ship. They were taken to Freetown, where they were landed on the morning of 5 March.

So ended the long and distinguished career of the *Helenus*, a career spanning twenty-nine years and two world wars, during which she had proudly carried the name of her Greek hero across so many oceans, bravely facing up to whatever trials and tribulations that lay in her path. It was a sad way for an old ship to go, her dignity destroyed, and her weathered hull blasted open to the sea by an unseen enemy.

Chapter Three

When, on the afternoon of 3 March, Karl Merten's torpedoes consigned the *Helenus* to her last resting place, *U-505* was some 370 miles to the north-west of Freetown, and pushing south-eastwards on the surface at a leisurely 7 knots. She was, as she had been for several days past, enjoying exceptionally fine weather, but with a light following wind just strong enough to negate any cooling breeze generated by the forward movement of the boat, the heat was oppressive. The watch in the conning tower, were stripped down to pith helmets and shorts, sheltering from the hot sun under a makeshift awning, and praying for the blessed relief that darkness would bring. Below deck, where the night would afford little relief, conditions were unbearable, even the slightest movement being enough to drench a man in his own sweat.

In the tiny box below the conning tower that passed as *U-505*'s radio room, her wireless operator, earphones clamped to his ears, stoically endured the sweltering heat and dripped sweat onto his message pad as he listened idly to the babble of Morse and static borne on the ether. The Morse consisting mainly of unintelligible traffic between French shore stations and ships on the coast, left him bored almost to the point of nodding off. Then, suddenly, a clear and urgent note broke through the static, and he was instantly wide awake. The transmission was brief but explicit:

SOS SOS SOS HELENUS TORPEDOED IN 06 DEGREES 01 MINUTES NORTH 12 DEGREES 02 MINUTES WEST. SINKING.

A cry for help, and proof that *U-505* was not alone in this war.

When he was handed the scribbled message form announcing

U-68's successful opening attack, Axel Loewe lost no time in communicating the good news to his crew. For some days now, the combination of the heat and the boredom of the long passage had brought morale on board to a new low. Now, it seemed that action was only just over the horizon. The overpowering heat was forgotten as the U-boat's diesels lifted a beat and she altered course fractionally to bring her on course for the target area. That night, and all the following day, she slipped silently through the calm waters, passing 150 miles to the west of Freetown on the night of 4 March. Throughout, although her lookouts scoured the horizon continuously with their powerful Zeiss binoculars, not even a lonely fishing boat came in sight. The old boredom was beginning to set in again as, on the morning of the 5th, *U-505*'s twenty-third day out of Lorient, the sun climbed into a cloudless sky, heralding an even hotter day to come. Then, and only then, did her fortunes change. Hastening north to put an end to *U-505*'s unbroken run of luck on her maiden patrol was the British cargo liner *Benmohr*.

The 5,920-ton steamer *Benmohr*, solidly built on the Clyde in 1928 by Charles Connell & Company, was one of the fleet of William Thomson & Company of Leith, better known as Ben Line Steamers, another of Britain's first-rate liner companies. Founded by the brothers Alexander and William Thomson in Edinburgh in 1839, Ben Line began with one sailing ship importing marble from Leghorn, and progressed to a fleet of twenty distinctive and immaculately maintained steamers running a regular service to Far East ports. Ben Line ships were Scotland afloat, Scottish-built, Scottish-owned, and almost invariably Scottish manned – the prime qualification for serving aboard a Ben Line ship was an Edinburgh address. They were proud ships – and, with good reason.

Commanded by Captain David Anderson, with a crew of fifty-five, the *Benmohr* was homeward bound with 8,539 tons of general cargo, which included a large quantity of rubber in bales, 2,000 tons of pig iron, and an unrecorded amount of silver bullion. Her last loading port was Bombay, and she sailed from Durban on 19 February after topping up her bunkers. Captain Anderson's orders were to proceed direct to Freetown, via the Cape, and there join a convoy, which would take them north to Oban, where further orders would be issued. There was little doubt in the mind of anyone on board that these orders would specify their first port of discharge as Glasgow. A homecoming considered long overdue.

Twelve months had passed since the *Benmohr* sailed out through the North Channel loaded down to her winter marks with cargo for the Far East. By then, the war was well into its second year, and German bombers were still laying waste to British cities, including Glasgow, with characteristic thoroughness. It was not easy for the *Benmohr*'s men, many of them with young families, to leave home, knowing that, under the terms of their engagement, they could be away for up to two years. But being merchant seamen going away was part of their life and no war could alter that. There were no hangers-back.

Britain had stood alone against the might of the German war machine when the *Benmohr* set sail on her long voyage, but she was not long at sea before there were momentous changes in the course of the war. On 22 June 1941 Adolf Hitler made his first great mistake by attacking his erstwhile ally, the Soviet Union. At first, with the Russians caught unprepared, Operation Barbarossa went without a hitch, German Panzers being at the gates of Moscow by the end of September. A month later, they had been brought to a standstill by the onset of the bitter Russia winter and were suffering heavy casualties at the hands of the fanatical Soviet defenders.

While Hitler's armies in the East were thus pinned down, Germany's new ally, Japan, carried out a surprise attack on the American base at Pearl Harbor. As with Barbarossa, the attack was a strategical masterstroke, most of America's Pacific Fleet and much of her air power in the area being wiped out at one fell stroke. However, the Japanese had underestimated the latent power of the huge American war machine, and were in the fullness of time to pay dearly for their temerity.

In the course of just six months, Britain's lonely isolation was ended, and Germany had acquired herself two powerful enemies, Russia and the United States of America, who would eventually bring to a bloody end her dreams of world domination.

Sailing independently, in fine weather and with little to fear from the enemy – the U-boats would not penetrate this far south for many months to come – the *Benmohr* rounded the Cape of Good Hope on 22 February and set course to the north. The weather continued fair, and as anxious as anyone on board to taste the salt spray of British waters again, David Anderson decided against zigzagging. A cooperative engine room obliged with a few extra revolutions, and the *Benmohr*, perhaps herself scenting the Clyde, surged forward for home.

The Equator was crossed on 3 March with not even a cloud in the azure blue sky to mar the euphoria prevailing aboard the *Benmohr*. 'Home in no time at all' was on everybody's lips – then the peace of the idyllic afternoon was shattered by the plaintive cries from the sinking *Helenus* coming in on the distress frequency.

They were still three days steaming from Freetown, and Anderson decided to carry on as before but, being alerted to the threat of U-boats up ahead, he doubled the lookouts, with the DEMS gunners standing gun watches at dawn and dusk. The boats were checked and life jackets kept handy, but under these untroubled skies, and with a calm sea disturbed only by the gentlest zephyrs of wind, it was difficult to take the threat of approaching danger seriously.

Twenty-four hours later, the reality of war was brought home to the *Benmohr* when a large aircraft appeared on the horizon to the north, and came roaring in at wave-top height. The gun crews raced to their guns, manning the 12-pounder and six light machine guns strategically sited around the ship in record time, but before they could open fire the oncoming plane was recognized as a Sunderland flying boat of the RAF.

The Short Sunderland, a magnificent, if superannuated aircraft based on the design of the old British Imperial Airways Empire-class flying boat was, in 1942, the only long-range aircraft available for patrol duties on the West African coast. Powered by four 890 hp Bristol Perseus engines, which gave it a maximum speed of 205 mph and an endurance in the air of 13.5 hours, the Sunderland was ideally suited for keeping a watch on shipping in these remote waters. At the same time, manned by a crew of ten, armed with nine Browning .303 machine guns and capable of carrying a bomb load of 4,960 lbs, the Sunderland was a formidable threat to marauding U-boats.

Luckily for this Sunderland, it was identified as British before it came within range of the *Benmohr*'s guns, otherwise its reception might have been very hot. It was flying at only a little above mast-top height, and the concentrated fire from the 12-pounder and the machine guns would most likely have brought it down. Apparently blissfully unaware of his narrow escape, the pilot calmly circled the *Benmohr,* his Aldis lamp flashing a demand for the ship's name and destination. Visibly relieved, Captain Anderson complied.

The Sunderland flew away again, but a few hours later, presumably soon after she returned to her base at Freetown, Anderson received a coded wireless message re-routeing him to the west. Previously the *Benmohr* had been steering directly for Cape Palmas to make her customary landfall before running up to Freetown. Her new orders were to steer due west for some 240 miles until due south of the port, and then to head north. This involved a considerable diversion, and would mean approaching Freetown directly from seaward which, as the high land was often obscured by mist at this time of the year, could be an operation fraught with danger.

When the sun came up on the 5th, heralding another long, hot day, the *Benmohr* was 380 miles south of Freetown and, aware that he was now in an area where at least one enemy submarine was at large, Anderson steered a zigzag course throughout the day. But he was anxious to make Freetown early on the 6th, and when darkness came again, soon after 18.00, he called on the engine room to give of their best and resumed a straight course.

The night, when it came, was intensely dark, the sky being almost completely overcast and the moon not yet up. There was no more than a gentle north-easterly breeze, and the sea was mirror-calm, over which the *Benmohr* appeared to glide like a shadowy ghost, her passing marked only by the phosphorescence of her bow-wave and regular thump of her engines. The zigzag dispensed with, she was speeding through the night at a good 12 knots. Captain Anderson, who had been on the bridge to watch the sun go down in an empty horizon, was satisfied that his ship was well prepared for the night, but decided to stay to see the change of the watch.

Unknown to Anderson and the others on the bridge, the *Benmohr* had been under surveillance for some time. A little more than a mile on the starboard bow, a white feathering on the smooth sea was all that was visible of *U-505*. Hovering at periscope depth, Axel Loewe was watching and waiting. His war diary records:

1836 Sighted steamer through periscope bearing 115 degrees, steering for Freetown and zigzagging. She is deep loaded. I work into position. The light is going, but he puts on his lights.

2000 Steamer dims lights and alters course.

2252 Wind NW 2, sea 1, NW swell, very good visibility, 9/10 high cloud.
    Fired 1 and 4 tubes. Depth 3 metres, range 600 and 800 metres. Both missed. There is a glare on the water.

2307 Fire again with Tube 2, depth 3 metres, range 400 metres. Hit amidships. Steamer stops and puts boats over side and throws over big life raft with light. Transmits SSS torpedoed, location and name *Benmohr* 5920 BRT frantically. Slowly sinking.

This differs somewhat from Captain Anderson's report:

Just before 1958 on 5th March I was on the bridge with the Mate and remarked to him how dark it was. I had a look along the ship to see if any lights were showing, but there was no sign of any light. I had just turned away towards the chart room when we were struck by a torpedo on the starboard side under the bridge.
    We were then in a position about 230 miles S 6 W (true) from Freetown, and were proceeding at a speed of about 12 knots. The sea at the time was smooth with wind NE force 1–2. The weather was fine and cloudy the visibility good, but very dark.

There are, in fact, a number of points on which Loewe and Anderson are at odds. Firstly, the time difference of the two reports is puzzling. Even given that the *Benmohr* will probably have been keeping local time (GMT+1), and *U-505* was on German time (GMT-1), as was customary, there is still more than an hour unaccounted for. Furthermore, Loewe logged two torpedoes fired at 22.52 that missed the British ship, but must have passed very close to her. The night was very dark and the tracks of the torpedoes will have been clearly visible in the calm and translucent sea. Yet Anderson makes no mention of being aware of this initial attack. Even more puzzling are the two differing reports regarding lights. Loewe said, 'The light is going but he puts on lights', and then, 'Steamer dims lights and alters course'. On the other hand, Anderson remarked, 'I had a look along the ship to see if any lights were showing, but there was no sign of any light'. Those who know the Gulf of Guinea well will swear that strange things happen in its warm fecund waters. It must have been so on this dark night that the *Benmohr* met her end.

Captain David Anderson takes up the story again:

The starboard bridge lifeboat was blown away and the concrete protection on the bridge and wheelhouse collapsed. A large column of water was thrown up which completely enveloped the ship. I was struck on the head by a piece of flying concrete. I managed to stagger across to the other side of the bridge and by that time the Mate and Third Mate were attending to the lowering of the boats. I rang the engine room telegraph 'stop' and then to 'finished with engines'. The three remaining lifeboats were lowered, but held above the water as the ship had considerable way on her. All the crew got into the boats with the exception of the Carpenter, Bo'sun and myself, who remained on board.

A wireless distress message was sent off immediately and an answer was received. The wireless operator was given our position every half hour and he sent off the message without further instructions, as I had given him previous orders to do this immediately in case of an emergency.

After the first torpedo struck the ship I saw two bright

30

lights some little distance away, one on each quarter. These lights remained steady and were of an orange colour. The Second Mate informed me that from his boat he saw these two lights and also saw submarine close to him on his starboard beam. I gathered from this that there must have been at least three submarines in the vicinity.

Although on this night, that had begun so serenely but ended in a terrible nightmare, Anderson's assessment was understandable, it was far from the truth. Post-war records reveal that *U-505* was quite alone in her attack.

Having done all he could to ensure the safety of his crew, Anderson turned his attention to his ship. She was noticeably down by the head, but appeared to be in no immediate danger of sinking. He sent Carpenter Gerrard forward to sound No.2 hold bilges, but within a few minutes of Gerrard leaving the bridge, Loewe, having brought *U-505* to within 300 metres of the ship, administered the *coup de grâce* with a torpedo fired from his No.3 tube.

The torpedo struck the *Benmohr* forward of her bridge house with catastrophic effect. Anderson later wrote:

> There was a tremendous explosion and a great deal of debris was blown into the air. A large amount of this debris fell into the port bridge boat and also filled the after starboard boat with water, but the occupants were able to bale this out and both boats got away safely from the ship.
>
> The decks amidships were blown open and badly torn. The carpenter, bo'sun and myself took shelter in the port amidship alleyway until the debris had fallen and then I sent the carpenter to sound No.2 hold and he came back and reported that it was full of water.
>
> The ship was settling steadily so I ordered the bo'sun to throw overboard some of the small rafts which we had stowed amidships and then the carpenter, bo'sun and myself left the ship.

Captain Anderson, Boatswain Christie and Carpenter Gerrard abandoned ship by shinning down the rope falls of one of the lifeboats which had already left the ship's side, waiting until the lower blocks entered the water before swimming clear. The ship had by this time lost all her way, but the darkness was so complete that they could see nothing around them, not even each other. It took a great deal of courage for these three men to consign themselves to the inky-black sea, where they were aware that the great hammerhead shark lurked, but they had no other alternative. Their mortally wounded ship was sinking rapidly.

Despite a sea temperature in the region of 85°F, the water felt cold, and the three men struck out with a will, swimming aft to where the small rafts they had earlier thrown overboard were floating. Hauling themselves aboard, one man to a raft, they paddled away from the ship, a few minutes later coming across the Fourth Engineer struggling in the water. He joined them on the rafts, and they drifted away into the darkness of the night, four frightened men with nothing between them and the wide ocean but a few planks of wood. Fortunately, they were not alone for long, being picked up by one of the *Benmohr*'s lifeboats which had been searching for them. Captain Anderson takes up the narrative again:

> Just after we got into the boat there was a shout from the water, 'Help, help, I cannot swim'. Without a moment's hesitation, the Bo'sun, who had only just been picked up from the water, dived overboard and swam off to the assistance of the man calling from the water. It was a very dark night, and we were not supplied with red lights on our lifejackets, but after about 5 minutes the Bo'sun, C. Christie, came back to the boat bringing with him one of the military gunners (name not known). I consider this was a very gallant action on the part of the Bo'sun.

The three lifeboats now came together, giving Anderson the opportunity to make a roll call. He was greatly relieved to find that all fifty-five men of his crew were accounted for, although there were some injuries. Their ship had by now gone down, and the boats were adrift some 150 miles from the nearest land, the coast in the region of Monrovia, but given that the weather held fair, Anderson estimated that under sail and oars, they could expect to reach that port in two and a half days. However, as their SOS had been acknowledged, he decided to remain hove-to for the night, in the hope that rescue might come at daylight. The three boats were lashed together, and the occupants settled down for the night.

As the hours went by, so the temperature fell steeply, and as most of the survivors were in light tropical rig, by midnight they were all so cold and miserable that it was decided to cast off the boats and take to the oars, purely as a means of keeping warm. No one was sorry to see the sun come up next day, even though it meant that within hours they would be sweltering in the torrid heat and begging for the cool of the night to return.

Although they were aware that the outside world knew of their plight, the survivors were also aware that their boats were only tiny dots in a very big ocean, and they were prepared for a long wait. Sails were rigged, more to give shade than provide propulsion, for what breeze there was – which was very little – was in the north-east, and the heavy wooden lifeboats would not sail close hauled. Any progress they made would have to be under oars, and the heat being so intense, Anderson decided to wait until the sun was going down again before attempting to row.

Fortunately, rescue came before he was obliged to put men on the oars. At around 11.00 that morning, as the sun was climbing towards its zenith and the boats' occupants were sheltering from its heat under makeshift awnings, the heavy drone of aircraft engines brought them to their feet. Minutes later, the clumsy bulk of a Sunderland flying boat appeared out of the heat haze to the north. Flying low, the huge aircraft circled the boats, its familiar red, white and blue roundels bringing cheers from the survivors. The cheers grew louder when the plane landed on the water some way off.

The Sunderland pilot seemed wary of approaching any closer, and signalled asking how many men were in the boats. When Anderson replied that there were fifty-six of them, there was no response. Then, to the great consternation of the survivors, the aircraft swung short around and taxied away. They were to be abandoned. But, fortunately, their fears were unfounded. When the plane was some two – three miles off, it stopped, released its depth charges, and came back.

Half an hour later, all fifty-six of the *Benmohr*'s men were packed into the flying boat and enjoying sandwiches and iced water. Then, the heavily overloaded aircraft, the throaty roar of her four powerful engines shattering the quiet of the day, began her take-off. Seven heart-stopping miles further on, she finally lifted clear of the water and slowly began to climb. Two and a half hours later, she flopped heavily into the still waters of Freetown harbour, having earned the doubtful distinction of being the first – and probably the last – Sunderland to take off and land with sixty-six persons on board.

Captain David Anderson and his men were repatriated to the United Kingdom in the Polish liner *Batory*, which coincidentally also had on board Captain Philip Savery and the surviving seventy-five crew members of the *Helenus*. Not surprisingly, they were all very happy men but, through no fault of their own, they were leaving behind a Gulf of Guinea in turmoil.

The sinking of the *Helenus* and *Benmohr* set the alarm bells ringing in Freetown. The favoured opinion was that at least two enemy submarines were at large in the Gulf, possibly with the support of U-tankers, and this was a threat not to be taken lightly. There was now a steady stream of Allied merchant shipping using the Cape route; ships carrying supplies and reinforcements to British forces fighting in North Africa and the Far East, others northbound with produce, ores and oils, without which an already hard-pressed Britain would be in dire straits. And all these ships, many hundreds in a month, were converging on Freetown, where convoys were formed and dispersed. Hitherto, it had been considered quite safe for ships to sail independently and unescorted between Freetown and the Cape; now the situation had changed dramatically, and there was no easy solution to the threat. Allied naval commitments, particularly in the North Atlantic, were so great that the defence of West African waters had for some years been a minor consideration. A few anti-submarine trawlers were stationed between Freetown and Lagos, and Sunderlands of 95 Squadron based at Freetown and Bathurst flew regular patrols over the Gulf. Beyond that, merchant ships were left to fend for themselves. If the U-boats were to come south in force, then a massacre would follow. And then there was the French question.

On 17 June 1940, the French Government had its nose rubbed in the dirt of the Forest of Compiègne when it was forced to sign an armistice in the very railway coach that had witnessed the ignominy of the German surrender in 1918. Thereafter, France was a divided nation, the whole of the western side of the country, including the vital Channel and Biscay ports, being under direct German occupation, while the remainder came under the control of Marshal Pétain's government based at Vichy. Pétain also had control of the French colonies in Africa and as the ageing Marshal, despite his impeccable record in the 1914–18 war, was openly pro-German, these colonies, particularly the West African states of Senegal, French Guinea, the Ivory Coast, Togo and Dahomey were a potential threat to British interests in the area. Two British ships, the *Gambian* and the *Takoradian*, both belonging to the United Africa Company, regular traders on the coasts, had already been seized and interned in Dakar. They were sailing in ballast to Nigeria and, as was their normal practice, had called in at Dakar to replenish their bunkers. Given no reason to do so – other than, perhaps, they were carrying out the wishes of their new German masters – the Vichy French authorities had interned both ships and sent their crews under escort to the Gambian border.

The German General Staff was no less concerned for the welfare of the French possessions. Early in September 1940, Admiral Raeder, Commander-in Chief of the German Navy, reported to Hitler:

> In the French possessions in Equatorial Africa there is an open break with Pétain's government and a swing over to General de Gaulle. There is a danger that unrest and revolt might spread to the French West African colonies. The situation in the colonies, particularly as regards foodstuffs, is used by Britain as a means of exerting pressure. An agreement between the colonies and Britain, and revolt against France would jeopardize our own chances of controlling the African area; the danger exists that strategically important West African ports might be used for British convoy activities and that we might lose a most valuable source of supplies for

Europe. The danger of an attack on the part of the USA is not entirely out of the question, in view of the possibilities for such action.

Far-sighted German measures are necessary to counteract any development of this kind. Therefore the Naval Staff agrees in principle to sending French naval forces to the areas threatened; to the resumption of merchant traffic between the colonies and neutral countries by means of French and neutral vessels, in order to alleviate economic difficulties; and to attempt to re-establish merchant shipping between France and her colonies.

Not unexpectedly, Raeder's wish to 're-establish merchant shipping between France and her colonies' had an ulterior motive, as later became clear. The traditional exports from French West Africa were timber, palm kernels and groundnuts, but exploration between the wars had unearthed considerable deposits of bauxite, manganese, iron and chrome ores, raw materials sorely needed by the Third Reich. If the French ships could continue trading between West Africa and France with these ores, then there was no doubt as to who would be the ultimate beneficiary – the German arms industry.

In London and Washington there had been for some time fears of a German occupation of the French colonies in West Africa, and that Dakar, with its naval base and airfield might be used to attack British convoys using Freetown. It was also suggested that the Luftwaffe could launch air raids on American cities from Dakar with long-range bombers. This was not stretching the imagination too far: the Italians were already flying a weekly commercial service from Africa to Natal in Brazil, a distance of only 1,600 miles.

The matter was brought to a head with the arrival in Dakar of three Vichy French cruisers and three destroyers, which had on board a number of Vichy troops and German advisors, sent, so it was thought, to stiffen the garrison. Winston Churchill concluded that, 'the whole situation at Dakar was transformed in a most unfavourable manner', and it was decided that the time had come to take action.

Operation Menace began on the morning of 23 September, and consisted of a force of 2,500 Free French troops led by General de Gaulle, carried in British ships, and backed up by a British fleet of two battleships, four cruisers and a number of destroyers. Unfortunately, the operation was doomed from the start. It was thought that the sight of such a formidable armada approaching Dakar would be sufficient to persuade those ashore that resistance was futile, but the weather took a hand. Instead of the fine, clear weather expected, Dakar and its approaches were enveloped in thick fog, and the British ships were not visible from the shore. When de Gaulle's emissaries entered the harbour in launches flying a flag of truce, they were greeted by a hail of bullets. With two of their number wounded, the Free French retreated back out to sea, bearing the news that Dakar was not yet ready to come over to the Allies.

The fog was now clearing, and the British fleet approached to within 5,000 yards, where they could clearly be seen. They were promptly fired on by the battery of 9.4-inch guns defending the harbour. The British ships returned the fire, and in the exchange the cruiser *Cumberland* and the destroyers *Ingefield* and *Foresight* were damaged and forced to retire, while a French submarine and a destroyer received hits.

The engagement continued for three days, with the battleships *Barham* and *Resolution* swapping 15-inch shells with the *Richelieu*, which was supported by the shore batteries. In the mêlée *Resolution* was hit by a torpedo from a Vichy submarine and two British destroyers were badly damaged by gunfire. On the French side, *Richelieu* sustained damage that would put her out of action for many months, two destroyers were set on fire and grounded and two submarines were sunk. In the end, the British fleet withdrew and the planned invasion by de Gaulle's Free French force was abandoned. The attack on Dakar had failed miserably, and did nothing to break the Vichy French hold on Senegal. De Gaulle eventually landed with his troops 2,000 miles further east in the French Cameroons, where he was received with open arms, but a Free French base in the far Cameroons was unlikely to influence the course of the war.

Perversely, after the fiasco of Operation Menace, the British

Government issued orders that French merchant ships – that is ships loyal to the Vichy Government – sailing under escort in the waters of the Gulf of Guinea should not be interfered with. Consequently, the ludicrous situation arose whereby Vichy French convoys, escorted by Vichy French warships, became a common sight on the coast. The loaded merchantmen were not allowed to go north of Dakar, but there was no check on the thousands of tons of ore landed in Dakar and shipped north in neutral-flag ships. Needless to say, much of this ore was ending up in Germany, the manganese for high-grade steel and bauxite for aluminium.

Chapter Four

When Germany invaded Norway on 9 April 1940, more than 1,000 Norwegian merchant ships were at sea or in port in various parts of the world. Oslo Radio, which quickly fell into the hands of the German military, broadcast a message ordering all these ships to attempt to return to Norway, or if that was impossible, to sail to a neutral port, preferably Italian or Spanish. Under no circumstances were they to enter a British port. This prompted London to send out a similar broadcast urging all Norwegian ships to make for the nearest British or Allied port, where they would come under the protection of the Royal Navy. By the time British forces withdrew from Norway a month later, almost 900 ships had reached Britain. There they were requisitioned by the Norwegian Government, which had taken refuge in London, and formed into the Norwegian Shipping and Trade Mission, or Notraship, the world's biggest shipping company. Sailing with Notraship was the 7587-ton motor tanker *Sydhav*.

The *Sydhav*, originally owned by Trygve Lodding of Oslo, and built in Sunderland in 1929, soon found herself engaged in feeding the insatiable demand of the British war effort with oil from the Middle and Far East. When the Japanese attacked Pearl Harbor, and then swept through the Pacific islands like a bush fire out of control, supplies of oil from the Dutch East Indies and Borneo dried up, and as Japanese submarines and surface raiders fanned out into the Indian Ocean, it became increasingly difficult to get oil through from the Persian Gulf. A number of Allied tankers, including the *Sydhav*, were switched to the West Indies, where there was ample oil that was, for the time being at least, more accessible.

It was thus that, in late February 1942, the *Sydhav* found herself alongside the loading berth at Point-à-Pierre, Port of Spain,

Trinidad. She sailed from there on the 24th carrying 11,400 tons of petroleum with orders to proceed to Freetown to join a convoy for the United Kingdom. Her master, Captain Nils Helgesen, conscious that he was in command of a floating bomb, was anxious to quit the area as soon as possible. He had good reason to want to do so.

When, on 12 December 1941, Germany declared war on the United States of America, Admiral Dönitz was quick to take advantage of the new pastures which became available to his U-boats. As the season of 'peace and goodwill towards all men' approached, five boats, *U-66, U-109, U-123, U-125* and *U-130*, all heavy with extra fuel and stores, set out from the Biscay ports to cross the Atlantic. The reality of war was about to be visited upon the Americas.

The U-boat attack force arrived on the east coast of the US in mid-January 1942 to find the Americans even less prepared for an attack on their coastal shipping than Dönitz had dared to imagine. Ships sailing between ports on the coast appeared to be completely ignoring the need for any precautionary measures. They were a blaze of lights at night, and used their radios with impunity, the ether being loud with incessant talk between ships, including names, positions and times of sailing and arriving. Lighthouses, beacons and buoys were still operating at full power, and no towns on the coast had made any attempt to dim their brilliant street lighting and advertising signs. The inevitable slaughter followed.

When the first ship was sunk, the 9,577-ton Panama-flag motor tanker *Norness,* torpedoed by *U-123* some forty miles off Long Island, she sent out a distress message saying she had hit a mine. This led to the US Navy warning all shipping to be on the lookout for mines which may have been laid off the coast. No was prepared to believe that an enemy submarine might be responsible.

The U-boats lay on the bottom in the shallow water offshore during the day, and moved in at night on the surface. The un-suspecting American merchantmen, conveniently lit, and often silhouetted against the shore lights, fell to the German torpedoes like ducks in a shooting gallery. By the time the US Navy woke up to the fact that the enemy was in their midst, 163,000 tons of Allied merchant shipping had been sent to the bottom.

Dönitz followed up this initial success by sending out another five boats to the Caribbean with orders to disrupt the supply of oil streaming across the Atlantic to Britain. The tankers were by now running darkened, but once again the United States Navy was caught unprepared.

Korvettenkapitän Werner Hartenstein in *U-156* opened the attack on 16 February by torpedoing the British-flag tankers *Pedernales* and *Oranjestad* and the American *Arkansas* as they were leaving Aruba fully loaded. He then went on to shell the oil tanks on the foreshore at Aruba, but was beaten off before he was able to cause any serious damage. *Kapitänleutnant* Albrecht Achilles was even more audacious. A little before dawn on the 19th, he took *U-161* right into the anchorage off Port of Spain, Trinidad, where a number of ships were anchored. His first target was the 7,000-ton American freighter *Mokihaha*, owned by Matson Navigation of San Francisco. The *Mokihana*, on her way from Baltimore to the Middle East with a cargo of Lend-Lease materials, was anchored two miles off the wharf in seven fathoms of water, silhouetted against the shore lights and with all her own lights blazing. Achilles' torpedo struck on the *Mokihana*'s starboard side, just forward of her bridge, blasting a 45 foot by 35 foot hole in the hull. Had the water been any deeper, the American ship would have sunk within a few minutes, but luckily for her forty-five man crew, she just sat on the bottom. There were no casualties, other than the ship herself.

Achilles now turned his sights on the 6,997-ton *British Consul*, anchored nearby. The fully loaded tanker erupted in a ball of fire but, once again, was saved by the shallow water. Both ships were later salvaged, but this attack resulted in Port of Spain being closed to the British troopships which had been in the habit of refuelling there on their way to the Middle East.

Three days after Albrecht Achilles' daring attack on Port of Spain, Jürgen von Rosenstiel's *U-502* sank the 9,467-ton Norwegian motor tanker *Kongsgaard* seven miles north of Curacao. On the same day, Nicolai Clausen, in *U-129*, sank the US-flag *West Zeda* off Georgetown, Guyana, and on the 23rd, in the same area, sent the small Canadian steamer *Lennox* to the bottom.

The war had been brought home to the *Sydhav* with a vengeance, and there was an audible sigh of relief from all on board when she finished loading at Point-à-Pierre and set sail for Freetown. None was more relieved than Captain Helgesen, who had been watching the U-boat war erupt in the Caribbean with a great deal of apprehension. He lost no time in clearing the coast and, as advised by the Admiralty, set an east-south-easterly course for a position about 250 miles south-west of Freetown. The *Sydhav* being deep-loaded and obliged to zigzag during daylight hours, was unlikely to break any speed records; averaging no more than 10 knots at best. Although Helgesen knew these waters were now clear of enemy surface raiders, and no U-boats had been reported, after the events of the past few days he was on his guard. Instead of the usual relaxed passage, with the north-east trades blowing light under a blue sky dotted with fair weather cumulus, perfect ship maintenance weather, it promised to be maximum readiness all the way, with chipping hammers and paint brushes giving way to extra lookouts and gun watches.

Eleven days later, early on the morning of 6 February, the *Sydhav* was approaching her alter course position 250 miles south-west of Freetown. Ten hours earlier, the wireless room had heard the *Benmohr*'s plaintive calls for help coming in loud and clear – the British ship had, in fact, been only 150 miles to the north-east. The night that followed had been uneasy, full of spooks and alarms as the tanker, deep with her lethal load of petroleum, crept through the darkness towards her destination. Those who were able to find refuge in sleep did so fully clothed and with lifejackets to hand.

It had also been an anxious night for *U-505*. Following his successful encounter with the *Benmohr*, Axel Loewe decided to stay put on the surface in the hope that others might come the way of the British steamer. The moon broke through shortly before midnight, and Loewe and his crew looked forward to passing a pleasant few hours idling on the surface, charging batteries and airing the boat. All went well until the small, grey hours of the morning, when all was quiet, and everyone had gone below leaving only the watch officer and the lookouts in the conning tower. At 03.00, without warning, a four-engined Sunderland came roaring

42

down the path of the moon, low on the water and heading straight for *U-505*. Fortunately, Loewe's men had been well trained, and the boat was below the surface and running deep before the enemy plane reached them. It seems probable that the Sunderland was not carrying depth bombs, for instead of the mind-paralysing crash of exploding charges they expected, *U-505*'s crew heard only the whine of the boat's electric motors as they carried her clear of the area.

When Loewe surfaced again at 04.25, the horizon was clear all round, and the sky to the east growing pale as the sun brought another day to the Gulf of Guinea. He decided to stay on the surface to see what that day might bring. He did not have long to wait, as his war diary records:

0930 ET 8320. Rain shower with rainbow. Good visibility.
   Sighted deep-laden tanker approaching 8–10 miles off. She is zigzagging. On approximate course for Freetown at about 10 knots. I close in.

1022 Dived to attack. Aim and shoot. Hit forward. Tanker sinks in position ET 8320. She was not flying ensign and no neutral markings. Believe she is *British Confidence*-type motor ship. Estimate 8000 BRT. Fired double shot, Tubes 5 and 6, range 170 metres. Only two detonations heard. Observe through periscope that tanker goes down in two minutes with white smoke cloud 400–500 metres high. Detonations heard for some minutes with hydrophones. Apparently she was carrying benzine.

The *Sydhav* had been heading into the sun, and no one on board, not even the lookout right forward in the bows, saw the stick-like periscope emerging from the flat calm sea or the streaks of foam and bubbles marking Loewe's torpedoes as they sped towards the ship.

Young Thorstein Schau was asleep in his cabin when the first torpedo hit. The shock of the explosion brought him rudely back to full consciousness and tumbling out of his bunk. Pausing only to slip on his lifejacket – he had been sleeping fully dressed – he ran for the boat deck. As he scrambled up the ladder from the main deck, the second torpedo slammed into the hull directly beneath him, and he was blown into the sea.

The *Sydhav* had been hit in the engine room and just forward of it, the double blast effectively opening up her largest watertight compartment to the sea. She sank so quickly that Captain Helgesen and eleven of his crew went with her.

When he came to the surface, still partly stunned and gasping for air, Thorstein Schau was able to pull himself aboard a life raft that was floating nearby. He was later joined by other survivors and, with their help, righted a capsized lifeboat which they then boarded and began to bail out. As they worked, they were horrified to find that the boat was surrounded by sharks. When they were at last able to ship the oars, they rowed around in the mass of floating debris – all that was left of their ship – looking for other survivors. They did come across one other man, who was floating on a mattress, but as they approached him, he was dragged screaming from his refuge by the voracious sharks.

Two hours after torpedoing the *Sydhav*, Loewe brought *U-505* to the surface. His war diary records:

> 1218 ET 8320 Surfaced. Approach the position of the wreck. Very large oil slick with two rafts and a lifeboat with 20 men, partly burned and covered with thick oil. I approach them and ask if they have sufficient water and provisions and offer help with their wounded. As I am asking the name of the tanker a Sunderland appears in the east at 8000 metres. I present narrow silhouette and the plane goes away without apparently seeing us, the oil slick or the boats.

Following this small act of mercy, the remaining survivors of the Norwegian tanker, twenty-four men in a waterlogged lifeboat, all in a wretched state, headed north for the West African coast. They were found in the early hours of 7 March by a British naval vessel and taken to Freetown.

Loewe now needed to reload his torpedo tubes, a lengthy operation, as *U-505*'s remaining spare torpedoes were stowed below the deck plating. During the night he moved to a position some 350 miles offshore, well away, so he hoped, from enemy air and sea patrols. Perversely, when the transfer of the torpedoes from their deck stowage began, the weather deteriorated, and the operation was carried out in driving rain squalls, and with a big swell running. The weather served to hide the surfaced U-boat from prying eyes, but it was early on the morning of the 8th before the job was finished.

While he was so occupied, Loewe missed the next ship coming north from the Cape, and also, perhaps, the attentions of a British warship. At 03.55 on the 8th, as *U-505*'s exhausted crew were manhandling the last spare torpedo below, the British steamer *Baluchistan* was ninety miles south of Cape Palmas and hurrying north to make her landfall. The weather with her was calm and misty, and out of the mist suddenly appeared a large unidentified, two-funnelled steamer, crossing the *Baluchistan*'s bows from port to starboard at some speed. An exchange of signals by lamp followed which almost resulted in a dangerous situation. The *Baluchistan*'s master, Captain Thomas Farrar, reported:

> . . . She signalled us and asked our name, I replied with the usual code signal which she did not appear to understand. She signalled three times asking our name and then asked where we were bound for. I replied with the code letters which she still did not understand. The ship then closed us and finally I gave the name of my ship and Freetown as our destination. He asked what position I was making for at Freetown. I again challenged him with our code to which he made no reply . . .

Captain Farrar's suspicions were now thoroughly aroused, and when the stranger suddenly altered course and closed on the *Baluchistan*, he ordered the wireless room to send out a QQQ signal (I am being attacked by an unidentified enemy ship) and sent his four-man naval gun's crew to man the 4-inch. This was a brave, but futile gesture, for the other ship was obviously heavily armed. She was, in fact, the armed merchant cruiser HMS *Ulster Monarch*, conscripted from her normal occupation, which in more peaceful days had been ferrying passengers and cargo on the Liverpool to Belfast run. Fortunately for Farrar, the AMC, after

45

circling the *Baluchistan* at a safe distance, appeared satisfied with her identity, and made off to the south. The contretemps had lasted for over an hour and Farrar waited another hour before cancelling his QQQ call. That being done, he was anxious to reach Freetown as soon as possible.

When she was challenged by the *Ulster Monarch*, the 6,992-ton *Baluchistan*, a cargo liner owned by F.C. Strick & Company of London, had been, with the exception of a brief stop at Cape Town for bunkers, continuously at sea for thirty-one days. She sailed from Basra, at the head of the Persian Gulf, on 4 February with a cargo of 8,000 tons of dates, a seemingly frivolous cargo to be carrying in wartime, but no doubt the Ministry of War Transport had a good use for them – perhaps a small boost for the morale of the luxury-starved people of Britain.

During the ten hour passage down the Shatt al Arab to the sea Captain Farrar had ample time to dwell on the voyage ahead. It was a long run to the Cape, 5,220 miles – three weeks at sea if the weather was fair – and with the south-west monsoon approaching, that was questionable. It was also something of a voyage into the unknown.

When the *Baluchistan* came north early in January, the waters of the Indian Ocean had yet to hear the drums of war, but while loading in Basra Farrar learned that at least one, perhaps two, Japanese submarines were at large in the Bay of Bengal. Their first unsuspecting victim had been the 5,049-ton American freighter *Florence Luckenbach*. Under the command of Captain Thure Eckart, she sailed from Madras on 29 January, bound for New York with a cargo of general and manganese ore. When she was only fifteen miles off Madras, she was struck by a torpedo in her No.1 hold. The explosion blew a great hole in the ship's side and sent her forward hatch covers and beams soaring skywards. She began to sink by the head, and Captain Eckart gave the order to abandon ship. No sooner had the thirty-eight crew members – all crammed into one lifeboat, as the other had been destroyed by the initial explosion – cleared the ship than a second torpedo delivered the *coup de grâce*. The *Florence Luckenbach* went down a few minutes later.

In the closing days of January 1942 the Japanese submarines –

it transpired that there were two of them, *I-162*, commanded by Takaichi Kinashi, and *I-164*, commanded by Tsunayashi Ogawa – sank another three merchant ships, two of which were off Ceylon. The enemy was moving deeper into the Indian Ocean.

Any fears Captain Farrar might have had for the safety of his own ship proved unfounded. The *Baluchistan* enjoyed a completely untroubled passage south to the Cape, but she had seen the last of peace in the Indian Ocean. Within a few weeks the Japanese fleet would move in to wreak havoc amongst British shipping, sinking the cruisers *Dorsetshire* and *Cornwall*, and eleven merchantmen in an unescorted convoy. The Japanese surface ships were followed by the 8th Submarine Flotilla, eighteen large ocean-going submarines supported by the armed merchant cruisers *Hokoku Maru* and *Aikoku Maru*. Overnight the Indian Ocean had suddenly become a high risk area for Allied shipping.

Sailing from Cape Town on 25 February, the *Baluchistan* moved north again on the penultimate leg of her long voyage home. Riding the swells under the blue skies of the South Atlantic the war seemed a world away until, on 7 March, when just south of the Equator, Farrar received a message from the Admiralty warning him of an enemy submarine operating in the vicinity of 05°- 00' N 12°- 00' W. The origin of this position is not clear, but it is most likely that it came from a patrolling Sunderland engaged in a sweep following the torpedoing of the *Sydhav*. It was presumed the submarine sighted was the same one that sank the Norwegian ship, that is Axel Loewe's *U-505*, but having completed reloading his torpedo tubes, Loewe was in fact then moving north towards Freetown. His place had been taken by Karl Merten in *U-68*, who for five days had been casting around for another victim. Merten's patience was about to be rewarded, for the *Baluchistan* and *U-68* were being inexorably drawn together.

On receipt of the Admiralty warning, which was followed by a recommended course to steer to avoid the danger, Farrar adopted the usual precautions, increasing the lookouts and having men handy to the guns. However, as the *Baluchistan* was then only just over twenty-four hours steaming from the Liberian coast he was not overly concerned. It was not until the brush with the then unidentified *Ulster Monarch* in the early hours of the 8th that he began to feel uneasy. But when the sun climbed over the horizon that morning, bringing with it the promise of yet another fine, warm day, Farrar's anxieties evaporated with the morning mist.

The *Baluchistan* was forty-five miles west of Cape Palmas, and approaching the coast in the region of the Liberian settlement of Grand Sesters when, at 10.05, the mirror-like calm of the sea was disturbed by a line of bubbles racing towards her starboard side. Merten's precisely aimed torpedo hit abaft her bridge, midway between Nos. 4 and 5 holds. Captain Farrar reported:

> There was not much noise from the explosion, it appeared to be more of a dull thud. I did not see any water thrown up nor any flame or smoke. The ship started to settle down very quickly by the stern. I ordered the four lifeboats to be lowered (all boats are kept swung out). I had one officer in charge of each boat. I was on the bridge at the time and the men lowering my boat let go of the after fall and the boat was suspended by the forward fall. We finally managed to lower this boat all right and all four boats cleared the ship successfully. By the time we were clear the after deck was level with the water. About ten minutes after being torpedoed we were all in the boats. I looked around the ship before leaving but did not see anyone, although I was told afterwards that there were two Lascars still on board who had refused to leave. We sent out an SSS signal on the main set before leaving the ship and took the emergency wireless set into the boat with us.

As the four lifeboats were rowing clear of the *Baluchistan*, Merten fired another torpedo with devastating results. The missile struck the abandoned ship in her boiler room, and was followed by a massive explosion as her three high-pressure Scotch boilers blew themselves apart. But still the crippled merchantman, a typical handcrafted product of John Readhead's yard at South Shields, failed to sink.

Merten now decided to surface, and motored towards the drifting lifeboats. Captain Farrar wrote in his report:

The submarine appeared to be in very good condition, and was newly-painted light grey. I could not see any holes along the superstructure. There was one gun mounted on the fore deck, not quite half-way between the conning tower and the bows, it seemed to be about the size of our 4-inch. Another gun was mounted on the after deck, this one was a lighter gun with a long, thin barrel, rather like an Oerlikon, and he had another smaller gun on the conning tower. The conning tower had a green clover leaf painted on its starboard side (Karl Merten's personal emblem), and the Chief Officer saw a black cross painted on the port side. The Captain was a shortish, thin, and young-looking man. He spoke to us in quite good English through a megaphone.

Karl Merten treated his defeated enemies with characteristic respect, chatting quite amiably with Farrar, asking only for the name, tonnage and nationality of his ship, and if he had any injured in the boats. In return for his answers, he advised Farrar of the course to steer for the land, which he assured him was only thirty miles away. Farrar was already aware of this from his charts, but he admired Merton's concern and shouted back his thanks. He was less pleased, however, when the U-boat backed away and fired another torpedo into the *Baluchistan*. Yet still the ship refused to sink, and Merten, anxious not to waste any more expensive torpedoes on her, resorted to his 105-mm deck gun, firing thirty-two shells into the ship before finally leaving the area. Thomas Farrar was left to watch his late command being consumed by fire. There was nothing he could do for her now.

As soon as the U-boat was out of sight, Farrar brought the boats together. A roll call was taken, which revealed three of the Lascar crew to be missing, presumably killed when the first torpedo struck. Then Farrar and his officers took stock of their situation. Although they had been able to get an SOS away before abandoning ship, as the land was only thirty miles to the north, it seemed pointless to stay put and await rescue. However, the wind was very light, no more than a gentle breeze from the east, and the heavy steel lifeboats, not designed for fast sailing under the best of conditions, would make painfully slow progress towards the

Liberian coast. Even the most optimistic among them accepted that they must be prepared to spend at least a day and a night at the mercy of the elements. Fortunately, with sixty-three men to four boats, the boats were not overcrowded, and while one boat had been slightly damaged in launching, all had a good supply of food and water. While others made preparations for the journey, Farrar and his chief officer discussed the course to be steered. There were no charts in the boats, but the best estimate was that they were some forty-five miles west of Cape Palmas, immediately beyond which lay the border of Vichy French-occupied Ivory Coast. As the Guinea Current was strong in this area, flowing eastwards at between twenty-five and thirty miles a day, the danger was that the boats, with only enough wind to just take the creases out of their sails, would be swept to the east, ending up on a French beach. If they were to escape internment, this must be avoided at all costs. It was decided to steer well to the west of north, using oars as well as sails.

They had been under way for only a few hours when the appearance of a Sunderland flying boat gave rise to hopes that rescue was close at hand. The aircraft was flying low and seemed to be searching, but the *Baluchistan*'s boats were not equipped with smoke floats or flares, and the survivors could only wave their shirts and shout impotently as the great plane flew past without seeing them.

Angry and disappointed, but far from downhearted, the survivors returned to their oars, and throughout the remainder of that day and the following night they rowed steadily, stopping to rest only when they became exhausted. The heavy canvas sails of the boats, while well suited to the blustery conditions of higher latitudes, were of little use to them in this area of calms and light winds. It was not until early morning on the 9th, when an onshore breeze sprang up, that they began to make any real progress, and soon after noon, a ragged cheer went round the little flotilla as the low-lying coast of Liberia came in sight. Captain Farrar later wrote:

The Chief Officer's boat landed first and we landed about an hour later. We had to pull through the surf, and as the boat

50

touched bottom we jumped out just before the boat swung broadside on to the beach. We took the painter and pulled the boat up on the beach as high as we could. It was now afternoon on the 9th March.

Despite the pull of the Guinea Current, Farrar and his men had landed on a sandy beach near Subbubo Point, in Liberian territory, and some thirty-seven miles to the west of Cape Palmas. They trekked the three miles to Grand Sesters, where there was a small factory for the production of palm oil, and were taken under the wing of the local magistrate. They were fed, and then distributed among the Magistrate's house, the Lloyd's Agent's house and the Chief's hut, where they slept the sleep of exhausted men.

Next day, Farrar sent two injured men by boat to the town of Harper, near Cape Palmas, where medical treatment could be had, but another week was to pass before the rest of the survivors reached Harper. After a few days there, they boarded the destroyer HMS *Wyvern* and were taken to Freetown, from where they sailed home as passengers on a ship that had crossed their path before, none other than the AMC *Ulster Monarch*.

Chapter Five

In 1928, as the last painful memories of the First World War were fading into history, the steamer *Baron Newlands* was nearing completion in the Ayrshire Dockyard Company's yard at Irvine, on Scotland's west coast. When she finally tasted the deep water, the world was moving into the deepest economic depression ever known, but her owners were well prepared for this.

The Baron Line, founded in 1870 by two canny Scots, Hugh Hogarth and Captain James Goodwin, began life with a 91-foot wooden brig named *Kate,* and painstakingly built up a moderate-sized fleet of sailing vessels trading mainly with Canada. In 1881, Hugh Hogarth – James Goodwin had by now left the company – moved into steam, but over the years that followed, Hogarth, frugal man that he was, resisted the trend towards bigger and faster ships. Baron Line steamers were small, none above 4,000 tons gross, and went about their business at an economical 9 knots on twenty tons of coal a day, offering near-starvation wages and conditions to their crews. It was with good reason that Baron Line throughout its long life was known as 'Hungry Hogarths'. But Scottish frugality paid dividends when the crash came in 1929. Throughout the long depression, while other fleets were laid up, the slow, tightly-budgeted Baron ships kept going, not one being put to a lay-by berth. At the outbreak of war in 1939, Baron Line, with thirty-nine ships, was one of the largest privately owned tramp fleets in the world.

Hogarth's 3,386-ton *Baron Newlands,* registered in the port of Ardrossan on the Firth of Clyde, was one of the survivors of the lean times, and in March 1942 she lay at the ore berth in Takoradi, on the Gold Coast, loading manganese ore for the United Kingdom. She carried a crew of thirty-eight, including six DEMS gunners, and was under the command of Captain William Ewing.

Takoradi, originally a fortified settlement founded by the Dutch West India Company in the seventeenth century had, over the years, grown into the Gold Coast's only enclosed deep water port, and in 1942 was the scene of a great deal of activity. Not only was the port handling the export of cocoa and timber from the plantations up country, for which reason it was built, but large quantities of manganese ore so desperately needed for the British war effort. At the same time, replacement fighter aircraft were being landed which were then serviced and flown north to airfields in the Western Desert, where British and Commonwealth forces were fighting a desperate rearguard action against Rommel's advancing *Panzers*. Loading and discharging facilities in Takoradi harbour were consequently stretched beyond their normal capacity, and many ships were being seriously delayed. And with daytime temperatures around 90°F, and a relative humidity on the same scale, Takoradi was not a place to linger. Certainly, Captain William Ewing had no regrets when, on the afternoon of 14 March 1942, he took the deep-loaded *Baron Newlands* out through the breakwaters of the port into the open sea, even though he was aware that U-boats were operating in the Gulf of Guinea.

While Ewing and his crew found temporary relief from the stifling heat in the cool sea breeze that greeted them as they crested the swells outside Takoradi, there was no such escape for *Kapitänleutnant* Karl Merten and the crew of the *U-68*. On the advice of BdU (*Befehlshaber der Unterseebooten* – U-boat High Command), Merten had decided to remain in the vicinity of Cape Palmas, patrolling up and down in sight of the tall white-painted lighthouse on a glassy calm sea undisturbed by even by the gentlest of gentle zephyrs. Off Liberia the dry, hot season was drawing to a close, but for the time being the sun was a red ball of fire suspended in a cloudless sky which made life below decks in the submarine intolerable. In the control room, the thermometer rarely dropped below 31°C (88°F), while the engine spaces were reporting 38°C (100°F). Merten had tried running submerged, but with the sea temperature at 28°C (83°F), the sealed hull quickly became like a sauna. Cruising on the surface, with the conning tower hatch open and the fans sucking air into the boat, was a dangerous game, but it provided some relief for those men working in the cramped conditions of the steel hull.

Sagging under the weight of her cargo of 5,000 tons of ore, the *Baron Newlands* set course to the west when she was clear of Takoradi. Her 240 nhp engine, lovingly cared for over the years, but no longer at its best, laboured manfully, but with the current running against her she could manage only just over 7 knots. The darkness was closing in when she rounded Cape Three Points and entered Vichy French territorial waters off Ivory Coast. Half an hour later, the twin-funnelled *Ulster Monarch* appeared out of the gathering gloom, her signal lamp flashing a challenge. The armed merchant cruiser, the only British warship of any size in the Gulf of Guinea, was engaged in combing the area for Vichy French ships attempting to beat the blockade, at the same time keeping a sharp lookout for the U-boat, or U-boats already responsible for the loss of four Allied merchantmen. Unknown to the *Ulster Monarch*'s commander, *U-68* and *U-505*, neither of which had had sight of an enemy ship for a week, were also diligently searching, and with the same frustrating result. Loewe and Merten were, in fact, by this time so despairing of coming to grips with the enemy that they had requested permission to look further afield, preferably on the other side of the Atlantic, off the coast of Brazil. As the Brazilians had recently broken off diplomatic relations with Germany, and Dönitz had no wish to antagonize them further, the request had been refused. The only boost to their morale came in a message from the Admiral congratulating all commanders on one million tons of shipping sunk in the past two months.

On the night of the 16th, having steamed westwards for another two days, sighting nothing afloat but the occasional untidy flocks of fishing canoes that came sailing out to scoop up the shoals of fish that abounded in the warm waters offshore, the *Baron Newlands* was nearly sixty miles to the west of Cape Palmas. The night was dark and sultry, with the pungent smell of the native cooking fires coming off the land and tall thunderheads gathering all around the horizon. Lightning flashed and thunder rumbled ominously. The West African dry season was coming to an end, threatening the arrival of the tornadoes with their violent winds and torrential rain. Captain Ewing, keeping the starboard wing of the bridge, sniffed at the night air and contemplated a rain squall bearing down on the ship from the west. It would pass. Freetown lay only 400 miles to the north-west, and all was well. He walked into the wheelhouse, checked the compass and spoke to the officer of the watch, before going below to take a well-earned rest.

While Ewing relaxed in his armchair with a book, lulled into a sense of wellbeing by the reassuring thump of the *Baron Newlands*'s engine, out in the darkness to starboard Karl Merten was carefully manoeuvring *U-68* into position for a shot. His torpedo ran true, slamming into the British ship just abaft her engine room.

The shock of the explosion was very heavy, and the *Baron Newlands* staggered, heeled to port, and then came upright again. Captain Ewing, catapulted from his armchair, grabbed his life jacket and ran for the bridge. He could feel that his ship was mortally wounded, and conscious that the dead weight of the ore in her holds would take her down quickly, he ordered the Chief Officer to launch all lifeboats and get the crew away as quickly as possible. He later wrote in his report:

> The engine room bulkhead was badly pierced and the vessel was settling rapidly by the stern. I rushed back to my cabin for my torch and pocket whistle and quickly returned to the lower bridge as the ship sank, and I went under with her, but my life jacket floated me to the surface again. I then noticed that the ship had disappeared, having taken only 30 seconds to sink. I saw a raft 10/15 yards away, swam to it, and found the Junior Wireless Operator and Gunlayer already on it.

> The crew attempted to clear away the port lifeboat but were unable to do so owing to the speed with which the ship was sinking. The gripes and falls were cut and as the boat struck the sea, it capsized and became swamped. No attempt was made to clear the starboard boat. Thirteen men succeeded in scrambling onto this upturned boat, sitting there until daylight. These thirteen men managed to right this boat by using the grab lines to lever it over. Fortunately the boat was a new one and these grab lines withstood the strain. By being very careful, they were eventually able to bale it dry

and the mast of the boat gear was found to be intact. I saw this boat with the red sail 3 miles from my raft as they were sailing in towards the shore, but apparently did not see us.

Ewing and his two companions, clinging to their flimsy wooden raft, were in an extremely dangerous predicament. Although they were only twelve miles or so from the shore, the darkness around them was complete, and they had no compass. Furthermore, they had by this time discovered that the raft's paddles were missing. Not deterred, however, they retrieved some planks of wood from the water and began paddling around, searching for other survivors in the mass of wreckage left by their sunken ship. They eventually picked up in turn a DEMS gunner, the First Radio Officer, the Second Engineer and the Cabin Boy. There were now seven men on the raft. Captain Ewing's report continues:

At daylight on the 17th we could see the land to the eastward, so with the help of my crew I commenced paddling towards it with the driftwood. The wind was favourable, being south-easterly, and we made some slight progress, the shape of the raft, which was square, not being helpful to our efforts. A red sail was sighted close inshore, which was the sail of the lifeboat, but I was unable to contact it. I did not use my red flares, as I wished to preserve them for use as I neared the shore.

At about 0900 I sighted a four-engined flying boat about 3 miles away, which was patrolling down the Liberian coast. Six hours later we contacted three native canoes, which took aboard the seven survivors, including myself, from the raft. Two of these canoes landed four men at Grand Cester (*sic*) and the other canoe landed two men and myself at Piccaninni Cess, which was 9 miles further up the coast. On landing we walked along the sandy beach, accompanied by guides, to Grand Cester, arriving there at 2200 hours. When we arrived at Grand Cester we met the other survivors and learned that we would have to remain there as it was impossible to accommodate us at Cape Palmas, where there were 165 survivors from other vessels. Most of my men were taken charge of by Mr Fey and Father Conway of the Catholic Mission, and to ease the situation five men were billeted at Barkleyville Methodist Mission, which was about 10 miles away.

Next day, Captain Ewing counted heads and found that eighteen of his crew, including the Second Officer, Third Engineer, Fourth Engineer and four DEMS gunners were missing. As the *Baron Newlands* had gone down so quickly that he feared these unfortunate men must have gone down with her, but given the remote chance that they might still be out there struggling in the shark-invested sea, he sent a cable to the Naval Base at Freetown requesting that a search be made. He also persuaded some of the local fishermen to search the area of the sinking. The canoes came back empty handed. Whether Freetown organized an air and sea search Ewing was unable to confirm, but nothing further was heard of the missing men, and he assumed the worst.

As a result of the activities of *U-68* and *U-505*, the situation at Cape Palmas was critical, survivors from sunken ships outnumbering the indigenous population by more than five to one. William Ewing and the remaining nineteen members of his crew remained at Grand Sesters, which itself was no more than a cluster of native houses grouped around a tin-roofed palm oil factory, until 30 March. Ewing was lavish in his praise for the treatment they received during their enforced stay at the hands of this small community. They were taken by surf boat to Cape Palmas on the 30th, where they remained until 16 April, again being very well looked after. On the 16th, they boarded a British corvette for Freetown, where they landed on 18 April.

Five ships and nearly 40,000 tons of cargo had gone to the bottom since Merten and Loewe turned the Gulf of Guinea from a quiet backwater of the war into a danger zone, and their next victim was already on the way. She was the 5,755-ton *Ile de Batz*, a ship with a chequered history.

Built in 1918 by the Skinner & Eddy Corporation in Seattle for Lykes Brothers of New Orleans as the *West Hobomac*, she spent the inter-war years trading in the Atlantic. In early 1940 she was handed over to the French Government, and was renamed *Ile de*

Batz. When France fell, she escaped to a British port and was taken under the wing of the Ministry of War Transport to be managed by the worldwide traders Andrew Weir & Company of London, who had suffered heavy losses through enemy action. Andrew Weir, better known as the Bank Line, had put their own British master and officers into the ship, while she retained ten of her original French African ratings and five French Navy gunners. Six British African and seven European ratings made up a total complement of forty-four.

Under the command of Captain A.S. Watts, the *Ile de Batz* sailed from Rangoon on 8 February 1942, less than three weeks ahead of the advancing Japanese armies. She was carrying 7,000 tons of Far East produce, including a large quantity of bagged rice. Calling at Cape Town to replenish her coal bunkers, she left Table Bay on 4 March, bound for Freetown and an unnamed British port.

On the afternoon of the 15 March, Captain Watts, who was following the recommended Admiralty route for Cape Palmas, received an urgent signal advising him to make for a position to the east of the cape before shaping up for Freetown. At dusk on the 16th, having obtained good star sights, which put the *Ile de Batz* some fifty miles to the east of Cape Palmas, Watts altered onto a westerly course to pass twenty miles south of the cape around midnight. Unknown to Watts, as a result of the sinking of the *Baluchistan*, Cape Palmas light, normally visible at over twenty miles, had been dimmed. At 00.20 on the 17th, nothing having been seen of the light, and the ship then being thirty miles to the west of the cape by dead reckoning, Watts altered course to 290°. Considering the ship to be then safe for the night, he handed over to the Chief Officer and went below to rest, leaving instructions that he was to be called if needed.

Captain Watts' rest was to be of short duration, for Karl Merten, after sinking the *Baluchistan* and *Baron Newlands*, had decided to remain in the vicinity of Cape Palmas in the hope that other ships were coming along. His hopes were realized when, at about 03.30, the *Ile de Batz* appeared out of the early morning mist now forming. Taking his time, Merten manoeuvred into position on the British ship's starboard side and at 04.03 fired his first torpedo, aiming for the ship's most vulnerable spot, her engine room.

Merten had chosen an opportune time to strike, for the watch was just changing on board the *Ile de Batz*, and no one on her bridge, or the lookouts posted fore and aft, saw the torpedo coming. It exploded with a deafening roar, throwing up a tall column of water that fell back and swamped the after well deck. Both starboard lifeboats were smashed by the blast. Captain Watts, rudely awakened from his short sleep, went immediately to the bridge. He reported:

When I got onto the bridge and the Chief Officer told me that we had been torpedoed, I ordered him to man the guns and then told the 3rd Officer to go to the boat deck.

I then had a look round the bridge, but as it was very dark at the time I could see nothing, and could just see the davits on the boat deck about 120 feet away. I tried the engine room telegraph and whistle, and also tried to telephone to the radio room, but was not able to contact either the engine room or the radio room as the apparatus was all broken.

I looked over the side and saw that the ship was stationary, listing slightly to starboard and settling slowly, also I thought the engine and boiler rooms were flooding. I therefore threw the confidential books overboard, with the exception of No.16, which I knew was kept in the radio room.

By this time it was not necessary to give orders about lowering the boats, as the Free French and other members of my mixed crew were not waiting for these instructions.

I then went into my cabin and collected the ship's papers and my lifejacket. After a few minutes the Chief Officer came and said that there were only two gunners standing by and that they were unable to see anything. There was a Norwegian sailor standing by the wheel. I gave him my case containing the ship's papers and told him to go to his boat. I went down the port side of the ship intending to cross over to the boat deck on the starboard side. It was very dark at the time and I was feeling along the rail with my hand, when suddenly the rail disappeared and I noticed that the deck under my feet was buckled. I decided to go round the other way and crossed over the fore part of the midship section, and went along the port side of the ship by the Engineers accommodation. As I came along I could hear the Chief Officer calling out.

Not wishing to get left behind, Watts made his way to the boat deck, where he was reassured by the First Radio Officer that repeated SOS calls had been sent out before the wireless room was abandoned. As the ship was now obviously sinking, he ordered both remaining boats to be lowered. The sea being calm, with only a slight swell, the launching was accomplished without difficulty, but when the boats cleared the ship's side and a head count was made, Watts discovered that four of his crew were missing. By this time the sea was lapping over the main deck of the *Ile de Batz* and there could be no going back. Watts was also concerned that at any minute the U-boat might decide to put another torpedo into the ship. He therefore ordered the boats to put as much distance between themselves and the ship as possible. At about 04.30, the boats were about 200 yards away and well separated when the water between them erupted as Karl Merten brought his boat to the surface. Captain Watts later wrote:

The submarine was only about 50 feet away from us, but the Mate's boat was seen first. I made a sign to the men in my boat and told them to keep quiet, but somebody on the submarine looked around and saw my boat. I could hear them asking for the Captain, so I called out and said where I was. Someone on the submarine called out and asked me to go alongside. This I did and they asked me the name of my ship. I could not make them understand the name so I was ordered on board the submarine. As I got on board the submarine I was greeted with 'Heil Hitler' by the officer-in-charge, this being said in a very self conscious tone. I took no notice of this greeting and again the officer asked me the name of my ship, so this time I spelt it out to him, and he wrote it down. The officer then asked the tonnage, where we had sailed from and what cargo I was carrying, to which I replied 'General'. He could not understand the word 'General' so I said 'Various' and he knew what I meant.

Knowing of the German habit of taking the masters of merchant ships prisoner, Watts decided it was time to go, and jumped back into his lifeboat, ordering his crew to pull away from the U-boat as fast as possible. Fortunately, his escape either went unnoticed, or was ignored, and at this point, Merten opened fire with both his deck guns on the abandoned *Ile de Batz*, which was then still afloat. Watts could only watch with silent grief while his late command, pounded by German shells, caught fire, broke in two, and finally sank.

The time was now 05.00, but it was still dark, the dawn being another forty-five minutes away. Watts had obtained a position from Merten, which put the boats twenty-eight miles south-west of Cape Palmas, and he now set course for Garraway, twelve miles to the west of the cape, making due allowance for the Guinea Current, for he had no wish to end up in Vichy French territory. The two boats became separated again, and were apparently not seen by a Sunderland which flew quite close just after 10.30. A long day followed as they made their way towards the shore under sail and oars. Captain Watts wrote in his report:

The Chief Officer's boat landed at Garraway about 1800 on 17th March, and about an hour before he landed I could see his sail. I sailed up to the spot where I had last seen his sail and by this time it was about 1900 and getting dark. As there was a heavy swell and as I did not know the coast I decided not to attempt landing in the darkness. My crew were a little disappointed but I decided that it was the best thing to do.

As I had been steering all day I put the Second Officer in charge and went to have a rest. No sooner had I done this than I saw a dugout canoe coming towards us with two natives in it. The canoe came alongside and to my surprise I found that the natives could speak quite good English. I asked them if we could make a good landing and for reply one of the natives came aboard and piloted us into Garraway, where several more natives were waiting for us.

Mr Mooney, an African, is the Town Clerk, who has the only proper house in the village, the rest being native huts, took us all into his house for the night. We were very much crowded together, but as there was no white man in the village we were glad of his hospitality. Mr Mooney was very short of food and could only offer us coffee, we took the stores out of the boats, including the tanks of water, as all water for the village had to be carried a distance of 1½ miles.

Mr Mooney told us that he had seen a submarine at various times ever since the previous December. He took me out to show me where he had seen the submarine, and this was in a position about 3 miles west of Garraway and 1 mile out to sea. Mr Mooney said that in this position the sea was shallow and the surface very flat, and that it would be quite easy for a submarine to lie on the bottom there.

Next morning Mooney introduced Captain Watts to the village Head Man, who arranged to send a runner to Cape Palmas to report the arrival of the survivors. A Mr Ramus sent back a message by runner to the effect that he would send a surf boat to take Watts and his men to Cape Palmas. This boat arrived twenty-four hours later, but Watts was not convinced that it would carry all forty men in safety. However, as there was no road between Garraway and Cape Palmas, and the food situation was becoming critical, he compromised, putting twenty-eight men in the surf boat and six men into each of the ship's lifeboats. It took the three boats six hours to cover the twelve miles to Cape Palmas.

At Cape Palmas, the *Ile de Batz* survivors met up with survivors from the *Baluchistan* and the *Scottish Prince*, which had been torpedoed within hours of the *Ile de Batz*. In all, there were now 144 survivors at Cape Palmas, and they were becoming an acute embarrassment for this desperately poor community whose normal population rarely exceeded twenty-five. When this became clear to Watts, he sent an urgent cable through the Firestone Tyre Company's wireless station to London and Freetown requesting early evacuation.

While at Cape Palmas, Watts received a great deal of assistance from Mr Ramus, who turned out to be an employee of the Firestone Company of Swiss/English extraction. Ramus, it transpired, was engaged in espionage for the British, obtaining information on happenings in the nearby Vichy French-controlled Ivory Coast using runners carrying legitimate letters, but with other more revealing correspondence sewn into their clothing. Ramus's outside contacts proved useful when Watts believed he had news of one of his missing men:

> After we had been in Cape Palmas a week a rumour started that one of my crew, a Free French Naval gunner, had been picked up. My gunners had been in the habit of sleeping on deck in hammocks by the engine room on the starboard side, close to the spot where the ship was struck by the torpedo. I had one of these gunners in the boat with me and he said that at the time of the torpedoing he was sleeping next to the missing gunner, and that when he was awakened the gunner was not there and there was a hole where he had been. The rumour came through that the missing gunner had landed 12 miles up the coast from Garraway. I traced this rumour back from one native to another. In the end I asked Ramus and he said that he thought it was more or less impossible that this man had fetched up, but that he was prepared to send a runner along the coast.
>
> The story grew, however, and the last time we heard of the man he was supposed to have a black dog with him.
>
> I reported the whole story to the Free French Officer in Freetown and he wired again to the Consul in Liberia. We learned in the end that the *Baron Newlands* had been torpedoed at more or less the same time as ourselves and that a mess room boy from that ship had landed in about the same place where my gunner was reported to have landed, so I think this is how the rumour arose.

The mystery of a lone survivor appears to be an example of the West African 'bush telegraph' at work. Captain Ewing made no mention in his report, which was filed on 14 May, of any of his missing men reaching the shore at a later date. It also seems most unlikely that it was any of the *Ile de Batz*'s four French gunners, who were almost certainly blown overboard when the torpedo struck below where they were sleeping. Even if one of them had survived the blast, he would have been faced with a fifteen to twenty mile swim ashore through shark infested waters.

After a week at Cape Palmas, towards the end of which food and drinking water supplies were running out, Captain Watts and his men were more than pleased to see the destroyer *Wyvern* anchor offshore. The *Wyvern* took them to Freetown, where they boarded the *Ulster Monarch* for home. Their long and eventful voyage ended in Greenock.

Chapter Six

Tuesday, 17 March 1942 was proving to be another good day for Karl Merten, for no sooner had *U-68* cleared the scene of the *Ile de Batz* sinking than her lookouts were reporting smoke on the horizon to the south. This time it was no superannuated coal burner, but the smart new British motor vessel *Scottish Prince*.

Built just prior to the outbreak of the war for the Mediterranean traders Prince Line, a subsidiary of Furness Withy, the 4,917-ton *Scottish Prince*, under the command of Captain William Hill, was through the exigencies of war a long way from her familiar waters. She was then nearing the end of a long voyage, homeward bound from Calcutta with a cargo of 6,400 tons of palm kernels, 600 tons of castor seed, and 900 tons of pig iron.

Sailing from Cape Town on the afternoon of 5 March, some eighteen hours after the *Ile de Batz*, the *Scottish Prince,* with her superior speed, had narrowed the gap between the two ships to a few hours on the passage north. On the 16th she had received a diversionary signal from the Admiralty similar to that received by the Bank Line ship, and was consequently sailing in her wake – and into the arms of Karl Merten. It is not on record whether she picked up the *Ile de Batz*'s SOS, but if she did, she appears to have taken no avoiding action.

Merten waited at periscope depth until the *Scottish Prince* was within easy range, and then fired a spread of two torpedoes. Captain Hill was on the receiving end:

At 1030 on 17th March, when in a position 13 miles SW from Cape Palmas, we were struck by a torpedo in the engine room on the port side. The sea was calm with a low swell and wind SW force 2. The weather was fine and hazy

65

and the visibility good. The degaussing was on at the time and we were proceeding at a speed of 9½ knots on a course of 301°.

When Merten gave the order to fire, Hill was on the starboard side of the lower bridge, gazing at the distant coastline and feeling justifiably pleased that he had come 3,000 miles from the Cape without sight of land to pick up Cape Palmas exactly as he had calculated. The day was fine, the flying fish were at play in the *Scottish Prince*'s bow-wave, and Freetown less than two days steaming away. Captain William Hill was at peace with the world.

He crossed over to the port side and leaned on the rail to scan the empty horizon. When he saw a black object break the surface of the glassy calm sea close to port, he took it to be lone porpoise homing in on the ship to scratch its leathery skin on her barnacled hull before joining the flying fish frolicking in her bow-wave.

Hill's peace was rudely shattered when the 'porpoise' became a torpedo, which flopped back into the sea and then sheered away, its delicate gyroscopic system thrown off balance by the impact with the water. But this did not mean a reprieve for the *Scottish Prince*. Behind it came a second torpedo, its track almost invisible, and this time heading straight for the ship. Hill also now became aware of the periscope of a submarine showing immediately behind the tracks and at a distance of about 500 yards. Merten had fired a double spread, one of which had broken the surface and sheered off course, but the other was running true.

As Hill ran for the nearest ladder the torpedo struck just abaft the bridge, the ship was rocked by a massive explosion and he was all but blown from the ladder. He recovered and clawed his way up to the bridge. As *Scottish Prince* settled by the stern, an assessment of the damage showed that Karl Merten had aimed well, hitting her squarely in the engine room. Both engine room bulkheads had collapsed, and the sea was pouring in to flood not only the engine spaces, but also Nos. 3 and 4 holds. The blast had also blown the port lifeboat into a thousand pieces.

Hill wrote in his report:

As the ship was no longer manoeuvrable and there was nothing in sight I decided to lower the remaining starboard lifeboat and abandon ship.

I ordered the rafts to be put over the side and then took a muster of the crew and found that the Fourth Engineer was missing. I think he must have been killed by the explosion because there was no trace of him when I looked down the skylight, the engine room being flooded to the cylinder tops which were just a broken and twisted mass of metal.

We took to the boats about 1045 and pulled away from the ship towards the shore, when at about 1100 we saw the submarine surface well astern and to port of the ship. The submarine immediately commenced to shell my ship, using her forward gun. Altogether about 30 rounds were fired, and it appeared to us that the submarine first of all fired at our gun and then at the superstructure which soon caught fire but went out again quite quickly. The ship seemed to be settling slowly by the stern and the submarine cruised slowly round to the starboard side after she ceased firing. She seemed to cruise the whole length of the ship twice when a heavy explosion was heard, which seemed to be in the vicinity of No.3 hatch on the starboard side, and I think that the submarine may have fired another torpedo into my ship.

It must have been with great reluctance that Karl Merten expended yet another of his dwindling stock of torpedoes on the *Scottish Prince*, for being nearly 3,000 miles from his base, he had no means of knowing when this would be replenished. Following the sinking of the *Atlantis* and the *Python* by the Royal Navy in November 1941, there were no German supply ships in the area, nor were any more expected. Neither could Merten expect to rendezvous with one of the new U-tankers, the first of which would not enter service until the end of April. These 1,700-ton Type XIV boats were designed to carry 700 tons of fuel oil, torpedoes, ammunition and provisions, each being capable of supplying twelve Type VIIs with sufficient to enable them to remain operational for an extra four weeks. However, first demand on these would go to the fifteen U-boats active off the east coast of the United States and in the Caribbean, who were busily sinking American ships as fast as they came along.

Despite being twice torpedoed and heavily shelled, the *Scottish Prince* was reluctant to die, and it was 13.00 before Captain Hill and his men, lying two and a half miles off in their crowded lifeboat, saw their ship sink, going down stern-first with her bow high in the air. When she had finally gone, and the U-boat had moved out of sight, they dipped their oars and set out for the shore, which had been clearly visible at thirteen miles from the ship. On the way in, they met a local fishing canoe, which guided them in to a safe landing on the beach near Cape Palmas.

Along with survivors from the *Baluchistan* and *Ile de Batz*, they remained at Cape Palmas, guests of the Firestone Tyre Company until taken off by HMS *Wyvern* and given passage to Freetown. They returned home on the *Ulster Monarch* in company with the rest of *U-68*'s victims.

Having disposed of the *Scottish Prince*, his fourth sinking in the space of nine days, and all within a few miles of each other, Karl Merten, not unexpectedly, opted to stay close to Cape Palmas. His next victim would not be long in arriving.

Coincidentally, the British steamer *Allende* had sailed from Calcutta only twenty-four hours before the *Scottish Prince*. She was carrying 7,300 tons of cargo classed as 'general' which, being loaded on the Indian sub-continent, was probably largely composed of chests of tea and bales of jute, a mundane enough cargo, but sorely needed in Britain. Leaving Cape Town after bunkering, she was leading the *Scottish Prince* by two days, but she soon fell behind, and was overtaken on the passage north by the Prince Line ship.

Built on the River Tyne in 1928 for Morel & Company of Cardiff, the 5,080-ton *Allende* was the archetypal, no-frills tramp of her day, designed to carry the maximum amount of cargo for the minimum cost. Morel, another family concern founded in the days of sail, had prospered in the South American trade, carrying coal out from south Wales to the River Plate and grain home. By the time the First World War broke out, they were operating a fleet of eleven steamers, but between the wars they fell on hard times. In 1939, the *Allende* was one of only four vessels carrying the

Morel house flag, and by then, as a result of eleven years of hard steaming and poor maintenance, she was old before her time. On a good day with a favourable wind, she would bowl along at a steady 9.5 knots, but more often than not she was hard put to reach 8 knots, adequate for an old tramp on a voyage charter in peacetime perhaps, but when the U-boats were on the prowl this was too much like tempting Providence.

Under the command of Captain Thomas Williamson, and carrying a crew of thirty-eight including two DEMS gunners, the *Allende* had sailed from Newport, Monmouthshire on 25 February 1941, and was into her second year away from home when she left Cape Town northbound. Not that this was unusual for British tramps in the 1940s. Crews signed two-yearly articles of agreement as a matter of course; if they reached home before the articles were up, that was considered a bonus, but all too often, their ships being slow and at the mercy of the charter market, they served out the full period. This was a long time to spend away from home and family, but that was the way it was then.

The first of the Cape autumn gales was brewing up when, on 3 March, the *Allende* quit Table Bay and headed north for Freetown, but she soon left the grey skies and stormy seas behind. Nine days later, sailing under blue skies, and with the following winds of the south-east trades urging her on, she was within a few days of the Equator when the radio officer on watch handed Captain Williamson a signal from the Admiralty warning him that the U-boats had returned to the Gulf of Guinea. The position given was twenty miles due south of Cape Palmas, and presumably referred to *U-68*'s attack on the *Baluchistan*. Williamson was, at this time, steering to make a landfall off Cape Mount near Monrovia. He later wrote in his report:

On 12 March we received a signal giving us the position of an enemy submarine, but this position was not on our track. On 14th March I received a wireless message from London diverting my course and taking me right over the position in which I had previously been told an enemy submarine was operating. When I received this message I naturally assumed that the submarine had moved away from the area.

It seems most peculiar that, following the sinking of the *Baluchistan* and the *Baron Newlands* off Cape Palmas, the Admiralty appeared to be then diverting all northbound ships not away from this area, but into it, with disastrous consequences for the *Ile de Batz* and the *Scottish Prince*. The waters in the immediate vicinity of Cape Palmas had quite obviously become an area of maximum danger, which should have been avoided at all costs. Meanwhile, Karl Merton, whose score since taking command of *U-68* now stood at nine ships of 52,000 tons, had learned that all he had to do was to stay put and, courtesy of the Admiralty in London, the ships would come to him. He was ready and waiting when, six hours after the *Scottish Prince* took her last plunge, the *Allende* presented herself on the horizon. The night was dark and moonless and *U-68* approached on the surface unseen by the ship's lookouts. Captain Williamson's report goes on:

> We proceeded without incident until 1900 ATS (Ship's Time) on 17 March when in a position 20 miles south from Cape Palmas (the position in which we had been told the enemy submarine was operating) we were struck by a torpedo on the port side in the engine room.

Merten, true to form, had struck at the very heart of the ship, with the usual disastrous consequences. The massive destructive power of his torpedo not only laid open the *Allende*'s engine room to the sea, but also split her high pressure boilers, which then blew up, sending a geyser of steam and scalding water high in the air. Williamson, who was on the bridge at the time, was quick to realize the gravity of the situation, and immediately ordered the boats into the water.

The *Allende* carried four lifeboats, two full-sized boats on the boat deck, and two smaller jolly boats equipped as lifeboats abreast the bridge, ample for her thirty-eight man crew. Unfortunately, when the time came to use them, it was found that the port lifeboat had been blown away by the explosion, and the port jolly boat was jammed in its davits, and could not be lowered.

The two starboard boats were launched without mishap, and Williamson ordered his crew to abandon ship and lay off.

Meanwhile, he made a hurried inspection of the ship, during which he established that the engine room, boiler room and cross bunkers were all flooded. Of the men on watch in the engine room when the torpedo struck, the Second Engineer and four firemen, he could find no trace, and assumed they must have been killed by the blast. He was of the opinion, however, that despite the flooding, the *Allende* was not yet about to sink. But as a precaution, he boarded the starboard jolly boat, which was waiting alongside for him, and then ordered both boats to row clear of the ship. This proved to be a wise move for, as soon as they were out of the way, Merten put another torpedo into the *Allende*'s No.4 hold. This was the final blow, for strongly-built though she was, the Cardiff tramp could take no more punishment. Four minutes later, she lifted her bow high in the air, and went down stern first, sending out a tidal wave that almost swamped the two lifeboats. Williamson's report reads:

> After the ship had sunk the submarine surfaced and closed my boat and ordered us alongside. There were several men standing on the fore deck and one of them asked the name of my ship, where she was from and her port of registry, also her cargo. The officer spoke in broken English, with what I took to be a German accent, although he always answered our questions with the French 'oui'.

Unexpectedly, when Merten restarted his engines and took *U-68* back into the darkness, Williamson's lifeboat suddenly capsized, throwing him and his men into the water. It has been suggested that the U-boat's wash swamped the boat, but the reality was different. While the jolly boat was lying alongside *U-68*, no one had noticed that it was directly under the submarine's cooling water outlet which, unseen in the darkness and masked by the slap of the waves against the hull, was quietly discharging into the boat. It was only when the submarine moved away that they realized their boat was full to the gunwales. A momentary panic was all that was needed to capsize it.

The jolly boat was not heavy, and the twelve survivors were soon able to manhandle it back into an upright position.

Unfortunately, immediately the men tried to climb aboard, the boat promptly overturned again. Over the next three hours, feeling the chill of the water soaking into their bones, even though the sea temperature was near 80°F, and conscious all the time that the sharks might find them at any moment, the survivors struggled to bring their boat right way up. Four times they righted it, and four times it capsized again. Then on the fifth attempt, by which time the men were losing heart, the boat remained upright when they boarded it. Unfortunately, most of the boat gear had been lost, leaving them with only a bucket and three oars. Using the bucket, they bailed throughout the rest of the night, and by dawn on the 18th the boat was finally dry.

Williamson rested his men for an hour, allowing then to dry off in the hot sun, then they took turns at the three oars, pulling for the land, which Merten had said was eighteen miles away. Being aware that they would probably come ashore very near to the border between Liberia and Vichy French controlled Ivory Coast, Williamson steered a course a little to the west of north.

By three o'clock that afternoon the men were exhausted but they had the land in sight at about five miles. Williamson was tempted to make a bid for the shore, but no more than three hours of daylight remained and, mindful of the heavy surf which habitually broke on the beaches in this area, he decided to lay off for the night. The night that followed was, if anything, even more miserable than the previous one. The survivors had been without food or water for almost twenty-four hours – the provisions and fresh water containers having been washed out of the boat along with the rest of the gear when it capsized – and they were not only cold and wet, but hungry and thirsty. At first light on the 19th they began to row again, this time buoyed up by the prospect of being ashore within a few hours. It was just after one o'clock in the afternoon when they beached their boat and scrambled ashore.

The *Allende*'s other lifeboat did not reach land until thirty-six hours later, running onto a beach some twenty miles further to the east near San Pedro. In this boat was Bill Haynes, a nineteen year old deck boy on his first voyage to sea, who some months later told his story to a reporter of the *South Wales Argus*:

1. The 4,564-ton *Criton* (Captain Gerald Dobson). Her crew ended up in the French prisoner of war camp at Timbuktu   *Bernard de Neumann*

2. One of the Vichy French sloops that stopped and seized the unarmed ex-French prize ship *Criton*.   *Bernard de Neumann*

AVISO   AIR FRANCE 1

3. *Allende*, 5,081 tons (Captain Thomas Williamson). Sunk by *U-68* on 17 March 1942 off Cape Palmas. The survivors, prisoners of the Vichy French, suffered a 1,000 mile trek inland to a camp in Timbuktu.

Bernard de Neumann

4. Seventeen year old Wilfred Williams sailed as mess room boy in the *Allende* and survived when she was torpedoed. Note that the entry in his discharge book records that he was 'Discharged at Sea'. This was the accepted jargon for a merchant seaman's ship being sunk under him.

Ken Williams

DIS A No R261869

	WILLIAMS	5	CERTIFICATE		OF DISCHARGE		6	WILLIAMS

5. Deck boy William Haynes *(right)* with other crew members. Photo taken on board the *Allende* in 1942. William Haynes lost his life in 1943 when his ship, *Empire Tower*, was torpedoed in the North Atlantic.

Western Mail

6. *Kapitänleutnant* Axel-Olaf Loewe, commander of *U-505*.

U-Boot Archiv

7. *U-505* is commissioned at Hamburg by *Kapitänleutnant* Axel-Olaf Loewe on 26 August 1941.   *Marineschule Mürwik*

8. *Oberleutnant* Harald Lange *(centre)* and his senior officers. This was taken before *U-505* sailed on her last patrol.   *Marineschule Mürwik*

9. The graves of Chief Engineer William Souter and Able Seaman John Turnball in Timbuktu. They were recently restored on behalf of the Commonwealth War Graves Commission by Dr Tim Insoll of the Department of Art, History and Archaeology at the University of Manchester.   *Tim Insoll*

10. N.V. Van Nievelt, Goudriaan & Co.'s *Alphacca* (Captain Reindert van der Laan). She was sunk by *U-505* on 4 April 1942.   *Bas Buitendyk Collection*

11. Italian U-cruiser *Leonardo da Vinci* (*Capitano di Corvette* Gianfranco Gazzana-Priaroggia). *Aldo Fraccaroli Collection*

12. Rotterdam South America Line's 5,483-ton *Alioth* (Captain Kornelis Dik). She was sunk by the *Leonardo da Vinci* on passage from Basra to Birkenhead. *Aldo Fraccaroli Collection*

13. U-cruiser arrives at Lorient at the end of a successful patrol. Note smaller Type VII C in the background.   *Photo No. 101 IIMW-4260 Bundesarchiv, Koblenz*

14. U-cruiser surfaces to assist and question survivors from the ship she has just sunk.   *Photo No. 101 IIMW-4287 Bundesarchiv, Koblenz*

15. Replenishing coal
    bunkers in India in
    1942 was a long,
    laborious process.
    The baskets were
    carried on board
    up a specially
    rigged gangway by
    young girls, often
    no more than
    twelve years old.
    S. Lawford

16. *Korvettenkapitän*
    Karl-Friedrich
    Merten, commander
    of *U-68*.
    U-Boot Archiv

I was at the wheel when the first torpedo struck the ship towards the end of the second dog watch. We were hit amidships and everybody below was killed. I was thrown off my feet, but not badly hurt. We took to the boats, and sixteen minutes later another torpedo hit the ship, blowing her stern off, and she sank almost at once. The boat had almost filled with water, and we were on our way back to the ship to get buckets to bail her out when the second torpedo struck. After that we bailed the boat out as best we could, with a bucket, a trilby hat and a fez!

All that night the boat was waterlogged, and it was suggested that we should lighten the boat by getting out and leaving the lightest man in her to bail, but the Second Officer would not let us do that – we hadn't thought of the possibility of sharks; he had.

After the ship had gone down, the submarine came up and stopped the other boat, the jolly boat (we were in the lifeboat), and asked for particulars of the ship: her cargo, destination, etc. Then he told them to 'beat it' and waited for them to clear off before he submerged. There were 19 in our lifeboat, 12 in the jolly boat, and two on a raft. An electric storm was raging at the time, and we could see the U-boat silhouetted against the sky in the lightning. Later we lost sight of the other boat.

We made the raft fast to our boat, and after we had bailed out sufficiently we hoisted a sail; we knew we were not far from the land because we had seen it from the ship a few hours before we were hit. All night long we drifted, and at about 3 p.m. the following day we sighted land, but could not make it. So we spent another night drifting, and the following day we made the shore, 42 hours after taking to the boat. Heavy surf was breaking on the beach, and we tried to follow one huge breaker and beach the boat before the next one came up. We failed, however, and a tremendous wave came up astern and swamped the boat, so that we had to swim for the beach. We found our way to a native village, and the French governor told us we were the first English people they had seen since 1910. The beach was blistering hot.

They fed us on chicken, yams, plantains and rice, but it was cooked in the native fashion, and none of us could stomach it. We had an Arab with us who could speak a little French, and he asked them to fetch us the food and let us cook it ourselves.

In spite of Captain Williamson's efforts to avoid landing in Vichy French territory, the jolly boat came ashore on a deserted beach a few miles on the wrong side of the border between Liberia and Ivory Coast. Unwittingly, they struck out to the east, and after a trek of seven miles under the blazing sun, they came to Tabou, a small village on the northern bank of the Rivière Tabou close to Pointe William. Tabou, the largest settlement in the area, was the seat of the District Officer, boasted a mission station and post office, and was connected to the general telegraph system. Williamson wrote in his report:

There are several white Frenchmen in Tabu, but none of them could speak English. In Tabu there are French representatives of a company run by Lever Brothers, 10 or 12 French military officers and a French commandant. The wireless operator at Tabu was in communication with the British authorities in Liberia and was very pro-British.

The Frenchmen in Tabu were not pro-British, but at the same time they were very anti-Vichy and had nothing good to say about the Vichy Government, but they all detested the name of General de Gaulle.

We were not at all badly treated and were fed quite well, and although we were not actually closely guarded we were only allowed to move about in a limited area. The Commandant's house was built on the beach and we were barred from all communication or contact with this beach.

To the French inhabitants of Tabou the *Allende* survivors were something of a novelty, for they were the first British people seen in the colony for over thirty years, and accordingly they treated them with a certain amount of respect. This helped to reinforce the opinion of the survivors that it would be only a matter of

74

completing formalities before they were taken to the Liberian border, only ten miles or so away, and released. And when, eleven days after they landed, they were put aboard the French gunboat *La Surprise*, they assumed they were on their way home. They were seriously deluding themselves. As it transpired, their real ordeal was only just beginning.

Chapter Seven

The *Allende* was the fifth ship to be sunk by *U-68* in the vicinity of Cape Palmas, and increased air activity in the area was a clear warning to Karl Merten that rich though the pickings were, he had overstayed his welcome in Liberian waters. It also seemed extremely likely that the warning was already out for Allied ships to keep well clear of the cape. He decided, therefore, to move his sphere of operation south-westerly to a position due south of Freetown, and there lie in wait for traffic north and southbound around the Cape of Good Hope, which in view of the deteriorating situation in the Far East, was on the increase.

The Japanese, with overwhelming sea and air power – something which many in the West still refused to believe – had swept like a forest fire out of control through the islands of the Dutch East Indies, into Malaya and Siam, and were now deep into Burma. India, jewel in the crown of the British Empire, would be next, and it was imperative that her garrisons were reinforced without delay. Many British merchant ships unexpectedly found themselves pressed into service for the carriage of troops and equipment, among them the 5,853-ton motor vessel *Muncaster Castle*.

The *Muncaster Castle*, owned by the Lancashire Shipping Company and commanded by Captain Harold Harper OBE was, like so many British merchantmen of the day, sailing in unfamiliar waters. Her normal run was between London and Continental ports to the Gulf of Mexico, but in early 1942 she was requisitioned by the Admiralty and fitted out as an auxiliary troop transport. This entailed converting her after tween decks to troop decks. On 18 March, while *U-68* with a string of new conquests to her credit was moving south, the *Muncaster Castle* was leaving Glasgow with 265 Navy, Army and RAF personnel and 3,000 tons of military stores on board. In keeping with her new role, she was heavily armed with a 4.7-inch anti-submarine gun, a 12-pounder HA/LA, four 20-mm Oerlikons, two twin Marlin machine guns, two Lewis guns, six depth charges, four PAC rockets, and several kites to ward off low-flying aircraft. This formidable armament was manned by twelve DEMS gunners, while Captain Harper, in addition to his crew of seventy-one, had the assistance of two Royal Navy signallers, a rare luxury in a merchant ship. The *Muncaster Castle*, while still flying the Red Ensign, was in many respects a man of war. Thus equipped, she was bound for Colombo via Freetown and Cape Town, a mammoth 13,000-mile voyage unlikely to prove comfortable for the men crammed into her improvised troop accommodation.

The practice of the day was for ships outward bound for the Cape to sail in convoy from British waters as far as Freetown, and to proceed independently from then on. The justification advanced for this was that the South Atlantic could be considered a 'safe area', free from enemy activity; in reality the Royal Navy was so stretched in other spheres that it had no escorts to spare for this route. However, as a result of the mayhem being caused by the two U-Cruisers, when the *Muncaster Castle* sailed from Freetown on the afternoon of 28 March, she was in company with seven other southbound ships, and escorted by a single corvette. As the ships, one by one, rounded the black conical buoy at the entrance to the harbour, setting its bell clanging mournfully with their wakes, and headed out into the open sea, momentous events were taking place far to the north.

In the small hours of that morning, Karl Merten, who had taken up a position 290 miles to the south-west of Cape Palmas, and was patiently cruising up and down across the Cape-Freetown route, received a strange radio signal from BdU. It was addressed to all U-boats, and read:

ENGLISH SHIPS APPROACHING NAZAIRE.

Three minutes later came a second signal:

TO ALL BOATS EASTWARDS OF 29 WEST MAKE FOR BF 6510 AT ALL SPEED.

Although *U-68* was to the east of 29°W, and was therefore included in this direct order from BdU, the grid position given, BF 6510, was in the approaches to the Biscay port of St. Nazaire, some 3,000 miles to the north, and she would obviously be serving no useful purpose by complying. Merten queried the order, and was relieved to be told to remain in position, but to keep a good listening watch. He complied, but was still in the dark as to what might be happening in the Bay of Biscay. His curiosity was partially satisfied when, later that morning, *U-68*'s wireless operator received a further signal addressed to all U-boats:

ENGLISH ATTACK BY DESTROYERS AND MTBs ON NAZAIRE REPULSED.

Admiral Dönitz, from his ivory tower overlooking the U-boat pens at Lorient, was putting a brave face on things, but the truth was that the German Navy had been dealt a very heavy blow.

For some time now, Hitler had been convinced that an Allied invasion of German-occupied Norway was imminent, and all available naval units had been sent north to oppose a landing. This left the Biscay ports Brest, Lorient and St Nazaire virtually undefended, except for a few MTBs. This allowed a British force of destroyers and light coastal craft carrying 250 Commandos to approach within a few miles of St Nazaire on the night of 27 March without being challenged. The force was led by Commander R.E.D. Ryder, VC, RN in HMS *Campbeltown*, an ex-American, First World War vintage destroyer. *Campbeltown*'s bows were packed with three tons of high explosive, the object of the raid being to ram and blow up the gates of St Nazaire's dry dock, one of the largest in the world, and the only one on the Atlantic coast capable of accommodating the German battleship *Tirpitz*. The 41,000-ton *Tirpitz*, currently in Trondheim, was a threat to Allied shipping in the Atlantic, and if she could be deprived of the repair facilities offered by St Nazaire, it was unlikely that she would ever venture out again.

Campbeltown went in first, flying a German ensign, and by using German recognition signals when challenged, she was able to lead the raiding force to within one and a half miles of the port before the deception was discovered and the shore batteries opened fire. Visibility was now down to between 200 and 400 yards, adding to the confusion, and *Campbeltown* had lined up on the dock and rammed the gates before the Germans could sink her. The Commandos swarmed ashore, their object to destroy the dock installations, but by this time the German defenders, who far outnumbered the attackers, had recovered from their surprise. All but five of the landing party were killed or captured, but the main objective of the raid was achieved. The fuses of the detonation charges aboard the *Campbeltown* were set before she was abandoned, but failed to detonate as planned. It was not until 11.00 next morning that the destroyer blew up, killing 380 Germans who were on board inspecting the ship at the time, completely unaware that she was mined. The dock gates were put out of action for the rest of the war.

Oblivious to the St Nazaire raid and the effect it might have on the war at sea, the eight-ship British convoy left the West African coast astern, intent on clearing this suddenly dangerous area as soon as possible. However, a zigzag course was being steered, and as the majority of the ships were run-of-the-mill British cargo carriers no records were being broken. As was the rule, the slowest ship was dictating the speed of the convoy, which was making forward progress at no more than 7.5 knots. This was particularly frustrating for Captain Harper, as the *Muncaster Castle*'s 953 hp diesel was capable of thrusting her along at almost twice that speed. Fortunately, just after noon sights on the 30th, when the ships were 300 miles south of Freetown, on the assumption that they had left the threat of U-boat attack behind, the escorting corvette gave the order for the convoy to disperse. It was with considerable relief that Harper was able to ring for full speed. Within two hours, the *Muncaster Castle* had left the other ships astern and out of sight.

Harper was on the bridge to see the sun go down, painting the sky red and gold as it slipped below the horizon. He kept the watch while Chief Officer Rylance took his evening star sights, which revealed the *Muncaster Castle* to be two degrees north of the Equator and making a speed of 13.5 knots, even though she was zigzagging. Harper was well pleased with this, but not being

79

entirely satisfied that the danger was completely past, he decided to continue zigzagging until after midnight. The weather was fine and clear, with just enough breeze blowing from the north-east to keep the ship cool. The night promised to be a pleasant one.

In these low latitudes the twilight period is very short, and half an hour after sunset it was almost completely dark, which was the signal for Karl Merton to bring *U-68* to the surface. Since early morning he had been shadowing the small southbound convoy, being initially attracted to it by a column of smoke emanating from the tall funnel of one of the coal-burning steamers in its ranks. The escorting corvette was very much in evidence, fussily dashing from bow to bow, quarter to quarter, its Asdic no doubt constantly searching for danger. Merton stayed well out of range and watched and waited, timing the convoy's zigzag pattern, which did not vary throughout the day. When the convoy dispersed, he picked out the *Muncaster Castle* as a worthwhile target. Unusually for a dry cargo ship of her day, her main accommodation was right aft, grouped around the funnel, while her bridge house, which contained the deck officers' accommodation, was amidships. She might easily have been mistaken for an oil tanker, and that was exactly how Karl Merten identified her. He followed in her wake.

When darkness closed in, the British ship, by this time 400 miles south of Freetown, continued to zigzag about her southerly course. The atmosphere on board was relaxed, the word having gone round that they were out of the danger area. It was a warm night, and many of the servicemen, glad to escape from their cramped quarters, were gathered on the midships' hatches yarning. Others stayed below, playing cards, writing letters home, ready to land at Cape Town, now only eight days away.

Captain Harper was on the bridge, chatting to Third Officer Moody, who had the watch. Overhead, the cloudless sky was black velvet, dusted with a million twinkling stars. The haunting strains of a mouth organ playing some nostalgic melody floated up from the hatch below. It was a night when all the world seemed at peace. Then, at 20.46, just as the helmsman put the wheel to port to begin the next leg of the zigzag pattern, Karl Merten's first torpedo struck. Harper wrote in his report:

The torpedo struck about 50 ft from the stem; there was a slight smell of cordite, but I did not see any flash or flame. It was a very loud explosion and a great deal of water was thrown up on the starboard side. The hatches were blown off No.1, and four big tanks 15 ft square were blown out of the hatch into the sea.

The ship immediately settled by the head on an even keel until the fo'castle head was awash, when she seemed to steady a little.

As soon as the torpedo struck the ship I ordered the engines to be stopped and ordered the Officers to get the boats away and to stand by to pick up the rafts.

Captain Harold Harper now found himself faced with a *Titanic*-like dilemma. The rules governing the number of lifeboats a merchant ship must carry are complicated, but in the case of the *Muncaster Castle* on her current voyage, with 265 extra people on board, they were quite specific. She had, in effect, become a foreign-going passenger vessel, in which case she was required by law to carry sufficient lifeboats to accommodate all on board, passengers and crew, a law that came into being as a result of the *Titanic* disaster, when 1,500 people lost their lives because there were no lifeboats for them. But the times were far from normal, and at sea in British merchant ships the rules were being bent to meet the demands of war. Ships often sailed with their Plimsoll marks submerged, and lifeboat capacity was arbitrary. As a normal requirement, the *Muncaster Castle* carried four lifeboats, which was ample for her eighty-five man crew. In addition, in acknowledgement of the new dangers she faced, she had four large wooden life-rafts mounted on quick-release chutes. To accommodate her servicemen passengers in case of emergency, the Admiralty had put on board twenty-five small wooden floats, which did little to enhance their chances of survival in tropical waters.

Captain Harper's report goes on:

We got the four boats safely away after one of the Indian crew had let one of the falls go with a run, but the boat was not seriously damaged. The boats stood by at a short distance and

81

I ordered the troops to abandon ship. . . About 12 men climbed on to each big raft and three men sat on the small buoyant floats. The four large buoyant tanks which were part of the cargo stowed in No.1 hatch had been blown through the hatchway and overboard and these proved a most useful addition to our life saving equipment. The remainder of those on board were accommodated in the boats.

Everyone left the ship with the exception of the Chief Engineer, Chief Officer, two Army doctors and the Chief Wireless Operator. They remained on board to try and help one of the soldiers who was asleep on No.2 hatch when the first torpedo struck the ship and was blown into the air. When he came down he became jammed between the topping lift wire and the end of the foremast. He was fully conscious although one of his legs had been blown off and he was shouting to us to get him down. I called to him to slide down the topping lift to the deck, but he said he could not do so as both his arms were broken. I sent for the Army doctors and one of them asked to be hoisted up to the man in order to give him morphia, but before he could do anything at 2110 a second torpedo struck the ship amidships on the starboard side, and at 2111, about a minute later, the ship sank.

As the *Muncaster Castle* started to go down, Harper and the five others who had stayed with him had to make the agonizing decision to abandon the injured man to his fate in order to save their own lives. They floated off the ship on the one remaining buoyant raft, and were no more than ten feet clear when she slipped below the waves.

Meanwhile Karl Merten had brought *U-68* to the surface, and called to the nearest lifeboat to come alongside. This boat was under the command of Cadet Bromfield, who was asked the usual questions; What ship? What tonnage? Where bound? How many crew? Although Bromfield answered truthfully, much to his credit, he omitted to say that his ship had been carrying 265 military personnel. Merten seemed satisfied with his replies, and before leaving gave Bromfield a course and distance to steer for the nearest land.

Captain Harper and his party of five, clinging precariously to their small raft, drifted for nearly an hour before being picked up by one of the lifeboats. Harper then transferred to his own designated boat and took stock of the situation. The four lifeboats, each with some fifty men in them, were hopelessly overcrowded, while there were fifteen men clinging to each of the large tanks from the cargo, twelve men on each of the big rafts and, so far as he could see, forty or so distributed around the small floats, two or three to a float. He also ascertained that one of his radio officers and four Indian crew members were missing, along with eleven Army other ranks, six RAF personnel and two Naval ratings. Merten's torpedo had exacted a heavy toll.

In view of the small fleet of heavily overloaded craft under his command, Harper decided against making for the land, which was 320 miles to the north. An SOS had been sent prior to finally abandoning the *Muncaster Castle*, so he deemed the wisest course of action was to stay put and await rescue. He distributed the men in the boats as fairly as possible, lashed the rafts together, and waited for the night to pass. Fortunately, the weather held fair, with only a light breeze, but the clouds had gathered, and there were frequent heavy showers. For the men on the rafts, in particular, the rain was a blessing. No one went thirsty, but the night was very cold and, as most of the survivors were in light tropical clothing and neither the boats nor the rafts had any protection from the rain, by the time the dawn came on the 31st they were all suffering.

As soon as it was light enough, Harper instituted a rota, by which those in the boats took a turn on the rafts, not a very popular move with those in the boats, but everyone cooperated. The lifeboats and the large rafts were well provisioned, but with so many men to feed, and there being no guarantee that rescue would come soon, Harper set the rations at one biscuit and one teaspoonful of pemmican per man in the morning, and one biscuit and a piece of chocolate at night.

With the sunrise, the clouds of the night melted away, and once more the Equatorial sun blazed down out of a hard blue sky. Those in the lifeboats made makeshift awnings from the boat covers, which protected them from the full heat of the sun, but the suffering of those unfortunate enough to be on the rafts increased as the day wore on. Harper did his best to ease their lot by bringing them into the boats for a spell, but this was a difficult operation, the smaller rafts being prone to capsizing.

As the day wore on and there was no sign of a rescue vessel, Harper began to give thought to trying to reach the coast, but the odds against success seemed too great. The lifeboats and the four big rafts had sails, but the small rafts would have to be towed. In any event, the wind was in the north-east, against them, and they would be unlikely to make much progress, let alone sail 320 miles. If, and when, the motley collection of boats and rafts reached the West African shore, it was unlikely that anyone on board would still be alive.

Another miserable night passed, and by the time the sun rose again on the first day of April, the survivors, lashed by the rains at night, roasted by the hot sun during daylight, and now suffering from lack of a good meal, were in a sorry state. Then came the first sign that their SOS had been heard and a search was in progress. Captain Harper wrote in his report:

On 1st April about 0840 we sighted an aircraft so burned one of the new red smoke floats, but the aircraft was far away on the horizon some 15 miles to the S.W. and travelling north-wards, so failed to see us. About one hour later at 0950 we sighted another aircraft and burned another red smoke float, but this aircraft was also a long way off and failed to see us. We sighted a third aircraft at 1115, also a long way from us, which failed to see us.

At 1240 we sighted an aircraft to the S.W. travelling in a northerly direction and we burned further smoke floats. This aircraft sighted our smoke floats and altered course towards us. He circled round the boats and rafts three times and then dropped some very small smoke bombs well clear of us to show the wind direction. Twice the aircraft tried to land, but the sea was too rough, so the pilot dropped a note saying that the sea was too rough for him to land and that he would send help to us.

84

For a brief while, as the flying boat circled them, the survivors felt that they were not alone, but when the plane flew away, the roar of its engines fading, and the silence of the open sea descending on them once again, they began to lose heart. Their fate was made worse by the arrival of the sharks. There may be those foolhardy adventurers and documentary film makers, who will swim with the sharks, but the average seafarer, the man who makes a living by the sea, has an abject fear of these loathsome creatures – and not without good reason. The sharks that found the *Muncaster Castle* survivors, great hammerheaded brutes, were quick to demonstrate. They surrounded the little flotilla, circling menacingly, then moved in to snap at the oars of the lifeboats as they rowed around relieving the men on the rafts. Unable to achieve anything by this, they turned on the buoyant floats, charging at them and attempting to capsize them. Only in one case did they succeed, and three terrified men were thrown into the water. Fortunately, they managed to scramble back onto the float before the sharks could attack them.

It was with immense relief that, at 18.00 that evening, just as the sun was about to set on them heralding the start of another miserable night, the survivors saw a ship approaching. She was the Greek vessel *Ann Stathatos*, bound for Freetown, which, purely by chance, had sighted the boats. She stopped and offered assistance. Captain Harper's first priority was to get the men off the rafts, for they were in a bad way, many of them badly burned by exposure to the Equatorial sun. In all, the *Ann Stathatos* took on board 239 men, leaving ninety men distributed between the four lifeboats. These men had volunteered to stay with Harper to await the arrival of the Royal Navy, as he was concerned that the Navy might rush to their rescue and find they had been brought out on a wild goose chase. While this might be a commendable attitude to take, it could well have ended in disaster for the men in the boats. Fortunately, the pilot of the Sunderland who had attempted to land earlier in the day was as good as his word. At 08.20 next morning, 2 April, the corvette HMS *Aubretia* found the boats. The remaining survivors were taken on board, and after sinking the four large tanks from the *Muncaster Castle*'s cargo, which were judged to be a danger to navigation, the corvette returned to Free-town, arriving on 6 April.

After the rescue, Captain Harper commented:

> The whole of the crew, with the exception of the officers, were Indians, they all behaved very well indeed. They soon settled down and took their turns on the rafts and gave no trouble at all.
>
> Chief Officer Rylance remained on board with me until we were struck by the second torpedo which sank the ship. Second Officer T.R. Jackson and Third Officer Moody both behaved very well indeed and were of great assistance to me; their conduct in the boats was a fine example to the men in their boats.
>
> Lieutenant Taylor, RNVR, who was in charge of the Naval ratings was also a great help to us. He kept the Service ratings together and showed great powers of organization and leadership – all Servicemen under his charge behaved magnif-icently.

In delivering the *coup de grâce* to the *Muncaster Castle*, Karl Merten had used up his last torpedo. He was also running short of fuel, and with no means of replenishing either oil or torpedoes, he was forced to make for home, arriving back in Lorient on 13 April. In a patrol lasting just sixty-two days *U-68* had sunk seven ships with a total tonnage of 39,350 tons gross. Taking into consideration the area in which she was operating, this was no mean achievement, and Merten and his crew were deserving of the warm welcome accorded them when they came alongside the quay in Lorient. But they would not be allowed to idle in port for long. There was much work for the Type IXC boats to do.

Following the tremendous success of his U-boats off the east coast of the United States and in the Caribbean – in the first two months of 1942 they had destroyed 350,000 tons of shipping, mostly American – Admiral Dönitz was anxious to strike swiftly, and as hard as possible in this area before the Americans recovered from their initial shock. This he was prepared to do even at the expense of neglecting the North Atlantic convoys – for a while, at least. To this end, he was pressing into service even the Type VIICs, which, by cutting down on fresh water and provisions in order to carry more fuel, and crossing the Atlantic at an economical speed, were able to operate off America for up to two weeks before returning home. This meant increased hardship for the U-boats' crews, but there was much glory to be won. In April 1942, to be sent to the American theatre was every German submariner's dream of the good life.

Although the United States Navy had been in the war for over four months, and prior to that had been unofficially escorting British convoys in the North Atlantic, it seemed unable to cope with the situation prevailing in its own waters. Dönitz's U-boats were reaping a ridiculously easy harvest on America's doorstep, sinking ships at will, and threatening to bring all shipping movements on the coast to a standstill. The Royal Navy had sent ten corvettes and twenty-four anti-submarine trawlers – which it could ill afford to spare – to assist in organizing and escorting convoys, and this was having some effect in easing the situation, but not one U-boat had yet been sunk.

The first sweet taste of success for the US Navy came on the night of 13 April, as Karl Merten, his last report written, was settling down for a welcome night of uninterrupted sleep in Lorient.

U-85, a Type VIIB commanded by *Oberleutnant* Eberhard Greger, was new to American waters and three and a half weeks out of St Nazaire, had found her first victim of the patrol, the 4,904-ton Norwegian motor vessel *Christian Knudsen*, within sight of Cape Hatteras. Encouraged by his success, Greger decided to move closer to the coast. On the night of the 13 April, *U-85* was idling on the surface near the entrance to Chesapeake Bay, when she was surprised by the US destroyer *Roper*. The water was very shallow, and a crash dive could have ended in disaster, so Greger opted to fight it out on the surface. This was a miscalculation, for *U-85*'s single 88-mm was no match for *Roper*'s battery of 5-inch guns. The submarine was sunk by the American destroyer's first salvo, leaving most of her crew struggling in the water. This should have been the end of it, but for some reason difficult to explain,

Roper charged in and dropped a pattern of eleven depth charges amongst the German survivors. This has always been regarded as an atrocity by the U-boat men, and although it was certainly, at best, an example of excess enthusiasm, it also signalled that the US Navy was in the business of killing U-boats. Although the tide was not yet turning against Dönitz's men in the Atlantic, it was certainly nearing the high water mark.

Chapter Eight

Four weeks had passed since the morning of 6 March, when Axel Loewe found the heavily-laden Norwegian tanker *Sydhav* in his sights. The sinking of the tanker only eleven hours after they had sent the *Benmohr* to the bottom led *U-505*'s crew to the premature conclusion that they had struck gold in the Gulf of Guinea. Not surprisingly, they looked forward with anticipation to more of the same thing, but they were to be disappointed.

U-505 was 450 miles west-south-west of Cape Palmas when she sank the *Sydhav*, and as soon as he had completed moving his spare torpedoes below, Loewe decided to go further south, and then begin an east-west patrol across the Freetown-Cape route. So began what transpired to be a long and fruitless search, full of frustration and boredom. At times, small French convoys were sighted close inshore, hugging the coast, but Loewe was under strict orders from BdU not to interfere with these ships. Crewman Hans Goebeler wrote some years later:

> All the built-in frustrations and petty feuds of the past few weeks would come flooding back. Suddenly, once again you became conscious of the heat and the noise and the stench of whatever shit our cook was preparing for dinner.

Loewe did his utmost to keep his men occupied with drills and maintenance, but there were factors beyond his control. An entry in his log for 9th March reads:

Temperatures at 1200.

Outside air 30.5℃. Sea Temp 28℃.
In boat 31℃, Diesel Room 36℃, Electric Room 38℃.

Running at 7 knots on diesel-electric. This gives better ventilation below and improves conditions for crew. In sunshine temps 1–2 degrees higher, at night 1 degree lower.

The days and nights dragged by, enlightened only by a signal from Dönitz to all U-boat commanders on the 14th congratulating them on over 1 million tons of enemy shipping sunk in the last two months. It was on that day that Loewe, despairing of the lack of likely targets in the area, and determined to join in this rich harvest, decided to move to the east and nearer to the coast. Next morning he received orders from BdU to remain where he was, to maintain radio silence, and to 'look for traffic'. He was only too happy to keep radio silence and to search for the enemy, but he had no intention of staying put. As it turned out, Loewe's decision to move nearer to the land paid early dividends. On the morning of the 16th *U-505* was approaching the coast of Liberia. Her war diary for the time reads:

16.3

0800 EU 4841 Very good visibility.

0805 Steamer appears from rain squall astern. On course for Freetown. Unfortunately it is too light to attack on the surface. Close in.

0843 Smoke cloud bearing 070 degrees 10 miles.

1200 EU 4475 Day's run on surface 210 miles.

1327 ET 6695 Dived to attack. Steamer makes large alteration of course and increases speed to 12 knots

1452 As I approach a favourable firing position the steamer alters course and comes beam on. Double shot Tubes 2 and 1, depth 5 metres. Both miss. Sea as smooth as glass.

1534 Surfaced. Steamer in view again for short time. Gave chase.

1840 Alarm. Attack frustrated by aircraft overhead. We are probably not seen.

1920 Surfaced. I am 1½ hours astern of the steamer, which is now out of sight.

2000 ET 6647 Smoke cloud still visible in the twilight, but no longer visible after dark.

The unexpected appearance of a patrolling aircraft foiled *U-505*'s attack on the unidentified ship, but served to warn Loewe that the game was up for the U-boats in the Gulf of Guinea, and that from now on they would not be allowed to operate against easy targets without repercussion. This was confirmed next day, when *U-505* was 200 miles further to the east, and running at an economical 8 knots on the surface. Only the sharp eyes of her lookouts saved her when a vengeful Sunderland roared in from the west. Surfacing after an hour, Loewe found himself within sight of an anti-submarine trawler and a corvette. The hunt was on in earnest for those who dared to bring the war to the quiet waters of the Gulf of Guinea.

Over the weeks that followed Loewe found himself chasing shadows. The British authorities in West Africa, shocked into action by the savaging of their shipping off Cape Palmas by *U-68*, had at last banned ships from sailing alone and unescorted. They began holding them in port while they tried desperately to arrange convoys. Given the scarcity of suitable escort vessels in the area, some ships were considerably delayed..

Constantly harassed by hostile aircraft, Axel Loewe continued to trawl determinedly back and forth across the Cape sea lane, remaining on the surface as much as possible to give his lookouts the maximum horizon. His search for the enemy proved fruitless. Only two ships came in sight, the Portuguese steamer *Quanza* on the evening of the 24th, and the *Pungue,* another Portuguese, shortly after noon on the 26th. Although they might well have been carrying cargo for the Allies, both these ships were flying a neutral flag, and Loewe was obliged to let them pass.

On the day that news came through of the attack on St Nazaire by British destroyers *U-505* was 220 miles south-west of Freetown. She was cruising on the surface at 6 knots in excellent visibility when Loewe's determination to search out enemy ships almost cost him his boat. The war diary reads:

28.3

1644 Aircraft bearing 300 degrees at 8000 metres on SW'ly course. I try to escape on the surface before he comes too close. Very good visibility. Isolated cumulus clouds.

1650 Dived to 40 metres. Aircraft drops bombs which are not well aimed. I go to 80 metres. Aircraft was twin-engined coastal scout type, probably Anson.

1900 Surfaced. It is pointless for me to remain in this area, as I have been spotted.

2030 Alarm. Aircraft at 8000 metres approaching from the north. He has probably not seen us.

2105 Surfaced.

2116 Alarm. Aircraft bearing 180 degrees. Passing by.

2156 Surfaced. Bright moonlight. Shadows on horizon bearing 090 degrees. Possibly destroyers. Alter course to pass 2000 metres astern. Another aircraft seen.

2246 Alarm. Fast revving engine heard by hydrophone. Uncertain bearing.

2325 Surfaced. Nothing in sight. Steered to the south.

29.3

0130 ET 9198 Shadow bearing 180 degrees. Freighter partially hidden in rain squall. I prepare to attack, but when she is abeam at 6000 metres she turns away. I dive. I fire and miss. There is an air of disappointment in the boat.

0550 Surfaced after moon has set. I intend to attack on the surface. Apparently, she has seen me, however, and sends out a call for help. Aircraft with Leigh Light dives, and is looking for me.

0620 Alarm. I go to 20 metres and run away. Asdic signals heard. I dive to 100 metres.

0648 At 40 metres four depth charges or bombs explode. I assume either from the aircraft or from the steamer, which may be an auxiliary or U-boat hunter. Asdic transmissions cease after 10 minutes.

0800 ET 9162 Surfaced to recharge batteries and air boat. The boat and crew behaved very well under their first baptism of fire. I decide to operate in the shipping routes further south. I must first reload.

There is no other record of *U-505*'s encounter, but it seems most likely that she had unwisely tried to sink an armed merchant cruiser which was operating in conjunction with a Sunderland. Loewe was very lucky to escape unscathed, and beat a hasty retreat to the south. He crossed the Equator on the afternoon of the 31st, and that night received a message from BdU warning him to look out for a convoy approaching Freetown from the USA between 1 and 3 April. *U-505* was by this time 500 miles from Freetown, and she was having trouble with her diesels. On the surface at full speed, she might have been able to intercept the convoy within thirty-six hours, but only at the expense of burning a great deal of fuel, and being seven weeks out of Lorient, her tanks were running low. Loewe estimated he had only fourteen days operational fuel left, after which he faced a 2,500-mile return passage with little prospects of refuelling. He opted to continue to move westwards at an economical speed in the hope that something might come his way. His patience was to be rewarded sooner than expected.

Although war had come to the United States of America, the San Francisco-registered *West Irmo*, owned by the American West Africa Line, was on her normal peacetime run, carrying 4,000 tons of general cargo from New York to Takoradi and Lagos. Under the command of Captain Torleif Selness, and with a crew of forty-five, which included eight Naval Armed Guard gunners, the 5,775-ton *West Irmo* had crossed the Atlantic alone, reaching Freetown on 31 March. She sailed again early next morning, but this time not alone. She was under escort by the 560-ton anti-submarine trawler HMS *Copinsay*. The trawler, armed with one 4-inch gun and with a top speed of only 11 knots, was not an escort to inspire great confidence but, Captain Selness consoled himself, she was at least equipped with Asdic and depth charges, and should be able to detect and scare off any attacking U-boat.

As was her usual custom, the *West Irmo* made a call at the anchorage port of Marshall, thirty miles east of Monrovia, where she picked up fifty-five cargo workers. In the 1940s, cargo handling facilities in the West African ports were primitive, and it was routine for ships to take on labour either in Freetown, or at a Liberian port. They were invariably members of the Kru tribe, more often than not the entire adult male population of a Liberian village, led by the village head man. While they were on board ship, they lived in tents on the hatch tops, carrying out ship maintenance at sea, and in port loading and discharging cargo and rigging cargo gear. For the predominantly white crews that manned the ships the boarding of the 'Kru Boys' signalled a welcome relief from heavy work in the excessive heat and humidity of West Africa. For the shipowner it meant cheap, willing labour and less overtime for the white crew. And for the Kru Boys themselves, normally un-employed for months on end, even though they were paid only shillings a day, it was an opportunity to earn a small fortune in Liberian village terms. It seemed that everyone concerned benefited from this arrangement – that is except the ship's deck officers, who found themselves working eighteen hours a day supervising the largely unskilled Kru labour.

The *West Irmo*, having anchored off Marshall for the night, sailed early on 2 April, bound for her first discharging port,

Takoradi on the Gold Coast, 600 miles to the east. The American freighter, although built in 1919, could still manage a credible 11 knots. Her escort, HMS *Copinsay*, on the other hand, was struggling to keep up. In view of the danger believed to be lurking off Cape Palmas, the ships were routed to pass some 120 miles to the south of the cape. This added another three hours steaming to the passage, but it seemed a wise precaution. Unfortunately, this turned out not to be the case. *U-68* was by this time long gone from the area, already half way between the Cape Verde and Canary Islands, and heading for Biscay. *U-505*, however, was 240 miles south-west of Cape Palmas, and moving east. Unknown to Axel Loewe and Captain Selness, they were on converging courses, and would meet very soon. Loewe's war diary for 2 April reads:

1622 FF 1318 Steamer sighted bearing 300°. Passing by on S'ly course. Very good visibility, sky completely overcast.
   I move nearer. Steamer passes ahead on approximately 150° course. She alters to 090°. Gives off clouds of smoke, and appears to be stopped. To port of her another smoke cloud, but cannot make out what it is.

It would appear that Loewe had sighted HMS *Copinsay*, then carrying out a sweep to the south of the *West Irmo*; a sweep which failed to sight the U-boat, probably because she was then too far off. Carefully, Loewe moved closer, remaining on the surface, but trimmed down so that the casings were awash, and only the conning tower above water.

1820 Steamer on course 090° to 100°. Will attack after dark.

2050 Begin attack on surface. Move nearer to the steamer then stop and wait.

2150 FF 1337 Double shot from Tubes 2 and 4, depth 4 metres, range approximately 1000 metres. Steamer still on 090° course. Making about 9 knots. Both torpedoes miss. Moon rises. It is full and it is very light. Prepare to attack again.

95

Unbelievably, both *Copinsay* and the *West Irmo* were completely unaware that they were under attack. Although it was dark, the moon was full, and visibility was very good. It may be that both ships were so far to the south of the normal traffic lane around Cape Palmas, that they had relaxed their vigilance. The weather deteriorated as the night wore on, and by midnight it was blowing south-south-west force 3 and rain squalls were closing in. But this did not deter Loewe, who was manoeuvring for another attack. This was a slow process, and it was early on the morning of the 3rd before he was in a favourable position.

> 0230 I get ahead of the steamer. For the last half hour she has been steering 110°. I have her in my sights when she is blotted out by a heavy rain squall. Now begins a hunt that will last for 2 hours. I see her at 100 metres, but lose contact again.

The chase went on throughout the night, and all the following day, with Loewe's patient efforts to get into a favourable firing position being constantly frustrated by poor visibility caused by heavy rain squalls.

All this time, the *West Irmo* and her escorting trawler were totally oblivious to the fact that they were being shadowed. When darkness set in again at about 19.00 on the 3rd, the two ships were on a course of 057° at about 10.5 knots, completely blacked out and maintaining strict radio silence. *Copinsay* was keeping station one and a half to two miles on the *West Irmo*'s starboard quarter. The weather had deteriorated further, the rain squalls being heavier and more frequent, the wind blowing force 4 and whipping up a rough sea that soon had the little *Copinsay* in trouble. An ex-Icelandic waters' fisherman, she was built for rougher weather, but her engines were giving trouble, and she was falling behind the American ship. As soon as it was fully dark, she signalled the *West Irmo* to slow down to allow her to catch up. The stage was set for a tragedy. A report issued by the Office of the Chief of Naval Operations, Washington states:

> The order was to proceed at top speed until about 1900 GMT when the *West Irmo* was ordered to reduce speed to permit

96

the escort to catch up with her. Speed was reduced to 7 knots. Thirty-five minutes later a torpedo struck the fore part of No.1 hold, starboard side and tore the whole bow out of the vessel. The hull in way of No.2 hatch was buckled and fractured. A hole 20 feet long and 18 feet deep resulted. The engines were immediately stopped and rudder turned right. The Second Officer saw the torpedo track and the Gunnery Officer stated he saw two tracks, one torpedo passing ahead of the ship. The *Copinsay* was immediately notified by Morse lamp that the *West Irmo* had been torpedoed. The submarine was estimated to be bearing 327° true based on the Second Officer's report. The *Copinsay* proceeded around the ship's bow to eastward then northward six or seven miles where depth bombs were dropped. No counter action was attempted by the gun's crew of the *West Irmo*.

U-505's war diary gives this version of the attack:

2132 Shoot from Tube 1 (3 metres) and Tube 3 (4 metres). Range of both 800 metres. Turn under full helm and shoot from Tube 5, depth 3 metres, range 700 metres. Hit observed beneath bridge. Steamer sinks quickly by the head. Two detonations heard on hydrophone.

Steamer radios SOS SSS, position and name *West Irmo* 5775 (American). I run away from the escort, and because of the rising moon the steamer has vanished in the dark.

I think she must have gone down very fast. Heard four heavy explosions. Not depth charges.

The CNO report states:
The *West Irmo* was abandoned at 2005 GMT by its 44 crew members, including the gun's crew, and 55 Africans (Kroo tribesmen from Liberia). Ten Africans who were seated on No.1 hatch were killed when the torpedo struck. The survivors were taken aboard the *Copinsay* at 2130 GMT. On April 4 an effort was made to tow the *West Irmo* stern first. She was finally abandoned at 1910. Her fore deck was awash

97

and her rudder and propeller out of the water. A depth charge was dropped after abandonment which resulted in her sinking in 2,500 fathoms. Confidential codes were thrown overboard in a steel box immediately after the ship was torpedoed.

The submarine was not seen at any time.

An investigation has been ordered concerning the protection afforded the ss *West Irmo* by HMS *Copinsay*.

To be fair to *Copinsay*, she had done her utmost to protect the *West Irmo*, but the circumstances had not been in her favour. It was dark at the time of the attack and, without radar, the trawler was totally reliant on the vigilance of her lookouts. Furthermore, *U-505* was trimmed down with very little showing above the surface, and would have been all but impossible to spot against a backdrop of rain squalls and tumbling white horses. And even if the U-boat had been seen, she could easily have outrun *Copinsay* – and perhaps outgunned her – if it came to a fight. The *West Irmo* was fortunate in that she did not lose a single man from her crew . But it had turned out to be a bad voyage for her Kru boys, who were only on board to earn a few pounds to take back to their families in impoverished Liberia. Ten of their number, who really had no part in this war, died on that dark, rainy night in the Gulf of Guinea.

After torpedoing the *West Irmo*, anxious to clear the area as quickly as possible, Loewe made off into the night at full speed on the surface. *U-505* was then 180 miles to the south-west of Cape Palmas, and with her fuel tanks running low, it was time to think about the long voyage back to Biscay. But Loewe was reluctant to return without adding to his rather meagre score, and he decided to turn west and make for a position 150 miles south of Cape Palmas, remaining in that area for a while before finally saying goodbye to the Gulf of Guinea. Running at 8 knots on the surface to conserve fuel, he reached that position at 14.00 on 4 March. To his surprise and delight, ten minutes later a thin pencil of smoke was seen rising from the horizon about thirteen miles to the south. Loewe altered course to investigate.

The Dutch coal-burning steamer *Alphacca* was bound northwest on the penultimate leg of what, in the midst of war, had been a not unpleasant voyage. Sailing from the east coast port of Hull in England at the end of December 1941, following in the wake of the lavender-hulled Union Castle liners around the Cape of Good Hope calling at the South African ports to discharge, turning round at Lourenco Marques in Portuguese East Africa, and loading again at the same ports westbound. At Cape Town, she had refilled her coal bunkers, for her boiler furnaces were hungry, consuming forty tons a day at sea, and sailed for Freetown on 23 March.

The 5,759-ton *Alphacca,* owned by Van Nievelt, Goudriaan & Co.'s Stoomvaart Mij., like so many of her Dutch sisters, was a fugitive from her own home port of Rotterdam, having escaped the clutches of the Germans to take refuge in a British port. There she had been taken over by the Netherland Shipping Committee, formed to look after the 800 Dutch vessels operating under British control. Commanded by Captain Reindert van der Laan, the *Alphacca* carried a crew of fifty, and on this northbound voyage had eight passengers on board.

The passage north from the Cape was marred by a tragic accident four days out of Cape Town, when an explosion in the ship's refrigerator room killed Chief Engineer Jacob de Vries and Second Engineer Pieter Kooy, and seriously injured Third Engineer Arie van Wijngaarden. The dead men were buried at sea the next day, leaving a pall of gloom over the *Alphacca* that would take a long time to lift.

The *Alphacca* was sighted from *U-505*'s conning tower at 15.00 on the 4th. She was steering a zigzag pattern around a westerly course at about 11 knots. Loewe dived to periscope depth, and gave chase, intending to attack after dark. He surfaced after sunset, and closed in on his prey in the short tropical twilight. Those keeping watch on the bridge of the Dutch ship were blissfully unaware of the danger. At 19.29, having closed the range to 800 metres without detection, Loewe aimed carefully, and fired one torpedo.

Twenty-nine year old Third Officer Aloysius Jansen describes what followed:

I kept the middle watch and went to sleep at 1900. Because of the fact that the West African coast in that period of the

99

war was riddled with U-boats, I slept fully dressed on the couch in my cabin. I always had my suitcase ready within arm's reach, filled with my papers, playing cards and 2000 cigarettes.

At about 1930 I heard a tremendous bang followed by loud noises and 'falling water', whilst the engine was racing like hell. I took my suitcase and went on deck to see what had happened. The ship developed a trim over the poop because the torpedo had hit us aft in Hold No.5. The lights went out, but the emergency system worked properly which was a good thing because it was pitch dark that night. The weather was fair, the sea calm, no wind. There was no panic and everybody went to their respective boats. The poor guys living aft in the poop deck quarters could not escape because the impact of the torpedo had destroyed the exits of the poop deck superstructure. They all must have drowned when the *Alphacca* foundered a few minutes later, stern first.

Meanwhile the ship was sinking slowly whilst the trim over her stern increased. We, the survivors owe much to the regular boat drills the Captain ordered. The four lifeboats were permanently hanging in their tackle, secured against bumping to the hull with lashings and pelican hooks for quick releasing. Seven minutes after the torpedo hit, the *Alphacca* disappeared under the waves. I herewith wish to state that owing to the fact that no panic arose and the fact that the lifeboats, davits and tackle were in very good shape, the ship abandoning procedures were carried out smoothly and quickly.

After the boats had been lowered into the water we tried to join the others, which we did by using our flashlights. Soon we were together and held a roll call, which revealed 16 men missing. They must have lost their lives in the poop quarters. All of a sudden the sub emerged as a result of which a little panic arose because we were afraid we would be shot, as unfortunately has happened so often. But everything went straight, they only asked us whether we needed something. They even offered us to take the wounded on board. It's understandable that no answers were given.

Of the sinking, Axel Loewe's war diary records:

> 2129 Shot with Tube No.1, depth 4 metres, range 800 metres. Hit on stern. Steamer begins to go down by the stern rapidly.
>
> Apart from tuning signals, ship has not transmitted anything. Later I approach lifeboats. It was the 5759 BRT Dutch ship *Alphacca* from Cape Town to Freetown with a cargo of wool. The crew, who have all abandoned ship safely, thank me for the help. The boats are well equipped. We speak first in English, then in German. It is a pity that we fight against people who speak our language. This is the irony of fate. We wish each other bon voyage.

A report lodged with the Netherlands Consul in Freetown, which was probably written by Captain van der Laan, gives another account of the meeting:

> After the ship foundered, the sub approached us and requested us to give the ship's name and nationality, and asked whether we had wounded men and whether we had sufficient water and provisions. Further, they wished to know whether we had a compass, and gave us the course for Cape Palmas. Prior to submerging, they wished us bon voyage.

Third Officer Jansen's report continues:

> The spirit in the lifeboats was rather low, but nevertheless decisions had to be made. We decided to group the boats two-by-two, the two motor boats each towing a lifeboat. Our position was known, i.e. about 150 miles south of Cape Palmas, a little village on the Liberian coast close to the border with Ivory Coast. We set course for Cape Palmas allowing for a strong westerly current. The first night we motored, and later we hoisted the sails when the weather was right. We strictly rationed the water and ship's biscuits from the beginning, as we did not know how long we had to sit in the boats. The cigarettes I had in my suitcase added very

much to the mood of the men; we even played cards! We rationed ourselves to one (Dutch) gin glass of water and one biscuit per day, which was not much, but sufficient to survive for a couple of days. Generally speaking, the spirit in the boats was reasonable, apart from a few incidents, whereby one of the seamen demanded to have as much water as a severely wounded man was given to ease his suffering. I made a quick end to this awkward misbehaviour by threatening the man with a boat axe.

At daylight, we threw all spare gear overboard in order to create a little more room for ourselves. Thanks to the splendid weather, the four boats were able to stick together. During the daytime the heat was almost unbearable. Before long men were suffering the misery of sunburn and blistering. The night hours lasted so long, that in the end we were happy when dawn came, in spite of the heat which we knew was soon to come. So we limped northward. A position could not be taken due to the absence of a sextant; the rapid abandonment of the ship had not left us time to snap up an instrument. After a few days we were all tormented by thirst, and I saw that some of the men were considering drinking sea water. I had to use all my persuasiveness to stop them doing so.

Very often I was asked 'Mister Mate, how long to go yet?', but only on the evening of the seventh day did I have the confidence to answer, 'I hope tomorrow.' On observing the swell I had noticed a certain backwash, but didn't mention this because I didn't want to raise false hopes. However, at daybreak next morning we indeed sighted a coastline ahead, which put us all in a good mood. I can assure you that this was indeed a great relief to all of us. Because the weather and sea were very calm, we started up the lifeboat engines again, and around 1500 we were approaching the coast. A surfboat with black oarsmen and a white man, who appeared to be a French officer, came out. They came from a tiny village on the coast called Tabou, which is in Ivory Coast, very close to the Liberian border. The Frenchman warned us that we should not land there as the country was occupied by the Germans, and that as a result we would be immediately interned and extradited to Germany. The French officer told us 'The Jerries are now enjoying their siesta', and advised us to put to sea again without delay and to shape a course for Cape Palmas, 30 miles to the west. I was very pleased that everybody, apart from the troublemaker, who wanted to go ashore, agreed to the officer's suggestion; I refused to let the thirsty seaman go. Thirty miles is quite a distance in an open boat, but with rescue imminent, morale improved considerably. I also increased the water and food ration.

That night we were confronted with adverse weather conditions. A thunderstorm and sudden wind and rain squalls made us anxious that the boats would take on too much water, but the good side of the situation was that we could collect and drink fresh water, which we needed so badly. So the next day came and another night. We couldn't find out how much progress we made, but finally we saw the faint lights of Cape Palmas. Immediately I signalled with the lamp – and got an answer! They asked us who we were and advised us not to sail too close to the coast because of numerous rocky patches. And so we approached Cape Palmas. They signalled that surfboats would come out in order to pick us up because it was too dangerous for lifeboats to enter the breakers. Do I have to explain how we felt when we stepped ashore on the beach? We were welcomed with cold drinks handed to us by terrific friendly and helpful people. There was a doctor for the wounded and a good bed for all of us. This was really a wonderful experience after eight days of sitting on hard wooden thwarts.

After staying about two weeks in Cape Palmas, we embarked on board a French destroyer, which brought us to Freetown, Sierra Leone. Some time later, on April 27th, we were ordered to join the Dutch ship s.s. *Meliskerk,* which brought us to the UK. We encountered much friendliness and cordiality from the residents of Cape Palmas, in particular one Dutchman and a number of Americans.

Emboldened by his success in finding two targets for his torpedoes in the space of twenty-four hours, and being assured that the

Alphacca had not used her radio before going down, Axel Loewe decided to remain in the vicinity of Cape Palmas. This proved to be unwise, for RAF Sunderlands were now overhead more and more frequently. On the morning of 6 April, *U-505* was caught unawares on the surface by one of these patiently searching planes, and forced to crash-dive in a hurry. As she was going down, one of her diving vents failed to open, and she developed a 40 degrees list. Loewe had to resort to blowing all tanks to bring her back under control, and ended up with his conning tower and stern out of the water. For five agonizing minutes the engineer, Fritz Förster, fought to free the jammed valve, *U-505* lay helpless half in and half out of the water. Incredibly, the Sunderland failed to see her.

A thoroughly chastened Loewe lost no time in quitting the area, moving to the east to set up a patrol off the Ivory Coast. After four days of barren horizons, with only one small Spanish freighter sighted, and his fuel tanks running low, he made the decision to begin the long trek home. *U-505* was continually harassed by Sunderlands until she was well north of Freetown, and on the whole of the homeward passage she was in a position to attack only one ship, and this turned out to be a neutral Swedish steamer. She reached Lorient on 7 May.

Chapter Nine

The *Alphacca* survivors escaped internment in Tabou only through the intervention of an unknown French officer, who put off from the shore in a surfboat to warn them to land further to the west. This they did, and so avoided the fate that befell the unfortunate crew of the British ship *Allende*, sunk by *U-68* when on her way home from India.

Having come ashore on 19 March on the wrong side of the Liberian border, Captain Thomas Williamson and his men made a seven-mile trek along the beach, unfortunately in the wrong direction, and walked straight into the arms of the Vichy French authorities at Tabou. They were well treated at first, being adequately fed and rigged out with fresh clothing to replace their salt-stained rags. In the eleven days they remained in Tabou, they were not closely guarded, and had been given to believe that they would soon be released and taken back across the border. On the basis of this, no one made any attempt to escape.

When, on 30 March, the French gunboat *La Surprise* anchored off Tabou, and the thirty-three men were taken aboard, they surmised wrongly that they were on their way home. The first indication that all was not what it had seemed came when *La Surprise* set course not to the west for Liberia, but to the east. Six hours later, the prisoners – for they now knew they were prisoners – were landed ashore under armed guard at Sassandra, the chief town of the district. Here they were confined in a compound for twenty-six days, during which time, it must be assumed, a decision was being made about their future. As merchant seamen, they were classed as non-combatants, and the logical solution would have been to repatriate them. But this was at a time when German fortunes were still in ascendance. In the Western Desert, the British

Eighth Army was falling back before Rommel's advance on the Egyptian frontier. In Russia, despite fierce resistance, Field Marshal von Bock's three army groups were creeping forward on a front 150 miles wide. In the Pacific the Japanese had reached their furthest point south yet, taking possession of Christmas Island, only 800 miles from the Australian mainland and at sea, in March, the Allies had suffered their worst monthly loss to date, 273 ships of 834,184 tons. It is not surprising that the Vichy French in West Africa assumed they were on the winning side, and were consequently anxious to impress their German masters.

On, or about 25 April, the *Allende* survivors, their morale at a very low ebb, were ordered to collect their few possessions and were marched out of their compound to be bundled aboard waiting open lorries. For the next five days they headed north, crawling along winding dirt roads that were little more than jungle tracks. Unprotected from the burning sun and the torrential rain that fell every afternoon, clinging to their hard wooden seats, and now under guard by a party of native troops led by two white French officers, the prisoners had no idea of their destination, and no one would enlighten them. They stopped each midday to eat a meal of half-boiled rice mixed with a few shreds of meat, then at night for watery soup and coarse black bread, before a few hours sleep under the stars.

By the end of the month they had reached the small township of Daloa, 200 miles inland from Sassandra, where they were housed in a barracks that had once been an outpost of the legendary French Foreign Legion. Now little more than a crumbling ruin, the barracks had nothing to offer but shelter from the sun, and as most of the men were now suffering from exhaustion and dysentery, they needed a lot more. After two days of incarceration in this hell-hole, fed on barely edible rice eaten with their fingers from a communal bowl, and lacking in even the most basic sanitation, the prisoners were given a cursory examination by a doctor, and passed as fit to travel.

That afternoon, they re-boarded the lorries, some of them now so weak that they had to be lifted on board, and the convoy set off again, heading first north, then east, making frequent stops to allow those stricken by dysentery to relieve themselves. For two

106

more days they swayed and rattled along unsurfaced roads, until on the evening of the second day they entered the township of Bouake, where they were disembarked at the railway station, and shepherded aboard a line of waiting railway trucks. Once more, as he had done at the beginning of each stage of what was turning into a nightmare journey, Captain Williamson demanded to be told where they were being taken but always his request was refused. Within the hour, an ancient steam engine was coupled to the trucks, and they were off again, still heading north. The trucks were filthy, with bare wooden seats, but they were covered, and their slow swaying movement was a welcome relief from the tortures of the open lorries.

Thirty-six hours later, the prison train pulled into Bobo Dioulasso, terminus of the railway and second city of Upper Volta (now Burkina Faso). Lying 450 miles inland from the Gulf of Guinea, Bobo Dioulasso boasted a mosque and a busy market, neither of which the *Allende*'s men were privileged to see. They were taken off the train and marched to the local military barracks, where a doctor gave them a cursory examination and pronounced them all fit to travel. This despite the obvious fact that they were tired and unwashed, and many of their number were wracked by dysentery or fever. They were then bundled aboard lorries, which set off heading to the west, therefore thoroughly confusing the navigators among them, who were trying to keep track of their journey.

Late that evening the lorries reached Sikasso, a town in the French Sudan (now Mali). Here they were locked up in the town jail compound for the night. Early next morning, they were aboard their lorries again, and for the next two days travelled west and then north, ending up at Bamako, capital of French Sudan, which stands on the River Niger and is notable for its cattle market and foul smelling open drains. The usual pattern of events followed, the survivors being herded into the local army barracks, which were filthy and insect-infested. As he had done on every occasion when they stayed overnight, Captain Williamson requested an interview with the officer in charge so that he might demand decent food and medical treatment for his men, but as always, his request went unanswered. It was at this point that the survivors, most of them now very sick and suffering acute malnutrition, began to suspect that French captors were hoping that they might die en route to whatever their final destination might be. Or was this the end of the line? No one would enlighten them.

After a poor night's sleep in their flea-ridden barracks and a breakfast of rice swill flavoured with rotten meat – and this in an area which abounded in fresh meat, vegetables and fruit – Williamson and his men, who had now been on the road for almost four weeks, were taken down to the river. There they embarked from a rickety pier into a fleet of small canoes, which were to be their mode of transport for the next ten days. The Niger at this time of the year – it being the dry season – was flowing sluggishly, and the heavily laden canoes made slow progress. Some nights they pulled into the bank to allow the prisoners to stretch their cramped legs and snatch a few hours sleep, otherwise the endless journey continued. They were now in country where mangroves lined the river bank, where mosquitoes swarmed, and malaria, blackwater fever and river blindness were rife. Miraculously, none of the men went down with any of these dreadful diseases, but they were all suffering bouts of fever, some had tapeworms, and most endured the debilitating horrors of dysentery. Those who had survived the sinking of the *Allende* were in a pitiful state – and they still had no idea of their destination, other than they were quite obviously not going home.

Four days, and 155 miles, down river from Bamako, the canoes reached Segu, where they stopped only long enough to change paddlers. They were under way again in less than an hour, gliding past low lying banks where crocodiles basked in the hot sun and herds of hippopotami cooled themselves in the muddy water. But there was no relief for the unfortunate wretches confined to their canoes. In the heat of the day the temperature was reaching more than 130°F, from which they had no escape, no shelter from the sun, and only a meagre supply of brackish water to quench their raging thirst.

The interminable voyage went on and on, the canoes progressing at only thirty or forty miles a day, the boredom of these days relieved only when they passed through the occasional small village whose inhabitants rushed down to the river bank offering fruit and vegetables for sale. The prisoners desperately needed a supplement to their starvation diet of rice and meat scraps, but they had no money and nothing to barter with. Their guards declined to help.

On the seventh day since leaving Bamako, the canoes entered a region of treeless marshland, and spent the night at Mopti. Lying 285 miles to the north-east of Bamako, Mopti is an unhealthy spot, a town built on three islands in the river which are joined by dykes. Once an important staging post for camel trains, the town had a tired and decayed air about it. The prisoners were allowed ashore for a few hours, but there was no attraction in this fever-ridden hole for them, and when ordered to they were more than willing to reboard the canoes.

The river passage finally came to an end four days later, when the prisoners were landed at Kabara, an unimpressive huddle of ramshackle buildings on the north bank 200 miles downstream from Mopti. Disembarking from the canoes which had been their homes for nearly eleven days, the forlorn group of seamen, their clothes in rags, and many of them barely able to stand, were formed up on the river bank by their captors and left in the full heat of the sun. They were tired and bewildered, for other than that they were somewhere deep in the heart of Africa, the *Allende*'s men had no idea of where they were. When the local guard commander, no doubt replete from a good lunch, at last arrived, his inspection was brief and cursory. He dismissed the prisoners with a wave of his hand, and the guards prodded them to their feet. The remainder of their journey was to be completed on foot.

Almost four hours later, after covering eight miles through rough scrubland, the pitiful band of British men staggered into the outskirts of a sizeable town. It was only then that they discovered that they were in Timbuktu, and that this was the end of the line for them.

Timbuktu, lies some 900 miles inland from the Gulf of Guinea, and is best known to most Westerners as the remotest spot on earth. It was founded in the twelfth century by the Tuaregs, and for hundreds of years was a major centre for the trans-Sahara gold and salt trade, as well as being a hub of Islamic culture. In 1942, it had abandoned all pretensions of greatness, and was just another drab Arab town clinging to a precarious existence in a barren land where no animals roamed, no birds sang, and an immense silence lay overall. The name, Timbuktu, meaning 'far away' in English, was very apt.

The gaggle of ragged prisoners entered the town and was led down narrow alleyways between the windowless houses, until a clearing was reached which contained a mud brick building surrounded by a barbed wire fence. A gate was opened, and the men were herded into their new home, surely the most god-forsaken prisoner of war camp that ever existed. To their great surprise, they found that the crew of the *Criton* had preceded them.

After their ship had been sunk in June 1941 by two French gunboats, the fifty-two survivors of the *Criton* had also endured terrible hardships on their long trek from the coast. Captain Gerald Dobeson later wrote in his report:

We were taken to a native concentration camp at Konakri which was enclosed with barbed wire. I remained at this place for six or seven days before being taken to hospital with an injured back. While at Konakri the French Authorities asked me if I had scuttled the ship. I said, 'No'. Then they said it would be much better for me if I said 'Yes', but I declined to do so. Whilst in this hospital they again visited me asking me to say that I had scuttled the ship; however I remained firm, saying that I had not done so.

Second Officer Bernard de Neumann described their treatment while at Conakry:

We were there for two months, crowded ten men in a mud hut. It was the height of the rainy season, and it poured through the grass roof. All that time we only had rice to eat and were continually drenched. The sanitary conditions were worse than the Black Hole of Calcutta.

We had a path 30 feet long and 7 feet wide for exercise. We were allowed one wash a day and the 52 of us had to get it over in five minutes.

110

We were not allowed to get in touch with anyone from the day we were captured in June until we arrived in Timbuctoo on October 10 1941. Every day men fell ill with malaria and dysentery. I must say that the French medical men did all that they could and were very kind.

While the *Criton*'s men were prisoner in Conakry, a French naval court martial was held to investigate the circumstances surrounding the sinking of their ship. Under questioning, Captain Dobeson still refused to agree with his captors' assertion that he had deliberately scuttled his ship. His denial was not accepted by the court, and as a result, he and his crew were declared to have committed an act of piracy. This was, of course, arrant nonsense, but it seems that the French were concerned that one day, perhaps in the not too distant future, they might be called upon to justify their unprovoked attack on a British merchant ship.

On 26 September 1941, Dobeson and his men, with the exception of the *Criton*'s African firemen and two officers who were still in hospital, were put on board a narrow-gauge railway, which took them on a two-day journey to Kankan, the eastern terminus of the railway from Conakry, 300 miles inland. There they transferred to lorries for another two-day drive to Bamako, where they were rested for five days, before going on to Koulikoro, fifty miles or so further inland on the north bank of the River Niger. At Koulikoro they boarded an open barge, one of four made fast alongside an ancient stern-wheeler. After a voyage down-river lasting five days, blissfully unaware that two of the accompanying barges were carrying a large quantity of ammunition, and during which they were driven almost insane by mosquitoes, they reached Kabara. Here, much to their relief, they were taken ashore. After a short rest, they were then marched inland to the camp at Timbuktu, which was to be their home for many months to come.

Captain Williamson of the *Allende* wrote in his report:

The crew of the British ship *Criton* were at Timbuctu and were regarded as prisoners of war, although the French authorities told us that we were not prisoners. We were put in the same camp as the crew of the *Criton*, which was surrounded by a 9 ft concrete wall and closely guarded by twelve native soldiers under the command of a French sergeant. We had to remain in this camp and were not allowed out. The house in which we lived was quite pleasant with walls about 4 ft thick and was a perfect protection from the sun.

We were given no breakfast, our first meal being at midday and consisted of native rice cooked in palm oil. We had another meal of kou-kous at 6 o'clock at night, in addition we were given about 175 grams of bread each day. This, without variation, was our diet for the whole nine weeks we were in Timbuctu.

The Chief Engineer, who was an elderly man, died of starvation. Everybody had been very sick whilst travelling in the canoes. On arrival at Timbuctu our first meal was rice and the Chief Engineer could not eat it. The Military Doctor came to see him and ordered him a milk diet, but the Military Commandant would not allow this, although there was plenty of milk available, as there were plenty of goats and milk in the town.

The French Commandant was a Martinique named Moreau, who was a despicable type of man and hated everything British. For the first two weeks in Timbuctu he came to visit us, but after that the captain of the *Criton* and myself had to report to his office every Monday morning. He encouraged us to grumble, presumably so that he could report the fact that the British were dissatisfied and discontented.

The crew of the *Criton* had collected about 20 books, and these we borrowed, this made some little recreation for us, otherwise there was absolutely nothing for the men to do. The *Criton*'s men were getting money through the American Consul in Dakar, but were not allowed to buy food with it, and their purchases were limited to 20 cigarettes each per day. We were not receiving any money, but the men from the *Criton* lent us some of theirs.

The French sergeants ate their meals in front of us, and I have seen one of them eat as many as eight eggs at one meal, apart from liver, bacon, white rice, and bread and butter.

The crew of the *Criton* had been a little better fed and had on occasions been given such delicacies as tomatoes in very small quantities, but when we left Timbuctu they were only living on rice and kou-kous.

There were iron bedsteads, straw mattresses and a sheet provided for us, but the sanitary arrangements were appalling.

The doctor at Timbuctu was French and was a very nice man, and did what he could for us, but he was completely overruled by the French military authorities.

There were 40 or 50 white sergeants and we had a different sergeant every day, the guard being changed every twenty-four hours. There were 10 to 20 white military officers and the rest of the troops were natives and desert nomads.

Captain Dobeson of the *Criton* was rather more critical of the regime at Timbuktu:

The treatment during the whole internment was disgusting. We lived for 140 days on rice and weak gravy for dinner with a meal of a very inferior type of bran for supper. One very special day we had one and a third sardines each, whilst on another day we actually had no food at all. As special treat when the survivors from another ship (*Allende*) joined us we were given boiled potatoes. The French said they were not interested in how they treated us so long as they kept us alive. Actually, three of my crew died during internment and a fourth died later as a result of their abominable treatment. These men were natives.

Captain Williamson and the men of the *Allende* were held in the Timbuktu camp for sixty-three days, during which time they were, in the words of one of their number, 'uncared for, unwanted and treated with complete indifference by the French authorities'. By the end of their second week of captivity most of them were so weak that they spent much of the time resting on their filthy, flea-invested mattresses. They had little water with which to wash,

113

their clothes were soon in rags, and without even a needle and thread for repairs, they resembled a bunch of emaciated scare-crows.

After two weeks in captivity, they began to die, first twenty-three year old Able Seaman John Graham, and three weeks later Chief Engineer William Souter, at sixty made old before his time. Both men were laid to rest in Timbuktu's tiny Christian cemetery, their only priest being Captain Williamson, who spoke a few half-remembered words from the burial service over their graves. The remaining *Allende* men now began to wonder which of their number would be next to end up in this barren patch of land in the wind-swept desert, for every day that passed they all became weaker.

About a month after William Souter died, the remaining *Allende* crew members noticed a dramatic change in the attitude of their gaolers, who began for the first time to treat them as human beings. This probably had much to do with the news filtering through that British forces had landed on Madagascar, and were engaged in wresting the island from Vichy French control. Suddenly, it must have occurred to Commandant Moreau and his guards that they might have backed the wrong side in this war.

A few days later, Williamson and his men were addressed by the camp doctor, who informed them that their imprisonment had been a mistake, and that they would soon be sent home. For the first time they were now allowed ample water to wash themselves, and were given new clothes to replace the filthy rags they had been wearing since their ship was sent to the bottom more than three months ago. Next day they boarded lorries, and left Timbuktu without a backward glance. Captain Williamson wrote of the return journey in his report:

> The first part of our journey was across 200 miles in motor lorries. There were no roads and poles sometimes had to be laid under the wheels to enable the lorries to get over some of the stretches of soft sand. It took us seven days to get to Mopti and two and a half days from there to Bamako.
>
> We were eleven days at Bamako, during which time we were given the most wonderful food which we were not

allowed to refuse. We were fed on rice, meat, eggs, liver and wine and cigarettes in abundance.

We saw General Richard who was in charge of the troops in the Vichy French Sudan. He appeared to be very pro-British and said he was very sorry that we had been so badly treated, stating that actually he was powerless to help us, as his family were still in France and if he showed his pro-British feelings too strongly he could not tell what would happen to them.

From Bamako we travelled for two days and two nights in a train to a place about 60 miles from the Gambian frontier. We were not taken into the railway station and were not told the name of the place. We got out of the train some distance away from the station and were immediately put into motor lorries which were waiting. We then crossed the border into Gambia where British lorries were waiting for us. I noticed that the French walked into British territory but the British did not cross onto French territory.

We were then taken to Bathurst and returned to England in the *Highland Monarch* and landed at Liverpool.

One of our firemen died in Bathurst but I do not know the cause of his death.

We were not given any clothes in Timbuctu until the day before we left, when the men were given a pair of shorts and shirt, but even then I was not given any clothes, as Commandant Moreau had taken a great dislike to me. We had not been provided with mending equipment during our stay, and my shirt and shorts were torn to shreds.

Possibly because they had been a prize crew on a French ship, and had at one time been regarded as pirates, Captain Dobeson and his crew appear to have received harsher treatment in Timbuktu than the *Allende*'s men. Certainly they were detained for much longer, not leaving Timbuktu until 5 August 1942. They then suffered a nineteen-day trek by road to Kankan, where they were held until 13 December, before being taken over the border into Sierra Leone. Volunteering to take the *Criton* home had earned them eighteen months in captivity, during which at the hands of the French they were subjected to treatment rarely seen outside a Japanese prisoner of war camp in the Second World War.

An interesting footnote to the internment of merchant seamen by the Vichy French in West Africa is provided by the narrative of Roy Thorne, a Canadian serving as mess boy in the Norwegian tanker *Malmanger*. The *Malmanger* was torpedoed by *U-68* some 900 miles west of Freetown on 9 August 1942. One of the tanker's lifeboats, containing eighteen men including Thorne, eventually landed north of Dakar eleven days later, and its occupants were made prisoner by the Vichy French, and taken to Conakry. In Roy Thorne's own words:

We were shipped another 1,400 miles inland to another big camp, a big tobacco plantation called Kankan.

In total it'd be around two hundred prisoners; that's the different crews. We were put into cattle cars and it took us, I think it was, a day and a half to travel it. You had two (French guards) in each car and this time their weapons were loaded. The stops we used to come to, the people in the villages knew there were prisoners being brought up and they would be cursin' us, spittin' at us, throwin' stones, callin' us names and everything. These are French people now! We'd just ignore them . . .

We were interned in this big camp with another bunch of British seamen, also Frenchmen, Lebanese, a bunch of Syrians. They had been plantation owners and business people who worked in the different towns and picked up because of their sympathies towards the British and Americans. They were there when we go there. In that camp there might have been around five hundred, that's all the different crews plus the civilians.

The invasion started in October 1942 and the Yanks and them swept right through Africa, cleaned them right out, didn't fool around. We were actually released in December 1942. We had three weeks of freedom before the French would let us out because of transportation (problems). We were demanding that they let us out because we were classed

116

as political prisoners of war because we were all civilians and all political prisoners of war were to be released immediately, which we weren't. That's when the Britishers went berserk. We burned everything that reminded us of the camp. We burnt all the beds and about half of those sheds and we even had half the stockade down before we left. There were bonfires every night. All we'd do is sit around drinking hot cocoa. They (the guards) were there but they wouldn't interfere, just let us go.

Then it came time they said so many of us could go into town, maybe fifty, where the canteens were. They would be taken in by an escort and then brought home. Jesus, when them Englishmen got into town, they cleaned everything. They raided their bars and there wasn't a woman safe on the streets. Some of them guys had been there since the war started, a good couple of years. They'd come down from Timbuktu, which was another big French prison camp during the war. You've heard the expression (Timbuktu) that's where it comes from. There was a big French prison camp in the French Sudan and up there they used to work, make them load sand, filling sand bags for battle emplacements and what not. How some of them got to the camp that I was in is because they were ill; a lot of guys had malaria, dysentery, beri beri and what have you.

Then it came word that we were goin' to be sent back to Conakry and from there to Freetown. On the way down there wasn't nothing the Frenchmen could (not) do for us. There homes were wide open, all kinds of booze, women, anything you wanted. Could have even slept with the mayor's wife. All cigarettes, clothes, they were throwin' the stuff at us . . .

After the war, the French Government awarded an ex-gratia payment of £30,000 to the crew of the *Criton* as compensation for the unwarranted hardship they suffered while in captivity. This money was accepted by the British Government of the day, but not one penny of it reached the *Criton* survivors.

Today, Timbuktu, now in the independent Republic of Mali,

has returned to its former obscurity, sought out only by the most intrepid 'adventure' tourists. William Souter and John Graham still sleep there, their graves carefully tended by the Commonwealth War Graves Commission, a monument to the inhuman treatment meted out to British merchant seamen by the Vichy French in the Second World War.

Chapter Ten

When Italy entered the war in June 1940, she possessed a large modern navy, which included a vast fleet of 112 submarines. The majority of these submarines were over 1,000 tons in displacement, heavily armed, and capable of long-range cruising. Under the agreement made between Hitler and Mussolini, these Italian U-cruisers came under the control of Admiral Dönitz, who welcomed them as valuable reinforcements which might tip the balance for him in the Battle of the Atlantic. By early August, a base had been set up at Bordeaux for the Italians, the first three boats entering the port in the following month. Dönitz was well aware that the Italians lacked experience in submarine warfare, and accordingly assigned them to patrol to the south of the Azores, where they were less likely to meet up with the Royal Navy, but might play a useful reconnaissance role and help tighten the blockade around the British Isles. He was soon disappointed with their performance, and by May 1941 was despairing of them ever becoming a fighting force to be reckoned with. It was his stated opinion that they,

> . . . 'are not sufficiently hard and tough for this type of warfare. Their way of thinking is too sluggish and according to rule to allow them to adapt themselves clearly and simply to the changing conditions of war. Their personal conduct is not sufficiently disciplined and in the face of the enemy not calm enough. In view of this I am forced to dispose the German boats and operate without regard to the Italian boats.

One of the few exceptions to the rule was the *Leonardo da Vinci*. The *Leonardo da Vinci* was a Marconi-class submarine of 1,489 tons displacement built in 1940. She carried a crew of fifty-seven, and was armed with eight 21-inch torpedo tubes, two 3.9-inch guns and four machine guns. Her 3,600 hp Adriatico diesels gave her a top speed on the surface of 18 knots, 8 knots submerged, and she had a cruising range of 10,500 miles. She first appeared in the Gulf of Guinea in May 1942 under the command of *Capitano di Corvetta* Luigi Longanesi-Cattani, having previously operated off the Caribbean with little success, sinking only two ships totalling 7,201 tons gross.

After casting about in the region of Freetown for several days, sighting nothing but the occasional Sierra Leonean fishing canoe, on the night of 2 June Longanesi-Cattani was idling on the surface forty miles to the south-west of Cape St Ann and contemplating moving deeper into the Gulf. It was a dark, moonless night without a breath of wind to disperse the oppressive heat of the day, and when the Italian commander saw the full-rigged ship drifting between him and the land, he at first thought he was hallucinating.

Longanesi-Cattani was not the victim of some West African voodoo spell. What he had sighted was the four-masted schooner *Reine Marie Stewart*, one of the few remaining commercial sailing ships engaged in ocean trading. The 1,087-ton *Reine Marie Stewart*, sailing under the Panamanian flag, owned by the Shepard Company of Boston, Massachusetts and commanded by Captain Paul F. Radeboldt, was on a voyage from New York to East Africa, when she had become becalmed off the coast of Sierra Leone. She was unarmed and carrying a cargo of timber ready-cut for fruit boxes, in her holds and stowed six to eight feet high on her decks.

The schooner was showing no lights, which led Longanesi-Cattani to assume that she must be an enemy ship engaged in carrying war supplies. In fact, she had no electricity on board, her only lighting being by kerosene lamps, which were probably not visible from the submarine. With her sails hanging limp, she seemed to be an easy target, and rather than waste a torpedo, Longanesi-Cattani opened fire with one of his 3.9-inch guns. Caught unawares – most of them were asleep – the eleven-man crew of the *Reine Marie Stewart* abandoned ship in their only lifeboat, a 16 foot wooden boat with an inboard motor.

The schooner caught fire as a result of the shelling, but with her holds and decks packed with buoyant timber she stubbornly refused to sink. In desperation, Longanesi-Cattani was forced to use a valuable torpedo on her, and only then did she reluctantly founder, sending up a great cloud of steam and smoke as the sea closed over her. Meanwhile, Captain Radeboldt and his crew were heading for the land in their motor boat. Before they reached the shore they were picked up by the British ship *Afghanistan*, which was bound south for Cape Town.

The *Leonardo da Vinci* had by this time been away from her Bordeaux base for nearly four months, and was running low on fuel, water and provisions. It was time, *Capitano* Longanesi-Cattani decided, to consider returning north. But first he was determined to improve on his score which, at two freighters and a schooner laden with boxwood, was not impressive. He moved further offshore and began to patrol up and down across the Cape-Freetown route. At that time the Danish ship *Chile* was some 1,200 miles due south of Freetown and bound north.

The 6,956-ton *Chile* was even older than the *Reine Marie Stewart*, being built in 1915 for the East Asiatic Company of Copenhagen. In an age when the big windjammers were still flogging their way around the Cape to Australia, and the coal-fired, steam reciprocating engine was only just becoming accepted as the ultimate means of propulsion for the merchant ship, the *Chile* was part of an embryo revolution originating in Denmark. She was one of the world's first motor vessels, a twin-screw ship powered by two Burmeister & Wain 6-cylinder, 4-stroke diesel engines which gave her a service speed of 11 knots. With no boiler room and no coal bunkers, she had much more cargo space than a coal-burner of her size, which compensated for her oil fuel costing four times as much as coal.

When Denmark fell to the Germans in April 1940, the *Chile* was in Singapore, homeward bound from the Far East. She was taken under the British flag, but retained her Danish officers and Chinese ratings, going into service between Burma and India to the United Kingdom carrying whatever cargo was on offer. On 2 May 1942, she sailed from Calcutta with a cargo of 6,380 tons of groundnuts, 2,500 tons of pig iron and 800 tons of cotton seed destined for Liverpool. In command was Captain N.E. Bom, with a crew of forty-three, which included a team of British DEMS gunners who manned the ship's armament of one 4-inch gun, two Hotchkiss machine guns, one Bren gun and a Holman Projector.

After making the usual call at Cape Town for bunkers, fresh water and stores, the *Chile* sailed late on 23 May for Freetown, where she would join a convoy for the UK. There were no enemy submarine warnings in force when she left Cape Town, which was just as well, for the Danish ship's twenty-seven year old diesels, although carefully maintained over the years, were not giving of their best. In the South Atlantic, even running before the south-east Trades, she was unable to exceed 10 knots. As he drew nearer to Freetown, Captain Bom grew increasingly anxious. As it transpired, he had good cause for concern.

On the evening of 7 June the *Chile* was 250 miles south of Freetown, and with the cooperation of his chief engineer Bom was hoping to arrive at the anchorage before dark on the 8th. It was a dark, but clear night, the silence of which was broken only by the steady beat of the two B & W engines as they urged the ship on. At a little after 21.00 Bom joined Third Officer Jargensen on the bridge, and the two men paced the port wing talking quietly and scanning the horizon

At 21.30, Bom turned to look aft, and was horrified to see two phosphorescent tracks approaching the port quarter at high speed. Acting instinctively, he ordered the helm hard to starboard, and the *Chile* vibrated heavily as she swung under the influence of full rudder. Seconds later, Bom saw the tracks of the torpedoes – for they were torpedoes – shoot across his bows, clearing the ship by no more than six feet. He later wrote in his report:

> I altered course and steered parallel with the tracks of these torpedoes for two minutes, afterwards altering course frequently, keeping the submarine astern. I had one lookout on the starboard side of the bridge and two on the port side with the 3rd Officer. The remainder of the crew were ordered to stand by their boat stations. Meanwhile I sent a message to the wireless room ordering them to send out a message 'SSS 4°17' N 13° 38' W *Chile* tracks of two torpedoes seen 2130 June 7th' and this message was sent out. We always kept all

watertight doors shut in danger areas and I am sure they were closed at this time. At 2150 we were struck by two torpedoes on the port side of the engine room. The ship was swinging to starboard and the torpedoes were apparently fired from abaft the port beam, but no one saw the tracks. The explosion was not very loud, and I did not see any flash but a terrific column of water and black smoke was thrown up on the ports side and the ship shook violently. I think the air bottles in the engine room may have burst and the bulkhead of No.3 hold must have collapsed as in one minute the stern was completely under water, and the after guns crews had to run over the hatches in order to escape. Both engines stopped immediately and all electricity failed. The port engine was completely wrecked but there did not appear to be any deck damage except that one of the davits of the port lifeboat was torn out from its socket. The wireless room was wrecked and out of action so we were unable to send out an SOS.

I was on the bridge with the 3rd Officer and ordered him to collect all confidential books including the wireless books and to put them in the weighted bag and throw them overboard while I collected a sextant and a chronometer. Meanwhile the boats were being lowered, we carried three lifeboats, one on the port and one on the starboard side and a small motor boat on the starboard side. There were 10 men in the port boat when it was lowered, as it became waterborne the seams opened up and it filled with water and became waterlogged and sank. This boat was right over the explosion and a lot of water and debris was thrown up and landed in the boat, probably damaging it. The remainder of the crew went over to the starboard lifeboat and were able to step into it from the deck. I left the ship about six minutes after being torpedoed by which time the boat deck was level with the water. The 3rd Officer, who had been throwing the confidential books overboard, had to jump to the lifeboat. Eight of the men from the damaged port boat swam round to the starboard lifeboat and we picked them up. We then rowed to the port side and picked up the other two men, who were Chinese. We were able to find them by the red lights on their lifejackets. The boat's emergency radio set was in the port boat and was lost with that boat. The ship sank at 2203 a few seconds after I left her.

The ship was equipped with three rafts each with a capacity for 28 men, and these floated off as the ship sank, one of them had automatic lights which flashed SOS. The boats kept together until morning in order that a search could be made for the missing men, and at daylight we were able to see all the rafts floating in the vicinity but we could not see any survivors on them. At 0838 HMT *Spaniard* came along and signalled that he would take us on board. Being in the motor boat I towed the other boat alongside and we all boarded the *Spaniard* by means of rope ladders. The *Spaniard* was about half an hour picking us up, after which she steamed round searching for further survivors until about 1400 when the search was abandoned and she started off for Freetown, arriving there on 11th June.

I consider that the Chief and 2nd Engineers and the greaser were killed by the explosion as they were on duty in the engine room. The 3rd Engineer and Chief Cook went to their cabins to collect some clothes and papers and I think they must have been trapped in their accommodation. The crew behaved magnificently and there was no sign of panic.

I wish to specially mention the gallant action of 3rd Officer Jargensen who gave valuable assistance throughout and he remained behind until he had collected and thrown overboard all confidential books and papers.

After sinking the *Chile*, Luigi Longanesi-Cattani, anxious to clear the area before British warships or aircraft arrived on the scene, moved south-west into the Atlantic. He was still optimistic that he might find unescorted ships, but mindful of his dwindling fuel supply, he realized that he must soon begin the long voyage home. He was 580 miles to the south-west of Monrovia, and heading north-west to pass outside the Cape Verde Islands when another unexpected victim came his way. This time it was no humble carrier of country produce.

The 5,483-ton *Alioth*, owned by the Rotterdam South-America

Line, and operating under the control of the British Ministry of War Transport was on her way to war, loaded to her marks with a cargo of military stores, her holds being packed with land mines, bombs and ammunition, while her decks were covered with twin-engined Avro Anson bombers. For such a ship to be sailing unescorted in these waters was tempting fate indeed.

The *Alioth*, a five year old motor vessel, was commanded by Captain Kornelis Dik, and manned by a crew of forty-three, of which thirteen, including her eight DEMS gunners, were British, while the rest were Dutch. She had sailed from Birkenhead on 21 May, bound for Basra in the Persian Gulf via Cape Town, and proceeded in convoy until abeam of the Straits of Gibraltar. While the other ships of the convoy peeled off for the Mediterranean, the *Alioth* continued on alone on a southerly course. Being a fast ship – 11.5 knots was considered fast for a merchantman of her day – it was assumed she would be safe on her own.

Continuing south in improving weather, the Dutch ship found herself in an empty ocean, with only the very occasional wisp of smoke seen on the horizon to indicate that she was not entirely alone in the world. But Captain Dik, a master with first-hand experience of the perils of war at sea, resisted the temptation to become overconfident. He remained vigilant, with lookouts posted at all times, the British gunners handy to their guns – the *Alioth* was armed with a 4-inch and a 12-pounder mounted aft, and four machine guns amidships – and a zigzag course was steered throughout the daylight hours. Meanwhile, the watches came and went, and the deck and engine room day-workers settled into their normal sea-going routine, scaling rust, painting, oiling and polishing anything that moved. War or no war, shipboard life goes on. The sheer normality of it all – and the shock that ended it is described by Bombardier Ted Robson, the senior DEMS gunner on board:

On the evening of the 10th June, we had played pontoon with some of the crew. At about nine o'clock, having made myself a cup of very sweet cocoa, with condensed milk and sugar, I also made a cheese and pickle sandwich before turning into my bunk for a couple of hours before turning-to again for the middle watch with Wally. Before getting into my bunk I ensured that my panic bag was to hand. My panic bag consisted of an Army issue haversack, inside of which was an oilskin wallet with my Army pay book, wallet and money, together with a few articles of clothing, such as a spare trousers and a blazer, which I thought might come in handy.

Sometime around 10 p.m. there was an almighty explosion, and Dan and his bunk collapsed on top of me. For what seemed an eternity I struggled to free myself. There were no lights, not until someone produced a torch. I grabbed my panic bag and somehow found my way up on deck. All the men who had been in the cabin had got out and I saw one of the naval gunners running, stark naked, towards the boat deck, carrying a large suitcase. I started to make my way to the gun deck aft but one of the gunners who had been on watch told me that the order had been given to abandon ship. The ship was by then settling by the stern and I thought at first that we had been in collision with something, reasoning that a torpedo would have set off our cargo of ammunition. It eventually transpired that we had been hit by a torpedo, low down on the propeller shaft, under the only hold that did not contain ammunition . Just how lucky can one be in such circumstances?

Capitano Loganesi-Cattani had adopted the usual attack procedure, approaching on the Dutch ship's quarter and aiming for her engine room, her most vulnerable compartment, but his aim had not been true. However, in exploding in her after hold, the torpedo had smashed the propeller shaft, which ran through the bottom of the hold. The blast had also blown open the watertight door between the shaft tunnel and the engine room, and when the engineer on watch abandoned his post, he reported that the water was pouring into the engine room. With the after part of her hull awash, and her means of propulsion gone, the *Alioth* was finished.

Captain Dik's insistence on holding frequent boat drills, which many on board had considered to be an unnecessary imposition, now paid dividends. Each man knew exactly what he had to do, and in spite of a heavy swell running, the *Alioth*'s two lifeboats were lowered safely, scrambling nets put over the side, and all forty-four crew abandoned the sinking ship without mishap. It was now imperative to clear the ship's side as soon as possible, as it was thought that the holds packed with explosives would blow her apart at any moment. The starboard boat, which was equipped with a motor, took the other boat in tow, and within minutes both boats were well clear.

By this time the *Leonardo da Vinci* had surfaced only a few hundred yards ahead of the *Alioth*, and her 3.9s were lobbing shells at the helpless ship. Unknown to *Capitano* Loganesi-Cattani, it would have needed just one of his shells to land in amongst the *Alioth*'s highly explosive cargo to blow her and the submarine into small pieces. Fortunately for him, the aim of his guns' crews was abysmal and the Dutch ship, unharmed by the shelling, eventually succumbed to the damage caused by the torpedo and sank slowly beneath the waves.

The two lifeboats were lying stopped some distance away, their crews silent as they watched their ship go down. They expected the enemy submarine to now approach them, but Loganesi-Cattani, having seen his victim sink, was not inclined to linger in the area. He secured his guns, closed the hatches, and followed the *Alioth* down.

After witnessing the dying moments of his command, Captain Dik brought the two lifeboats together to take stock of the situation. A quick roll call revealed that, mercifully, the only casualty of the attack was the ship's pet monkey, which only a few hours before had been locked in the paint locker for misbehaving himself, and was assumed to have gone down with the ship. It was also established that before leaving the ship the British radio officer, W.H. Rees, had succeeded in transmitting an SSS (I am being attacked by an enemy submarine) message. While the call for help had not been answered by any ship or shore station, there was a good possibility that someone had picked it up. To the forty-four men now adrift in two tiny lifeboats 600 miles from the nearest land this was a small hope to cling on to, but the only one they had.

The first night was not a comfortable one for the survivors. In the heavy swell the boats rolled horribly and most of them were sea sick, but fortunately they were kept occupied in bailing out, for the seams of the wooden boats had opened up in the hot sun of the tropics, and it was a constant battle to keep the water at bay.

When dawn came at last, the boats came together again and a plan of action was decided upon. As, thanks to the foresight of Captain Dik, both boats had sextants on board, it would at least be possible to establish the daily latitude correctly, and it was agreed that they should avoid the danger of ending up in Vichy-controlled Ivory Coast by heading directly for Freetown. No.2 boat, under the command of Chief Officer Pieter Gnodde, was lighter than the motor boat and would, therefore, sail faster, so it was decided that Goode should press on ahead during daylight. After sunset, Captain Dik would use his engine to catch up with the other boat, and then take it in tow for the night. In this way the two boats would stay in company and although their progress might be slow, it would at least be constant. Before they parted company, a case of tinned condensed milk, which with great fore-sight, had been put aboard No.1 boat by Chief Steward Blyenburgh before they left the ship, was shared out between them. Bombardier Robson takes up the story:

In charge of our boat was the Chief Mate and amongst the remainder were the 2nd Officer, 3rd Officer, Chief Engineer, a Sparks, an Assistant Steward, various deck and engine room crew, the two Ordinary Seamen RN gunners, and my four gunners. Once the boat had stopped leaking we made ourselves as comfortable as possible by fixing an awning over the forward end of the boat and with the floorboards and oars rigged a flat area. This made quite a snug cuddy where the watch below could get some sleep. We had by now been split into three watches, which meant we did four hours sailing and keeping lookout, four hours sitting amidships, and four hours in the cuddy trying to get some sleep. Blankets were on hand and were much needed when the temperature plunged at night. Some parts of the cuddy were more comfortable than others so we moved a place at each sleep watch. Thanks to the 2nd Officer, we became very well organized. He had taken over from the Chief Officer who was much older and had become ill.

We had three containers of water, one small keg in which the water was dirty, one tank of rusty water and one of clean water. The rusty water was OK after you left the rust to settle. We had only three cups for drinking out of, but as we emptied the cigarette tins they were used, and you then had your own mug with a lid in which you could save your water and sip it slowly to stave off the thirst pangs. Water was rationed out twice a day, morning and evening, and the ration amounted to about half an inch in a fifty-fag tin. Not a lot on or near the Equator under a blazing sun, but it was nectar.

For solids we had two concentrated oatmeal biscuits a day and there was also some really hard tack old ship's biscuits, very dry and the last sort of food one could eat when so deprived of liquids.

The 2nd Steward found a 7lb tin of corned beef amongst the stores, a real luxury, but of course there was no opener, so my Army issue jack-knife came into use for this and also the milk. After each time of using it was religiously returned to me, and I still have it in use today. Having opened the corned beef we had to eat the lot as in that temperature it would have gone off. Have you ever eaten warm corned beef out of your not too clean hands, which had been given to you by hands that were also not too clean? I can assure you that not a crumb was wasted. This feast took place on the fourth day. We got a ration of Carnation milk each day and although this was sustaining it made one thirsty.

For the next six days the two lifeboats crept northwards. They enjoyed a following wind, and under sail during the day, the motor boat acting as a tug for the other at night, progress was slow but steady, averaging between sixty and seventy miles a day. Noon sights were taken every day, which gave them a latitude, but without a chronometer their longitude was only a dead reckoning figure. However, as they were on a northerly course, the latitude gave them a fair idea of where they were each day. The wind held fair until dawn on the 17th when, without warning, it suddenly dropped away to nothing. With their sails hanging limp, and the sea a glassy calm, they drifted in the manner of Coleridge's Ancient Mariner's ship, 'As idle as a painted ship upon a painted ocean'. But this was only the calm before the storm, which struck on the night of the 19th. By their reckoning, they were then getting close to the land. Ted Robson had good cause to remember that night:

> That evening it was our turn off watch in the cuddy when we were aroused by a very fierce wind and we seemed to be heading for tall black cliffs when suddenly the wind changed and we were forced to down sails and get out the oars to bring us around. I was on an oar with a big beefy second cook and seemed to spend more time in the air than on the sea. It was a nightmare but we got her around with a struggle and the other boat got a line over to us. During the night we festooned the mast and sails with the small red battery operated lights from our lifejackets so that we could be seen by any passing vessel, and this looked nice and cheered us up.
>
> Shortly after the above incident we hit the mother and father of a tropical storm with waves as big as a house. I do not know to this day which was the worst, being on top of such a wave and looking down, or being in the trough and looking up at the wall of water which you are sure is going to swamp you. I cannot remember much about the wind except that it was a continuous roar and the lightning, both sheet and forked, played around us with St Elmo's fire in the rigging. The rain hit us in squalls and I have never been so wet in all my life – that storm put a new dimension to the word 'scared'. When the storm had passed and the rain fell steadily for hours we collected water in sheets and refilled all our now empty containers. From being hydrated we were now waterlogged and everything was soaked, clothing, lifejackets and blankets.

It was the beginning of the rainy season in the Gulf of Guinea, and the *Alioth*'s survivors had been victims of a West African tornado,

130

a small but very intense depression in which the rain comes down like bullets, thunder cannonades all around, and the lightning is blinding and continuous. In a large ship a tornado can be frightening, but for those men, already weakened by lack of adequate food and water, and crammed into small boats with only an inch or two of freeboard, it must have been a terrible ordeal. Fortunately, this ordeal was short-lived. By dawn next day the storm had moved on; the skies cleared and the hot sun shone down again, putting new heart into the wet and demoralized survivors. Bombardier Robson's report continues:

We were sailing on a course which should have taken us to Freetown, with the Mates bringing out their sextants each day for a midday shot of the sun and setting our course allowing for drift etc. I and the others in the boat owe our lives to those Dutchmen, and I will be eternally grateful to them for the way in which they organized the boats and for their disciplined and skilful navigation.

We had our light moments such as the day we had a steady light rain storm which seemed to come from nowhere. Most of us stripped off and let the shower soak into us, it was not enough to catch for drinking, but we must have looked a fine sight, it was a pity we had no camera handy.

By this time our biscuits were running low but we had a box of very stale chocolates, one each was the ration. The condensed milk was also running to a low level, in fact everything was dwindling except our hopes. I suppose everybody prayed in their own way. I did and was convinced that my prayers were being heard. I cannot even now explain the feeling but it was like throwing a dart at a dartboard and knowing that at the very moment the dart leaves your hand that it was going to hit the bull's eye. I have never felt the same with prayer since, though I am still a great believer in it; the answer these days seems to be 'No'.

On the 8th day we began to see signs of floating vegetation and a few sea birds appeared, a sure sign of nearing land, and we were also getting frequent tropical rainstorms with visibility almost nil. We now had plenty of water, in fact more than we needed and I remember the Chief Engineer courteously offering me a tin full to the brim with water and myself in a like vein politely refusing it. A couple of days previously such an action would have been impossible.

On the evening of the 20th, survivors knew from their daily sights that they must be very near to the land and when, during the night, a flashing light was sighted right ahead, their hopes were realized. But even at this juncture the officers navigating the *Alioth*'s boats were cautious. Their exact longitude was still a matter of educated guesswork, and while they hoped that the light seen was the lighthouse on Cape Sierra Leone, it also might well be that on Cape Verde. If it was the latter, then they were in danger of coming ashore in Vichy-controlled Senegal, which could possibly end in internment for them. After surviving the Italian torpedo and a 600-mile voyage in open boats, this was something they feared more. After consulting with his officers, Captain Dik decided that it would be best to heave to for the night, and wait until daylight, when he hoped to be able to positively identify the land.

When dawn came at last, the boats found themselves at the entrance to the Sierra Leone river, with the white lighthouse on Cape Sierra Leone and the tall radio mast on Aberdeen Hill easily recognizable. There were various other small craft around, mainly local fishermen, but although they tried every means, the survivors failed to attract their attention. They continued on into the harbour, but soon found that they were fighting the full ebb tide of the river, which was swollen by recent heavy rains. Their progress was painfully slow, and their plight made worse by a sudden rain squall, which blotted out the visibility completely. When they emerged from the rain, it was to find a huge slab-sided bulk bearing down on them from astern. It was the escort carrier HMS *Archer,* inbound for Freetown. Although they shouted until they were hoarse and waved their shirts, it seemed that the carrier was intent on running them down. Then, at the last moment, *Archer*'s lookouts spotted them and she sheered away under full helm. Minutes later, the carrier had the two lifeboats in tow, and when she reached her berth, the survivors were taken aboard. Ted Robson describes their reception on board:

The crew of the *Archer* were marvellous, loaned us shaving kit, soap, towels and took us to the showers, absolute bliss, and I just wanted to stay under the shower for ever. Having been cleaned up, we donned what was left of our clothing and they brought us trays of food. I felt that perhaps we should not eat so much after ten days on a starvation diet, but with no doctor to advise us, and I doubt if we would have paid heed if we did have one, we fell to on generous helpings of eggs, bacon, sausages, fried bread, tomatoes and bread and butter. In fact the whole lot went down in no time at all, washed down with gallons of nice hot coffee. God, what a feast! It was the finest meal I have ever had, before or since. We really enjoyed it, and no after effects.

It was thanks to the firm discipline and leadership of Captain Kornelis Dik, and a well-maintained lifeboat engine, that all forty-four men of the *Alioth* survived the 600-mile voyage and lived to sail another day – which, of course, they did.

Chapter Eleven

Returning to Lorient on 13 April 1942 after her successful cruise in the Gulf of Guinea, *U-68* was not allowed to rest idle in port for long. Essential repairs were carried out, her crew given a short leave and, refuelled and reprovisioned, she put to sea again four weeks after her arrival. With Karl-Friedrich Merten still in command, *U-68* was bound for the Caribbean, where the US Navy, seriously depleted by the demands of the Pacific theatre, was fighting a losing battle against the catastrophe threatening their coastal shipping. The U-boats were enjoying their second 'Happy Time'.

After running the gauntlet of the increasing number of British aircraft patrolling the skies of the Bay of Biscay, *U-68* put into El Ferrol in Northern Spain. Here, in a supposedly neutral port, she refuelled from the German supply ship *Max Albrecht* and carried out a few essential repairs before setting out to cross the Atlantic.

Reaching the blue waters of the Caribbean in early June, Merten lost no time in joining in the great American turkey shoot. Arriving off Aruba on the night of 5 June, he met up with the US-flag tanker *L.J. Drake*, on her way to San Juan, Puerto Rico, with 72,961 barrels of gasoline. One torpedo was sufficient to create a blazing funeral pyre for her crew of forty. A few hours later, the 13,000-ton Panamanian-flag *C.O. Stillman* followed the *Drake* to the bottom with her 126,000 barrels of fuel oil.

Over the following three weeks, *U-68* sank another five ships, including the 9,242-ton Vichy-French tanker *Frimaire*, which was unfortunate to stray unidentified into Merten's sights. Before he left the Caribbean to return to Biscay, Merten learned he had been awarded the Knights Cross of the Iron Cross, a fitting reward for his mounting toll of enemy ships, which now stood at a very substantial 113,821 tons. *U-68* reached Lorient again on 10 July.

Increasingly aware of the steady stream of Allied ships using the Cape route – his agents in South Africa reported that on a regular basis up to fifty ships were to be found at anchor off Cape Town – Dönitz formed a new hunting pack, code named *Eisbär* (Polar Bear), to go south to the Cape. The pack was to be made up of four Type IXCs, *U-68*, *U-156*, *U-172* and *U-504*, with the U-tanker *U-459* in support, a powerful self-contained unit with the potential to inflict immense damage on the Cape to Freetown route.

Eisbär set out from Lorient on 20 August, the five boats sailing in formation to provide mutual protection from marauding Allied aircraft. On the 27th, when 180 miles north of Madeira, they sighted the northbound convoy SL 119 and Werner Hartenstein's *U-156* sank a straggler, the British steamer *Clan Macwirter*. Continuing south in company, they reached the Cape Verde Islands on 4 September, where they split up, proceeding independently from then on.

Merten's run of luck continued with the sinking of the British motor vessel *Trevilley* off Ascension Island on the 12th, and the Dutch steamer *Breedijk* on the 15th. He established his position with a brief sighting of the tall peak of St Helena on the 19th and 600 miles further south, in an empty part of the South Atlantic, met up with *U-459* again and *U-68*'s fuel tanks were topped up.

The *Eisbär* boats arrived off Cape Town in early October to find Table Bay completely empty of ships. The Admiralty had got wind of their coming, and had cleared the bay. The area was also being heavily patrolled by anti-submarine trawlers and aircraft. The U-boats moved away from the land, out into the shipping routes.

On 8 October, Merten was scouting some eighty miles south of the Cape of Good Hope, when he found the missing ships. In a hectic twenty-seven hours he sank the Greek steamer *Koumoundouros,* the Dutch ship *Gassterkerk*, the American tanker *Swiftsure*, the British *Sarthe*, the American *Examelia* and the Belgian steamer *Belgian Fighter,* all sailing independently and blissfully unaware that they were being stalked. And there Karl Merten's run of good luck came to an end.

Spring was now giving way to summer off the Cape. Up until

135

then the weather had been predominantly fair but, without warning, a series of deep depressions began moving in from the west, bringing gale force winds and rough seas. *U-68* was a big boat, 253 feet long and 22 feet in the beam, but the heavy seas, riding on the back of a long South Atlantic swell, forced Merten to heave to, the search for new targets forgotten in the fight to avoid damage to his boat.

For more than two weeks *U-68* rode out the gales, powerless to do more than keep steerage way with the wind and sea on the bow. When, eventually, the weather relented, Merten resumed his quest for enemy ships, but the sea lanes of the South Atlantic were empty, while in the skies above there was increased activity by aircraft of the South African Air Force. On the 29th, feeling uncomfortably vulnerable, and increasingly aware of the fact that he was 6,000 miles from home, Merten began to move north again. On the same day, the *City of Cairo* arrived in Cape Town.

Built in 1915 at Earle's shipyard in Hull, Ellerman Line's 8,034-ton, coal-burning *City of Cairo* had been well maintained over the years, but her best days were past and, no doubt, had Adolf Hitler not made his bid to take over Europe, she would have been long consigned to the knacker's yard. She was a hybrid, a cargo/passenger ship, one of many to be seen criss-crossing the oceans before the era of mass air travel. As a means of travel, these ships could offer neither the speed nor the comfort of the luxury liners, but they were the cheapest and most convenient link with home for the vast army of British expatriates, government officials, planters and engineers, that kept the wheels of the Empire turning. The long, leisurely voyage in these ships stole three or four weeks of a man's precious home leave, but as a means of unwinding after a stressful year-long tour of duty, they had no equal. There was none of the pomp and ceremony of the liners; an informal dress code, few rules and regulations, no 'organized' entertainment, just lazy days in steamer chairs, culminating in duty-free gin and tonics at sundown. Most of the big shipping companies operated cargo/passenger carriers on the main routes to Africa and the East. They were the direct descendents of the East Indiamen of the eighteenth century.

The *City of Cairo*, under the command of forty-six year old

Captain William Rogerson, sailed from Bombay on 2 October 1942, having on board a cargo of 7,422 tons of pig iron, manganese ore, timber, wool, cotton, and 2,000 boxes of silver coin. In her passenger accommodation she carried 136 passengers, including twenty-seven women and eighteen children, many of whom had escaped from Malaya and Burma ahead of the advancing Japanese armies. In addition to a crew of ninety-eight, she had on board fifty-seven Lascar seamen, on their way from India to join ships under construction in Britain. Her armament consisted of a 4-inch anti-submarine gun, two Oerlikon 20-mm anti-aircraft guns, and four machine guns, two twin-Marlins and two twin-Hotchkiss, all of which were manned and maintained by seven Naval and four Army DEMS gunners. She was equipped with seven full-sized lifeboats and two jolly boats, the whole with a rated capacity of 338 persons. Additionally, she had a number of life rafts stowed on deck.

At that time, the Mediterranean was still closed to Allied shipping, and the *City of Cairo*, bound for an unspecified British port, faced the long run around the Cape of Good Hope, a distance of 11,500 miles from Bombay to British waters. With stops at Durban and Cape Town to top up her bunkers, the voyage promised to run into forty-five days or more. On the passage to the Cape the ship would be on her own, but there was a promise that from the Cape northwards she would either be in convoy, or have an escort of sorts.

The first of Captain Rogerson's problems arose soon after sailing from Bombay, brought about by the notoriously poor Indian coal the *City of Cairo* had filled her bunkers with before leaving. The maximum speed she was able to maintain was no more than an uncertain 9.5 knots, and this at the expense of a column of dirty black smoke rising from her tall funnel that must have been visible far beyond the horizon. This was bad news for all on board, for apart from the danger posed by the smoke, Rogerson had been warned that unless his ship was capable of more than 10 knots, he would not be allowed to carry his passengers beyond Cape Town. They would have to disembark there and wait for a faster ship to carry them through the Atlantic. Rogerson had words with his chief engineer, Robert Faulds, but no matter how hard the ship's Lascar firemen laboured, she continued to dawdle, advertising her presence to her enemies.

Fortunately, no enemy appeared and, it being the season of the north-west monsoon in the Indian Ocean, the weather was kind. Zigzagging by day and steering a straight course in the hours of darkness, the *City of Cairo* reached Durban in twenty days, having averaged a speed of 9.37 knots. She would have to do better.

With her bunkers replenished with South African coal, the *City of Cairo* brought back a smile to Captain Rogerson's face. After sailing from Durban, he hauled out well off the coast to catch the west-flowing current, and the old ship responded by averaging in excess of 12 knots. However, although the South African coal burned better than that taken on board in Bombay, it was just as dirty, throwing out clouds of black smoke that went rolling back from the funnel as far as the horizon. Rogerson had been warned that German U-boats were active in the area, and he was greatly relieved when, three and a half days after leaving Durban, he picked up the pilot in Table Bay.

Rogerson's relief was short-lived, for while alongside in Cape Town bunkering, he was told that neither convoy nor escort were available for the passage north. Once again the *City of Cairo* would have to plough a lonely furrow, and that furrow would be a very long one. In its wisdom, the Admiralty had routed her across the South Atlantic to Pernambuco, Brazil, where after taking bunkers she was to head north for Halifax, Nova Scotia, there to join a convoy for the run across the U-boat infested North Atlantic. While this route might have been considered safer, it also added more than 3,000 miles to the homeward passage, which involved another eleven days at sea. That in itself was an added hazard.

The *City of Cairo* spent three days alongside in Cape Town taking on coal, fresh provisions and fresh water. This gave her passengers ample time to explore the old colonial city, while her officers sampled the products of the local vineyards and renewed old female acquaintances. It was also an opportunity for some serious Christmas shopping – the war had not yet reached the shops of Cape Town, which were full of luxuries unobtainable at home. The Lascars, not welcome in this strictly white man's country, wisely stayed on board.

Shortly before 10.00 on the morning of 1 November the *City of Cairo* cleared the harbour breakwaters and breasted the long Cape rollers as she headed out into the South Atlantic. Captain Rogerson then opened his sealed orders, which instructed him to steer north, maintaining a distance of forty-five miles off the African coast, until reaching the Tropic of Capricorn, in 23.5 degrees South. Thereafter, he was to head west until he was in mid-Atlantic, before setting course to the north-west for Pernambuco. After years of peacetime sailing, when the shortest distance between two ports was always in as straight a line as possible, Rogerson was loath to make such a wide diversion, but he was obliged to comply with the Admiralty's orders. As it transpired, he might have been wiser to follow his own instincts.

On 3 November, the *City of Cairo*'s radio operators intercepted a message to all ships warning of U-boats operating in her vicinity, but as the message was not addressed specifically to his ship, Rogerson continued on course. He was already zigzagging during daylight hours, and had extra lookouts posted. He could do no more. Early on the 4th, the Tropic of Capricorn was crossed, and course was altered to west-north-west, as per the Admiralty's orders. In complying with these orders Rogerson put the *City of Cairo* on a converging course with *U-68*, and so condemned her to a watery grave.

Tired of his long battle with the southern gales, and mindful of his dwindling stock of diesel, Karl Merten had set course for Biscay on 29 October, running on the surface at an economical speed. Eight days later, on 6 November, *U-68* was some 500 miles south of St Helena when, at 19.21 in the last of the dying twilight, her lookouts reported smoke on the horizon to starboard. Merten immediately altered course and increased speed to close the range.

For some days, sailing in fine, clear weather, with only a light breeze blowing, Captain Rogerson had been concerned at the amount of smoke climbing skywards from the *City of Cairo*'s funnel, but no amount of pleading with the engine room to make less smoke produced any result. No matter how many times the boiler fires were cleaned, and however carefully they were stoked, the dirty South African coal continued to advertise the ship's presence, and enabled Karl Merten to home in on her.

The night, when it came, was dark and moonless, warm with only a gentle breeze ruffling the waves and the distant horizon clearly visible in the light of a million stars twinkling in the black velvet sky overhead. The *City of Cairo* was deep in the Atlantic, with the African coast 1,250 miles to the east and the coast of Brazil 2,000 miles to the west. The general consensus of opinion amongst her crew and passengers was that they were now in relatively safe waters, and that they might sleep well that night.

An hour after first sighting the *City of Cairo U-68* had approached undetected to within 500 metres of her. At 20.26 Merten fired a single torpedo from his bow tubes, which slammed home in the British ship's hull twenty-nine seconds later. The story is taken up by Jack Edmead, Third Steward/Writer in the *City of Cairo*:

The first torpedo struck the ship in No.4 deep tank on the port side with a heavy dull explosion. A column of water was thrown up but no flash or flame was seen. All electricity failed, the accommodation aft was wrecked, but the main engines remained undamaged. The ship listed slightly to port but quickly righted herself. We carried nine lifeboats which the Captain ordered to be lowered. While the crew were lowering the boats I went forward with the 2nd Engineer and released four rafts. All the lifeboats were lowered safely alongside the ships, and most of the crew were away, when at 2040 a second torpedo struck the ship amidships, again on the port side. This was a loud explosion, a large column of water was thrown up, and there was a brilliant flash. All the accommodation amidships was shattered, two of the lifeboats in the water on the port side were capsized and a third one was badly damaged.

I was in one of the lifeboats which was capsized by the explosion from the second torpedo. Whilst in the water I sighted a raft a short distance away. At 2050, before swimming towards it I turned and saw the ship sinking very quickly stern first, and as she disappeared I swam to the raft and climbed on board. During the next hour, 20 more of the crew found their way to this raft and at daybreak there were

24 men on it. I heard the Captain shouting to the lifeboats to tie up together for the night and to put out their sea anchors.

At daybreak on the 7th November the Captain called a muster; it was found that 3 passengers and a Wireless Operator were missing. I then heard that the 2nd Wireless Operator had transmitted an SOS message and had received an acknowledgement from Cape Town before the ship sank. *(This was in fact a cruel deception. Merten had instructed his radio operator to answer the* City of Cairo's *SOS, posing as the Walvis Bay shore station. In this way he obtained full details of the ship, her cargo and passengers.)*

When it became light I, accompanied by several of the crew, swam to the capsized lifeboats. We succeeded in righting one of these boats, but on bailing it out we found it was leaking badly through one or two seams. I cut a hole in my lifejacket, pulled out some kapok, plugging this with some white lead into the seams. Finally, 54 of us managed to get into this lifeboat with the Chief Officer in charge.

During the morning we collected all the food, water and gear from the four rafts, dividing it amongst the other lifeboats. The Captain ordered all the boats to set sail and steer NNE, keeping together during daylight and tying up in line ahead at night. As our boat was still making water it was necessary to maintain 2 hour pumping watches, day and night, to prevent the boat from becoming waterlogged. On the 8th November the Chief Officer asked permission from the Captain to leave the other boats and proceed to St Helena as our boat was the fastest sailer. The Captain was reluctant to agree, but on the following day, realizing that our boat could indeed sail a great deal faster than the others, he agreed to let us sail for St Helena, which we estimated to be about 220 miles distant. The Chief Officer reckoned that we could make this island in about 12 days.

Accordingly, on the evening of the 9th November our boat left the other six and continued independently. There were 54 men in the boat, including the Chief Officer and 6th Engineer, 31 Natives and 12 passengers, including a doctor, a captain Royal Navy, and one woman. The Chief Officer took charge

141

of the lifeboat, ably assisted by Captain MacCall, Royal Navy, and we sailed through very fine weather with slight seas for about 9 days without incident.

The Chief Officer rationed food and water, allowing 3 meals a day, each meal consisting of 4 oz of water, biscuits, pemmican, chocolate and Horlicks tablets. There was plenty of food with more than 30 gallons of water in the lifeboat, and it was estimated that with these rations we could exist for about 3 months. After about the 10th day, as land was not sighted the Natives grew very low spirited, becoming unwilling to assist in bailing the boat, consequently the Europeans had to do twice as much work. Some of the Natives began to drink salt water about this time, which made them more thirsty, and from the 10th day onwards several Natives were delirious. From noon until about 1800 each day the sun beat down on us unmercifully and it was impossible to keep cool. An old flag was torn up, each man was given a small piece to put over his head. On the 11th day the first Native died, and during the next few days they died two and three at a time. It was about this time that some of the Europeans began to lose heart, several of them dying at various intervals. Death in each case appeared to follow an attack of delirium lasting about 3 hours. From this time onwards the crew gradually lost their appetites and the water situation became very grave. On the 14th day the Chief Officer died, so Captain McCall, RN took charge and carried on with the steering. Some of the men gargled with salt water while others used a solution of iodine and salt water, but after the 15th day several of them suffered from acute sore throats. One of the quartermasters developed a high fever which lasted for three days before he died; just about this time Captain McCall died during the 16th day. The men now died on various days until on the 28th day there were only 6 of us left, the water had practically given out and there was only one more ration remaining for each. We were all feeling very tired and disinclined to work but the boat had to be bailed out morning and night in order to keep her afloat. During the evening of the 29th day we experienced a heavy rain storm.

We all drank as much water as we could then caught some rain in the jib, finally collecting about ¾ of a gallon which was put into one of the empty water breakers. Three more of the men died during the night, leaving only Angus MacDonald, Quartermaster, one woman passenger and myself.

We carried on during the next week, the water ration being so small that we could not eat any food. I used to bail the boat out for one hour in the morning and 1½ hours at night, but on the 36th morning the water was up to the thwarts, and I was unable to do any further bailing. At 0830 on the 36th morning – 12th December – I suddenly heard the noise of an engine, which appeared to be very close to the lifeboat; at first I thought it must be an aircraft, but I was too weak even to hoist the red sails, so I burned a flare and shouted loudly. Immediately a voice answered me 'All right'. I then realized slowly that there was a ship very close to us, so I lay back in the lifeboat and waited. A few minutes later the ship came alongside, lowered a ladder and a seaman came down into the boat. He put a sling around each of us and we were hoisted on board. I thought it was an American ship, but on asking one of the crew I learned she was the German blockade runner *Rhakotis*. Apparently she had stopped for about 5 hours with engine trouble, and had just restarted her engines as we drifted by. We were taken straight to the sick bay and put to bed. The woman passenger was in a serious condition and continued to get weaker, the German doctor told me that all the tissues in her throat had collapsed and she was unable to eat anything. She died on the 17th December and I was taken on deck to attend her burial on the 18th. The Quartermaster and I were kept in the sick bay for nearly three weeks before being allowed to walk. During this time the German doctor was most attentive, visiting us three times a day. He kept us on strict diet of milk and light food for 10 days, then gradually allowed us to eat the ship's normal food. My legs and thighs were very painful whilst in hospital, I had a number of sores on my legs, and my feet were blistered, the toes and nails having turned black.

After three weeks we were allowed to walk about the ship. I found there were also 12 Norwegian seamen on board who had been rescued in the Indian Ocean and had been on board for about three months; they were being taken to Bordeaux to be repatriated and sent back to Norway. This German ship flew a number of flags, I particularly noticed that a Dutch flag was frequently flown forward. We were allowed to wander about the ship as we liked but whenever action stations were sounded we were shut up in the hold forward with the Norwegians. Every night U-boats would surface near the ship and on one occasion three submarines surfaced all at the same time; the *Rhakotis* stopped and orders were shouted to her through a megaphone.

At 0230 on New Year's morning the ship was suddenly lit up by flares and we were promptly sent below. I asked the guard what was happening as I could hear machine-gun fire. The guard told me that the ship was being attacked by a single British aircraft, unfortunately, he said, the plane got away undamaged. At 1500 on New Year's day a British warship opened fire on the ship. Again we were rushed below as the first shell struck amidships. Realizing the ship was going to be sunk, a German Marine officer with 2 ratings dashed into the hold, driving us and the 12 Norwegians before them, just as we were about to make an effort to get up the ladder. They then mounted two machine guns and trained them on us, with every intention of murdering the lot of us. Had it not been for the timely arrival of the Chief Officer, who kicked away the supports of the machine guns, there is little doubt that we should not be alive to tell the tale. The Chief Officer informed the Marine that the Captain had ordered us to go on deck and to take our chance in the lifeboats with the rest of the crew. We went up to the boat deck with the Chief Officer, and saw that the shells were coming over very fast now. The two starboard lifeboats were lowered and I believe the crew in these two boats were rescued by a submarine later in the day. Angus MacDonald, the quartermaster, was in one of these boats, and I understand this man is now a prisoner of war in Germany. I remained with the German

144

chief officer who abandoned the ship in one of the port lifeboats with 37 of the crew. He set a course for Spain, knowing it was not far away. The boat had plenty of food and water, I found the German biscuits much softer than ours and much easier to eat, also instead of pemmican they had tins of bully beef which is much more palatable. Besides the usual water supply this lifeboat had a number of bottles of soda water. The German officer did not take much trouble to ration the food as he expected to reach Spain within a few days. On the 5th January we were picked up by a Spanish fishing trawler which towed the boat to Corunna arriving at 1500 on the same day. The Captain's lifeboat had arrived on 4th January. I had barely recovered from my first trip in a lifeboat, consequently I was feeling very weak and tired when I arrived at Corunna. The British Consul was informed that there were no English people in the lifeboat, and had not sent anyone to meet me. However, on learning I was British he immediately came down and at 1930 took me to a hotel where I stayed for 5 days, before being sent by rail to Madrid; from there I proceeded to Gibraltar, and finally returned to the United Kingdom.

I would like to specially mention the outstanding behaviour of Quartermaster Angus MacDonald. This man took full charge of the lifeboat after the death of Chief Officer Britt and Captain MacCall. He was very experienced in small boats and took charge of the steering while I looked after the rations and kept the natives in order. Whilst in the lifeboat I kept a log of all the events but on being rescued by the s.s. *Rhakotis* this log was taken from me, in fact everything was stripped from our lifeboat and taken on board.

Jack Edmead's lifeboat was one of six which survived the sinking of the *City of Cairo* – two boats had been destroyed when the first torpedo struck. They were all grossly overloaded, carrying between them 294 survivors. One of the boats, with fifty-four persons on board, lost touch with the others during the first night adrift, which proved to be a blessing, in that it sailed into the path of the southbound British ship *Bendoran*. The *Bendoran* rescued all fifty-four and took them to Cape Town. Another fifty-four survivors were not so fortunate. Their boat also lost touch with the others, and was never seen or heard of again. A third boat, this time with fifty-six on board, lost touch after a week, and continued sailing north for another six days, before being picked up by the British ship *Clan Alpine*, which was heading for St Helena. The remaining two boats performed an amazing feat of navigation covering a distance of 590 miles under sail, sighting St Helena, a tiny speck in this vast ocean, on 19 November, thirteen days after leaving their torpedoed ship. They were also picked up by the *Clan Alpine*, which landed a total of 156 survivors on the island. Unfortunately, eight of these died in hospital after landing.

Under the command of Chief Officer Sidney Britt, Edmead's boat also attempted to reach St Helena, but after fourteen days without sight of the land, it was accepted that they must have sailed past the island, and the decision was made to sail west to South America. Rather than trying to find St Helena, this must have seemed the most feasible alternative, for they were in the south-east Trades, and both wind and current would be behind them, urging them on. The distance was great, however and after 1,500 miles in an open boat, with no protection from the burning sun during the day and precious little to shield them from the chill of the long nights, it is not surprising that the majority on board did not survive to see the land again.

It was a cruel trick of fate that led Jack Edmead to be picked up by the German blockade runner *Rhakotis,* then bound for Bordeaux from Japan. But although the *Rhakotis* was carrying Edmead into certain captivity, it was even more ironic that his rescuer, then less than thirty-six hours from port, should be sunk by a British ship, the cruiser HMS *Scylla*. However, his fellow survivor, Angus MacDonald, was even less fortunate. MacDonald, along with roughly half of the *Rhakotis*'s crew, was rescued by the German submarine *U-410*, and was landed in St Nazaire. He spent the rest of the war in a prisoner of war camp.

When the final count was made, it was established that of those on board, four were believed lost with the ship, 100 died in the boats or after rescue, while 207 survived. The fate of the ship's cat, a stray ginger tom that boarded in Bombay, is unknown. It was last seen in No.8 lifeboat, where it had taken refuge to avoid the attentions of Chief Officer Britt who, following complaints from some of the passengers of the tom's loud meowing, was trying to remove it to another part of the ship. The cat refused to be enticed out of the boat, and in desperation Britt attempted to smoke it out with a sulphur candle. It has been said that it was the smoke from this candle that was sighted by *U-68*, and although this makes a good story, it seems far more likely that the tell-tale smoke came from the *City of Cairo*'s funnel.

Chapter Twelve

On 2 November 1941, General Bernard Montgomery's 8th Army, backed by 800 guns and six armoured brigades, smashed through the German lines at El Alamein and sent Rommel's mighty *Afrika Korps* into a headlong retreat all the way back to the frontiers of Tunisia. Four German and eight Italian divisions were dispersed in confusion and 30,000 prisoners, 350 tanks and 400 guns were captured. Five days later, in the small hours of 8 November, 90,000 British and American troops, carried in 600 ships, stormed ashore on beachheads from Casablanca to Algiers. The last great battle for control of North Africa had begun. A steady supply of men and equipment was required to sustain this operation, and among the many ships involved was the trooper *Empress of Canada*.

The 21,517-ton *Empress of Canada*, built in 1922 for the Canadian Pacific Railway Company, and requisitioned by the Admiralty in 1939, made two voyages carrying American troops into Mers el Kebir, then, in January 1943, left the Clyde with 3,000 British servicemen on board. Under the command of Captain George Goold, she sailed in convoy with other troopships around the Cape, through the Suez Canal to Alexandria, where she landed her troops. Homeward bound again with several hundred 'walking wounded' on board, she diverted to Bombay to pick up 200 Polish and Greek refugees, who had been released from Russian prison camps following the German attack on Russia.

Calling at Durban on her way south, the *Empress of Canada* took on a token cargo of 800 tons of sugar, and her passenger list was swelled by the addition of 200 British naval personnel and 499 Italian prisoners of war. The latter, captured by the 8th Army in the push from Alamein, joined via a camp in Ethiopia. Including her crew of 362, on sailing from Durban on the evening of 3 March, the trooper had on board a total of 1,892 souls. As she was able to maintain a speed in excess of 18 knots, and was armed with a 6-inch gun, two 12-pounders, a Bofors, eight 20-mm Oerlikons and two twin-Browning .5-inch machine guns, the Admiralty considered the *Empress of Canada* was capable of sailing unescorted, at least until she reached Freetown. However, as it was believed that U-boats were active off Cape Town, she was routed south from Durban, reaching down almost into the Roaring Forties, before turning west, then north in mid-Atlantic to pass within sight of Tristan da Cunha. This extensive detour added more than 1,000 miles to the passage, but was considered to be prudent.

Coincident with the 8th Army's breakthrough at El Alamein on 2 November, was the return of the Italian U-cruiser *Leonardo da Vinci* to the Atlantic. On her way north after sinking the *Alioth* in the previous June she had sunk one other ship, the 6,471-ton *Clan Macquarrie*, before returning to her base in Bordeaux in early July. She did not venture out again until October when, under the command of *Capitano di Corvetta* Gianfranco Gazzana-Priaroggia, she appeared off the lonely St Paul's Rocks, a cluster of five craggy pinnacles covered in bird droppings 600 miles off the coast of Brazil near the Equator. Lying in wait for ships taking the mid-Atlantic route, Priaroggia sank four, one British, one Greek, one American and one Dutch, in nine days. Apparently satisfied with his success, he then returned to Bordeaux. The *Leonardo da Vinci* was now the top scoring Italian submarine of the war, having sunk nine ships totalling 51,242 tons in two years of operations. These were high figures for one of Mussolini's boats, but insignificant compared with the average German U-boat, which was sinking more in a single three-month patrol. After the usual long lay-up, the *Leonardo da Vinci* left Bordeaux in late February 1943 to return to the Gulf of Guinea. Capitano Gazzana-Priaroggia's finest hour was yet to come.

The *Empress of Canada*'s northward passage up the South Atlantic was in good weather and without incident, the boredom of the long days being relieved for the passengers by frequent boat drills and practice gun shoots. Captain Goold had wisely put the British naval personnel in charge of passenger discipline, a move that paid dividends. Charles Roberts, one of the naval party, later recalled:

> A very friendly atmosphere had developed on board and, despite the many nationalities, communication was quite good and very few people resented the policing role the Navy had to exercise. The many Polish passengers were very easy to get on with and as a few of them spoke English, they acted as interpreters, translating the various orders which had to be observed to ensure the smooth running of the passenger section of the ship. The ship's company of the *Empress of Canada* had their own normal duties to carry out.

On 12 March, when the *Empress of Canada* was to the east of Ascension Island, and a day's run south of the Equator, Captain Goold received orders to make a call at Takoradi to pick up another 300 Italian prisoners of war. This was not welcome news for Goold, the ship's lifeboats already being totally inadequate for the number of people on board. The only concession to his swollen complement was a number of large balsa wood rafts, which had been put on board in Durban. Goold fervently hoped that these would never be used.

The next day dawned fine and clear, the sea a flat calm and as the sun rose, the accommodation of the crowded troopship quickly became like the inside of a hot oven. Those who were able to sought out the shade on deck, and all movement was kept to a minimum. The *Empress of Canada* was zigzagging around a mean course of 062 degrees at 18.5 knots with her bow-wave foaming and the dog-leg pattern of her wake stretching back to the far horizon. She was less than a day's run from Cape Palmas, her long voyage around Africa drawing to a close, and there was a feeling of quiet confidence in the air. Having sailed nearly 12,000 miles, much of it in dangerous waters, without so much as a scratch on her paintwork, in the opinion of those who knew – and there were many on board – she could come to no harm now. No one gave thought to the fact that this was Friday the 13th, and the devil that

150

rides the backs of seamen on this day was at work. Over the horizon, and patiently patrolling right in the path of the liner was Gianfranco Gazzana-Priaroggia's *Leonardo da Vinci*.

When, after a long, hot day, the cool of the night descended on her again, the *Empress of Canada* pressed on under the light of a full moon, confidently eating up the miles and altering course each time the bell of the zigzag clock in the wheelhouse pinged. As the night wore on, the sky clouded over, and a gentle south-easterly breeze urged her on her way. At a quarter to midnight, Captain Goold came onto the bridge to write up his night orders before turning in. He was chatting to the officer of the watch when, at 23.56, Priaroggia's torpedo erupted in the bowels of his ship. Goold later wrote in his report to the Admiralty:

The torpedo struck in way of No.4 stokehold on the starboard side. There was a dull, heavy explosion, but very little effect was felt on deck, no water was thrown up and no flash. The track of the torpedo was not seen by any of the official lookouts, but later some of the Greek passengers said they saw it. The main steam pipe in the engine room was shattered by the explosion, putting everything out of action, the engineer on watch was blown off the platform, the engines stopped immediately, all lights failed, and having no power the steering gear was out of action. One boat became unhooked and fell into the water. I ordered the Wireless Operator to send out an SSS message, which was done immediately, and although we received no reply, I learned later that it was picked up by everybody in the vicinity.

I then gave the order for emergency stations, and 10 minutes later the Chief Engineer reported that the engine room was filling rapidly, it was impossible to keep the water down, so I gave the order to abandon ship; she had now taken a list of 15–20 degrees to starboard. We carried 10 boats fitted with Wellin gear, one of which had fallen into the water as described, but we lowered the other 9 boats without difficulty. The remaining boats were fitted with Wylie gear, and as we had no power we could only manage to launch three of these by hand, making 12 boats, which were filled to capacity and pulled clear of the ship. At 0200 we made a signal stating that we were abandoning ship. Meanwhile, the Naval party took charge of the Italian prisoners, helping them down the scrambling nets into the water. We had 499 Italian prisoners of war and an Italian doctor to look after them. They behaved very well, were not at all panicky, but disliked the idea of taking to the water and were very slow in doing so; I promised to pick them up in the boats and rafts as soon as possible. We all had our lifejackets on, including all passengers, but only the crew had the red lifejacket lights.

We were still trying to launch some of the Wylie boats when at 0050, roughly an hour after the first, a second torpedo struck the ship, again on the starboard side, in way of an oil tank immediately under the bridge. The track of the torpedo was not seen, but a Naval signalman on watch said he had seen the submarine pass across our stern soon after the first torpedo was fired. This explosion was also dull and heavy, a huge column of water was thrown up, damaging one of the boats and throwing all the occupants into the water; many of the Naval party who were helping the prisoners over the side were lost at this time. We launched all the rafts and buoyancy floats – 4 large Fleming rafts, which were very good indeed, being fitted on special skids on the after deck, 12 or 14 Carley floats of various sizes, and 50 small buoyant floats.

The ship took a further heavy list to starboard, which increased to about 40°, making it impossible for me to walk from the lee side of the deck, and at 0110 I was able to step off the ship into the water, accompanied by the Chief Officer, J.S. Clarke, and Chief Engineer, Mr Cowper, we three being the last to leave. The vessel then slowly righted herself, rose vertically by the bows, and plunged straight down by the stern at 0115, about 5 minutes after we were clear. I swam round for about 2 hours, the Poles and Greeks made no attempt to help me into a boat, so I swam away until a little later I was hailed by a young RNVR Lieut. O'Brien, who had found the waterlogged boat which had been damaged by the second explosion. He managed to haul me into it, although he was nearly as exhausted as I was, both of us having swallowed a good deal of fuel oil. A short distance away we sighted an upturned boat with two men clinging to it, we called out to them, and they swam over to help us. These two men, Petty Officer Hunter, and my 5th Officer, Mr Bullock, were both young and hefty, and together they bailed out the water from the boat, which was down to the gunwales. The water tanks had been blown out of the boat by the explosion, and the pump in the bottom could not be used with the water at its present level, but we continued to bail, using a bucket, the sea anchor, boots and shoes, in fact everything we could find, then we got the pump working, until we completely emptied the boat, which we found almost undamaged.

Then Commander Begg came along with a Carley float having some 60 people on it, all of whom were eventually taken into the boat, after which we collected a crowd from another raft until we had between 96 and 100 people in it. Commander Begg's party were mostly Italian prisoners of war, and he had a Marine Officer and 2 ratings in charge with him. Daylight was breaking, the boats had drifted a good deal to leeward of the rafts, and the two motor lifeboats were going round collecting survivors from rafts and wreckage. Both these boats had a fitted wireless set, one would not work as the batteries were flooded, but the other worked most efficiently and I learned later from various naval craft that the signals we sent out from this set were picked up. The motor boats found it impossible to tow the rafts, so they towed the boats back to the vicinity, then transferred many of those who were struggling in the water, and others from the rafts and floats. All my Deck Officers, except one who went away in charge of his boat, left the ship at the last moment and were swimming round for some 12 hours before being rescued, and so were most of the Naval party, who stayed on board as long as possible to look after the Italian prisoners. A lot of people were bitten by sharks; I was not bitten myself during the 2 hours I spent swimming round, but I was smothered with fuel oil which probably kept them away, as they don't like the taste of it. Several people were suffering from barracuda bites;

I think the sharks are worse, but the barracuda are more annoying as they bite slowly.

Other survivors described their experiences in abandoning the sinking ship. Charles Roberts, one of the Royal Navy party:

Grabbing a pair of shorts and my shoes I made my way as fast as possible up the two stairways to the upper deck, and sat down for a brief moment to put on my shoes and proceeded to my boat station. By this time the ship had ceased to list and was lying quite steady. There was little sign of panic, but everyone was in a hurry to get to their boats and rafts.

Our lifeboat was quickly filling up with people, and luckily I had a leading seaman RN and two merchant seamen to help me get the boat lowered into the water . . .

On (the boat) reaching the water the four of us who had lowered the boat quickly shinned down the main ropes to join our friends below. The slips holding the boat to the falls were quickly released and we drifted slowly away from the ship's side.

Just before we pulled away a Polish woman jumped overboard from the liner's deck, and landed in the water by our boat striking her legs on the gunwale as she fell. We dragged her aboard quickly, but there was no time to discover how badly injured she was. Our main concern at this time was to put as great a distance as possible between the lifeboat and the ship to avoid being sucked down when the *Empress of Canada* sank . . .

A few minutes later the second torpedo hit the liner immediately beneath a lifeboat full of passengers, who were just about to draw away from the ship. The awful sight of the boat disintegrating in a large column of water with bodies flying in all directions is one I can never forget . . .

Joe Clark, laundry boy, and youngest member of the crew:

As any seaman will tell you, the boat deck of a 21,000-ton liner is a long way above the waterline. I could make out the rafts below me in the water but at this stage I was very reluctant to go over the side. This problem was solved by one of the ship's firemen telling me he would help me when I reached the water, but I never saw him again.

The water was quite warm and I swallowed quite a bit, along with a mixture of fuel oil, before I was grabbed by the hair and one arm and lifted into a life raft. We must have looked like members of a minstrel group and the smell of oil was everywhere. One of our group, an AB who, on previous trips had told us he was an atheist, recited the Lord's Prayer from start to finish.

We could hear a lot of shouting and some screaming all around us and we heard voices in Italian coming from a megaphone or something of this nature. I know now that it was from the submarine that had sunk our ship . . .

Charles Cusack, one of the *Empress of Canada's* crew:

There was a lot of confusion and shouting to each other. I just grabbed my lifejacket and bolted through the door, making my way to the main hallway, where there was an emergency exit. It was a steel spiral staircase leading to the deck . . .

I managed to get into a boat before it was lowered away. As soon as we hit the water we pulled clear of the ship, knowing that as she was sinking we could be sucked down with her.

The night was filled with all the cries and calls for help. We pulled as many people as we could out of the water and filled the boat up as much as we dare. We also had to keep bailing the water out of the boat constantly. We were extremely lucky that the weather was calm or else we would have sunk because the boats were very overcrowded. With so many different languages being spoken the confusion continued into near chaos. I'm sure there was many a prayer said that night for the weather to stay calm . . .

Daylight came on the 14th to reveal a sea of wreckage, all that remained of the crack ocean liner *Empress of Canada*. Amongst

155

the flotsam drifted a forlorn flotilla of lifeboats, life rafts and buoyancy floats, packed with humanity, while dozens of other survivors clung to bits and pieces of wreckage around them. Sharks and barracuda were at work, and the cries of those attacked were pitiful, but there was no one to help them. One by one they succumbed, either through sheer exhaustion or taken by the predators. In the lifeboats the tight discipline exercised by Captain Goold still held sway. The boat of which Charles Roberts found himself in charge was perhaps a typical example.

> At daylight I was able to take stock of the situation and discovered I had a boat load of 75 survivors, including 45 Polish soldiers, 18 Polish women (one with a broken leg), a naval leading seaman and a drunken colonial civil servant who must have consumed a bottle of whisky before he abandoned ship, and was something of a liability until he sobered up. All he wanted to do was lay down and sleep, which was practically impossible when you have 75 people packed into a boat with a life-saving capacity of 50! He recovered after a few hours, and later apologized for being such a confounded nuisance.
>
> We quickly sorted ourselves out, and the women were moved to the fore end of the boat. There was a first-aid box in the boat, and with a rudimentary knowledge of first aid I was able to bind up the lacerated leg of the Polish girl and make her reasonably comfortable. A canvas screen was stretched across the boat dividing the men from the women to give the women a certain amount of privacy . . .

When the sun came up, Captain Goold instructed all the lifeboats to hoist their red sails and fly the large yellow distress flags they were all equipped with at the mast to make them more easily visible. His initiative paid off that afternoon, when a patrolling Catalina flying boat spotted them, and flew low, signalling with its lamp that help was on the way. Hearing this news, the spirits of the survivors soared, but their hopes were premature. Charles Roberts reports on his boat:

The first day dragged on. There was little to do except to look around the horizon hoping for a ship to turn up, and for us to talk to each other.

The fierce heat of the sun, especially when at its meridian, was a great discomfort to those with no head-gear and bald heads. I was one of these, my clothing consisting of a pyjama jacket and shorts, and I soon began to feel dizzy and sick, and my head began to blister. One of the Polish women, noticing my discomfort, took off her cotton petticoat, tore it into squares and knotting the four corners, made me a hat (I remember the colour – white with red polka dots). I probably looked like one of the 'Pirates of Penzance', but this head-gear undoubtedly saved me from severe sun-stroke. The temperature plummeted at night, and most of us shivered with the cold . . .

After another long, gruelling day in the sun, help finally appeared for the survivors at dusk on the 15th, when the British corvettes *Boreas, Crocus* and *Petunia* came steaming over the horizon. They lost no time in picking up those in the boats and on the rafts, *Boreas,* being first to arrive, was soon full to capacity and returned to Freetown, leaving *Crocus* and *Petunia* to finish the job. Once they had taken everyone off the boats and rafts, the two corvettes spent the rest of the night and all next day searching the surrounding waters, rescuing those who remained alive clinging to the buoyancy floats and pieces of wreckage. The armed merchant cruiser HMS *Corinthian* arrived on the morning of the 16th, and took on board all those who had been rescued, leaving *Crocus* and *Petunia* free to continue the search, which was finally abandoned on the morning of the 17th. Captain Goold later reported:

Our own Naval losses were heavy, chiefly because the men stayed to the last helping the Italian prisoners of war to get away, and they also assisted my crew in every way they could. The Italians were not panicky, but acted rather like sheep and were very slow; unfortunately, the Greeks – about 200 ratings and 20 officers – and the Poles were the worst offenders for being panicky. It is significant that all the Greek officers were saved, and most of the Polish officers, whilst our losses amongst Naval officers were high. I cannot speak too highly of our Naval men, they were wonderful throughout.

I should especially like to mention Petty Officer Hunter, and also my 5th Officer Bullock. These two men were hanging on to the keel of an upturned boat when they spotted the waterlogged boat in which were myself and Lieut. O'Brien, RNVR. They immediately swam over to our boat, and it was only through their strenuous efforts that the boat was eventually dried, after which we were able to rescue nearly 100 people. Hunter was particularly good all the time afterwards until picked up; O'Brien and I were both exhausted and ill from swallowing so much fuel oil, so Hunter took complete charge of the boat, and had the Italian prisoners so well trained that he brought the boat alongside *Petunia* just like a naval cutter; it was a great credit to him.

My Chief Officer, J.S. Clarke, was responsible for the organization of the ship, and I consider it was his efficient handling of the abandoning ship which helped to save so many lives. Chief Engineer Cowper went below to shut off the fuel pump, well knowing that a second torpedo might strike the ship at any moment, and another man worthy of mention is Doctor Miller, our ship's doctor, who attended to the wounded without rest or thought for himself.

With so many diverse nationalities on board, and so many different languages being spoken, the evacuation of the *Empress of Canada* after she had been torpedoed was by no means a 'text-book operation'. Mercifully, the weather was good, but it was largely due to discipline and courageous action of the liner's crew and the British naval party on board that it was a success. The ship sank twelve minutes after the second torpedo struck, but even so, of the 1,892 people on board, 1,499 were saved. Forty-four crew members, eight DEMS gunners, fifty men of the naval party and 290 passengers lost their lives. Their executioner, Gianfranco Gazzana-Priaroggia, who came to the surface and went alongside one of the lifeboats, taking off an Italian doctor, was well aware that a large number of his fellow countrymen were struggling in the water, yet he made no attempt to help them. He quickly moved off to the south, where five days later he came upon the British merchantman *Lulworth Hill*.

The 7,628-ton *Lulworth Hill*, a 14-knot steamer owned by the Counties Ship Management Company of London, was under the command of Captain William McEwan, and on passage from Cape Town to Freetown with a cargo of 10,000 tons of sugar destined for a British port. She was manned by a crew of forty-five, which included seven DEMS gunners, and was armed with a 4-inch anti-submarine gun, four 20-mm Oerlikons, two twin Marlins, two Lewis guns and, unusually for a merchant ship, carried three depth charges on a ramp at her stern.

At dusk on 18 March, the *Lulworth Hill* was about 250 miles to the south-east of Ascension Island, and zigzagging on a northerly course at 13.5 knots. Captain McEwan was aware that he was approaching the position where the *Empress of Canada* was torpedoed and had extra lookouts posted; the 4-inch was manned by the DEMS gunners. It was one of these extra pairs of eyes that saw the track of a torpedo approaching from the starboard quarter, and raised the alarm.

The torpedo missed, passing within a few feet of the ship's stern, and minutes later the *Leonardo da Vinci*, rather foolishly, surfaced about 250 yards off the starboard bow. The *Lulworth Hill*'s gunners reacted immediately, getting off two rounds from the 4-inch. Their aim was accurate, but the submarine was so close that the gun could not be depressed sufficiently, and the shells went over the Italian. But they were close enough to persuade Capitano Priaroggia to crash dive. Captain McEwan, acted with equal promptitude, swinging the ship under full helm to put her stern to the submarine. Ringing for maximum speed, he zigzagged away into the approaching night.

Half an hour later, when it was fully dark, the beam of a searchlight was seen sweeping the sea on the *Lulworth Hill*'s starboard beam. Priaroggia had surfaced again and was looking for his potential victim. Ordering his gunners to hold their fire, McEwan once more put his stern to the submarine and zigzagged away. An hour later the horizon astern was lit up by snowflake flares as

159

Priaroggia continued his hunt. The flares were at least five miles away, and McEwan had good cause to hope that they had made good their escape.

The watches came and went, and with her engines beating out an urgent tattoo, and her hull vibrating to their beat, the British ship raced on, trying to put as much distance between herself and the enemy as possible. The sky was now overcast, obscuring the moon, and a fresh south-easterly was whipping up a choppy sea, all of which was in the *Lulworth Hill*'s favour. At around 02,30 on the 19th, four hours having elapsed since the last sighting of the enemy submarine, Captain McEwan decided it was safe enough for him to go below to snatch a few hours sleep.

McEwan had underestimated Priaroggia's determination. The Italian had taken his boat down, and had begun a careful search with his hydrophones. Listening conditions were ideal, and by midnight he had found the *Lulworth Hill* again, and was creeping up on her. At 03.45 he was close on her starboard beam, and fired a spread of two torpedoes, which went home in the merchantman's forward holds.

The explosion of the first torpedo to strike blew the ship's carpenter Kenneth Cooke out of his bunk. He had hardly scrambled to his feet when the second torpedo struck. Snatching up his lifejacket, he ran out on deck to find that the ship, her back broken, was sinking rapidly. The boat deck was already level with the water, and the base of the funnel awash. He ran to the rail and hurled himself over the side, just as the ship sank under him. Twice he was drawn down deep by the suction, but each time his lifejacket brought him to the surface again.

> I swam around until I found a lifebuoy to support me; I could see the red lights on the lifejackets of other members of the crew in the water. I was wearing my lifejacket, but in my great hurry I had put it on inside out, consequently my red light was next to my body and could not be seen. I could see a red light bobbing not very far away, so I swam towards it and found DEMS Gunner Hull. The sea was rough enough to make swimming unpleasant and conversation difficult, but we discussed what was to be done under the circumstances.

160

We knew none of the lifeboats had been lowered, but thought we might be able to find a raft, if any had floated off. We then saw some other red lights in the distance, and were just going to swim towards them when the U-boat surfaced and switched on its searchlight. I thought our best course would be to swim to the U-boat, so we made towards it. My lifebelt hampered my movements, consequently Gunner Hull reached the U-boat about four minutes before me. I saw him being pulled on board by two of the crew, and by the time I reached the side he had been taken below.

I therefore put my arm through a hole in the submarine's superstructure to support myself, and when the U-boat Commander saw me, he put the searchlight on me and asked a number of questions, e.g. the name of the ship, where from, where bound, our cargo, tonnage, etc., and also wanted to know where the Captain was. He spoke in broken English with a definitely German accent. It was too dark for me to see him clearly, and in any case only the top half of his body was visible, but I could see that he was clean shaven, and wearing a naval uniform cap with gold braid. Three or four other members of the crew were with him on the conning tower, but I did not hear them speak.

When the Commander had finished questioning me, he flashed his searchlight around and sighted some other members of the crew on a raft; he then steamed towards them. He did not give me a chance to release my arm from the hole, consequently my arm was badly wrenched; the wash of the U-boat eventually flung me clear, but nearly drowned me.

By the light of the submarine's searchlight I saw what appeared to be six survivors on a raft, so I started swimming towards them. As I neared the U-boat I could hear the Commander talking to the men, and when I got to within 20 or 30 yards I heard him shouting something about the RAF blasting Germany, and heard him say 'Now you will drown!' He then switched off the searchlight and steamed away. I could hear his engines for five or six minutes, after which there was silence.

Cooke tried to contact the six men on a raft, but without success, and he soon found himself alone, drifting on this dark sea with the tiny wavelets created by the departing submarine lapping at his face. Not without good cause, he felt frightened and vulnerable. He swam around, shouting to attract the attention of other survivors, which he felt sure must be out there somewhere in the darkness.

After about half an hour, with only the silence of an empty sea answering his calls, Cooke at last heard another voice, and found Able Seaman Colin Armitage sitting on a raft which had floated clear when the ship went down. Cooke joined Armitage on the raft, each man overjoyed to have found the other. Some hours later they came across Chief Steward Herbert Thornton and hauled him onto the raft. The dawn came and the three men paddled through the floating debris that was all that remained of their ship, looking for other survivors. They soon came across Chief Officer Basil Scown, who had been swimming around all night. He was completely exhausted and retching violently, having swallowed a great deal of fuel oil. They were now four on the raft, and becoming more confident that their survival was possible. They found another life raft, larger and newer than the one they were on, so they transferred to it, taking the smaller raft in tow while they looked for other survivors. By nightfall, the four had become fourteen, and they were distributed ten to the large raft, and four on the smaller one. They set the small square sails carried by the rafts, and using the stars, as they had no compass, attempted to steer a course to the north-east, towards the land which they believed was around 900 miles away. It was a daunting prospect, but they had the heart for it – and what else could they do?

Writing on a piece of canvas with a small stub of pencil provided by Chief Officer Scown, Kenneth Cooke kept a day-by-day log:

We drifted with the current, finding the sun very hot during the day, but the nights were cold. We expected to be picked up at any time during the first week, and kept a continual lookout, but as the days went by and we saw nothing, the men began to get very downhearted. The Chief Officer was

162

ill from the very first day, and very quickly lost hope; he appointed me as his successor, and I took full charge after 6th April, when he became delirious, and died, after some eighteen days on the raft. I had the responsibility of rationing out the water and food, varying it as much as possible throughout the whole period, according to the condition and numbers remaining . . .

Our greatest problem was water, all of us suffered from intense thirst, and after a while I noticed some of the survivors drinking salt water. Six of the survivors were boys under the age of 18, whom I found taking occasional drinks of salt water, so I warned them that they would die a terrible death if they persisted. They obeyed me for a day or two, but I soon found them taking surreptitious drinks of sea water. As they drank more and more, they rapidly became delirious, imagining they could see rivers of water and snow. One man became very troublesome, and had to be forcibly held down until he became too exhausted to struggle any more; I threw water over him with an empty biscuit tin to subdue him. Three of the men jumped overboard shortly after drinking salt water, until eventually, by the 21st April, after 33 days on the raft, all the survivors had died except myself and Able Seaman Armitage.

Some died from drinking salt water, others from exhaustion, and I think in many cases the men gave up hope, and lost the urge to struggle on for their lives. Their relative degrees of fitness did not seem to have much bearing on the sequence in which men died, this seemed to depend more upon the mental outlook of each individual. We were all having the same rations, so had equal chances of survival. The Chief Steward said right at the beginning that he thought he could hang out for thirty days at the most, and strangely enough he did actually die about this time. After ten or twelve days, everyone suffered from salt water boils, and we were all covered with them. The 2nd Engineer developed gangrene in his feet, which had been injured when the ship was torpedoed, and one of the young boys also suffered from gangrene . . .

With only himself and Armitage alive, Cooke was able to increase the daily ration of food and water, which gave them the strength and fortitude to hold on. On 2 May, after forty-four days on the raft, they were sighted by a patrolling aircraft, but they would have to endure six more days adrift, during which their raft was harassed by a number of very large sharks, before they were finally picked up by the destroyer HMS *Rapid*.

When they were picked up, Cooke and Armitage were around twenty miles south of the Equator, and 430 miles from the nearest land, despite the prevailing winds and currents, both of which should have been carrying them further away from the land. That they survived at all was undoubtedly due to the firm hand exercised by Kenneth Cooke who, although only a carpenter more used to sounding bilges and repairing hatchboards than taking command, had shown exemplary leadership and seamanship.

Chapter Thirteen

The *Leonardo da Vinci* continued south after sinking the *Lulworth Hill*, rounding the Cape of Good Hope into the Indian Ocean. She then began to cruise in the approaches to the port of Durban, one of the main bunkering stations for ships bound to and from the Middle East and India. Gianfranco Gazzana-Priaroggia had chosen his location well, for in the course of seven days he sent four Allied ships to the bottom. On 17 April he sank the Dutch steamer *Sembilan,* the British steamer *Manaar* on the 18th, the American Liberty ship *John Drayton* on the 21st, and the British motor tanker *Doryssa* on the 25th, adding another of 23,327 tons to the *Leonardo da Vinci*'s already impressive total. But this proved to be her swan song. Returning to her base at Bordeaux, on 23 May, when 330 miles to the west of Cape Finisterre, she fell in with the destroyer *Active* and the frigate *Ness*, outriders of a British hunter-killer group, and was herself promptly sunk, taking Priaroggia and all his crew with her.

By then, time was running out for the Italian submarines. Sicily was soon to fall to the Allies, and on 3 September British and American troops landed on the mainland. The Italian army, with no more stomach for the fight, crumbled before them, and although German troops continued to fight on, the Italian Government decided to throw in the towel. An armistice was signed, and eight days later, on 11 September, what remained of the Italian fleet surrendered to the Allies.

Overall, the war record of the Italian submarines did not match up to their potential. Only two, the *Leonardo da Vinci* and her sister U-cruiser type the *Enrico Tazzoli*, had made any real impression on Allied shipping, sinking between them thirty-two ships totalling 210,000 tons. By and large, the others had little success, although their claims were often extravagant. Enzo Grossi, in the *Barbarigo,* for instance, claimed to have sunk two American battleships, and became an Italian hero. His 'battleships' were later revealed as the US light cruiser *Milwaukee,* which Grossi missed completely with two torpedoes, and the British Flower-class corvette *Petunia* of 925 tons, whose lookouts reported a torpedo passing beneath the ship, and was also undamaged. Carlo Feccia di Cossata, in the *Enrico Tazzoli,* displayed similar incompetence when he attacked the Elder Dempster motor vessel *Sangara.* The 5,445-ton *Sangara,* which had been earlier torpedoed by *U-69* while discharging at anchor, sank in shallow water leaving much of her upperworks exposed. Three months later Cossata came along, and taking the wreck of the *Sangara* for a ship under way, fired a torpedo at close range. Incredibly, he missed, yet he claimed to have sunk a 5,500 ton ship. In fact, the *Sangara* was later refloated and towed home, returning to sea after the war to continue trading for Elder Dempster until 1960.

The thirty-two Italian submarines which operated against the convoys in the North Atlantic were credited with only 109 ships between them, totalling only just over half a million tons. The remainder of Italy's large submarine fleet, which did not stray outside the Mediterranean, accounted for a mere fifteen merchantmen and ten small warships.

It was the opinion of Admiral Dönitz that the ineffectiveness of the Italian submarines was due largely to poor training and the inability of their officers to inspire their crews. Mussolini's boats were not run like the British and German submarines, where rank mattered little, and officers and men worked as a team, sharing the same quarters, the same food, and taking the same risks. The Italian submarines tended to act as though they were big ships, with officers and men strictly segregated, the officers enjoying better quarters and better food. This was not an atmosphere in which an efficient fighting team could develop.

With the Italian submarines out of the fight, it was the turn of another U-cruiser, *U-515,* to harass Allied shipping off the west coast of Africa. *U-515,* a Type IX C commissioned in February 1942 and under the command of *Oberleutnant* Werner Henke, was sent south in the spring of 1943, and on the night of 30

April was 130 miles south-west of Freetown. At around 21.00, Henke was delighted to see shadows approaching from the south-east. He was about to rendezvous with Convoy TS 37.

TS 37, a convoy of eighteen deep-loaded ships, was a new innovation on the West African coast. As a result of activities of the U-cruisers off Cape Palmas, the Admiralty had belatedly decided to fall back on a tried and tested system, ordering ships coming north from the Cape to call first at Takoradi, where they would be formed into convoys for the 800-mile passage to Freetown. While this may have been a wise precaution, West Africa was not high on the Royal Navy's list of priorities, which is why TS 37 was escorted by only a corvette and three anti-submarine trawlers, none of which was capable of any great speed, and mounting just four 4-inch guns between them.

By 22.50, Werner Henke had manoeuvred *U-515* into a position on the port side of the convoy, apparently undetected by the escorts' Asdics. He turned stern-on, and at 22.56 fired two torpedoes from his after tubes. Both found targets, one in the 5,236-ton British steamer *Bandar Shahpour*, loaded with 6,768 tons of manganese ore and produce from India and the Persian Gulf, while the other hit another British steamer, the 5,682-ton *Corabella*, loaded with a full cargo of manganese ore. Both ships sank within minutes, their ore cargoes dragging them down. The survivors were picked up by the trawler HMS *Birdlip*, the *Bandar Shahpour* having lost one man, and nine went down with the *Corabella*.

With the escorts steaming in frantic circles, Werner Henke followed up with another torpedo at 22.57. This hit the British India ship *Nagina*, 6,551 tons, carrying a cargo from India which included 2,750 tons of pig iron. She also sank quickly, and two of her crew of 113 were lost, HMS *Birdlip* rescuing the others.

Henke fired three more torpedoes, two of which missed, but the third found the 7,295-ton Dutch motor ship *Kota Tjandi*. She was nearing the end of a long voyage from Haifa with 5,000 tons of potash and 1,000 tons of tin in her holds. Six of her crew were lost, and once again *Birdlip* came to the rescue.

U-515 had fired six torpedoes in the space of five minutes, and had sunk four ships without coming under attack from TS 37's

167

escorts. Henke now retired to reload his tubes, but he was back again just before dawn on 1 May. He attacked at 05.40, firing three torpedoes in quick succession. The first hit the 6,555-ton British ship *City of Singapore,* carrying 9,025 tons of cargo from India, including 2,700 tons of pig iron. She caught fire and burned fiercely, but all ninety-seven crew members survived to be picked up by *Birdlip* and another trawler, HMS *Arran.*

Henke's second torpedo slammed into the Belgian motor ship *Mokambo* of 4,996 tons. She also caught fire, but reached Freetown under tow. Her next in line, the 6,940-ton *Clan Macpherson,* was less fortunate. She also had a large quantity of pig iron on board from India and sank, taking four of her crew with her, when Henke's third shot went home in her hull. HMS *Arran* picked up the others.

When TS 37 reached Freetown the next day, its Senior Officer Escort had a sorry tale to tell. He had lost seven ships and their valuable cargoes at the hands of one U-boat without being able to retaliate. It was later revealed that a U-boat had been heard transmitting early on the 31st – this was Henke reporting in to BdU – but instead of breaking radio silence to report this to Freetown, the SOE had signalled the sighting by lamp to a patrolling Hudson, expecting the aircraft to alert Freetown. This was not done until the Hudson returned to base. Destroyers sent out to help TS 37 did not arrive until Henke had completed his work and fled the scene.

Meanwhile, *U-68* had returned to sea to create havoc amongst Allied shipping with her characteristic efficiency. She was now under the command of *Oberleutnant* Albert Lauzemis, Karl Merten having left her when she returned to Lorient from the South Atlantic in December 1942. This marked the end of Merten's operational career in the U-boat arm, which had begun in May 1940. During his time in command, he had earned a reputation as one of Dönitz's top 'aces', being responsible for sinking a total of 170,151 tons of Allied shipping. He left *U-68* in January 1943 to apply his considerable experience and expertise to commanding the 26th Training Flotilla, based in the Baltic Sea. It was with this flotilla that new U-boat crews received their final training before they were sent into battle. Merten left *U-68* in good hands. At the age of twenty-five Lauzemis was very young to take command of an operational U-boat, but he had learned his trade well, having served in *U-68* under Merten until April 1942, firstly as second watch officer, and then first watch officer.

Lauzemis's first patrol, leaving Lorient on 3 February 1943, took *U-68* to the Caribbean, and was only moderately successful. By this time the Americans had their defences in order, and all ships were sailing in escorted convoys, with aircraft constantly patrolling overhead. In an attack on Convoy GAT 49 on 13 March, Lauzemis sank the 2,680-ton Dutch steamer *Ceres* and the 7,506-ton US-flag tanker *Cities Service Missouri*, but this was the only blow struck by *U-68* in a thirteen-week patrol. Following that, on four separate occasions she was surprised on the surface by aircraft of the USN 204 Squadron, being slightly damaged on the fourth occasion. This was enough to convince Lauzemis that the Caribbean was becoming too dangerous, and on 2 April he decided to make for home. *U-68* arrived back in Lorient on 7 May.

On 12 June, *U-68* set out from Lorient in company with *U-155, U-257, U-600* and *U-615*. Allied air activity over Biscay had risen to a new peak, and the five boats, all equipped with a formidable array of anti-aircraft weapons, were sailing together for mutual protection. At 09.00 on the 14th, they were spotted by four rocket-firing Mosquitoes of RAF 307 (Polish) Squadron, who immediately attacked. The U-boats scattered and while the others were able to dive quickly and escape, *U-68*, being a Type IX C, bigger and slower to submerge than the others, was caught on the surface. She received substantial damage and at the same time one man was killed and two injured, and Albert Lauzemis took a bullet in the jaw. His first watch officer assumed command of the boat, and brought her back to Lorient.

Lauzemis, by then recovered from his injuries, had resumed command when *U-68* once more left Lorient on 1 August, this time sailing unaccompanied. She was back again two days later, having been under attack from the air. On the 14th she set off again to cross Biscay, but was beaten back soon after she was out of sight of the land. She made another attempt to break out on 8 September, and this time was successful in reaching the Atlantic. Lauzemis had orders to take her back to the Gulf of Guinea, where it was felt his U-cruiser would once again fulfil her full potential. In addition to her standard type torpedoes she had on board a number of the new FAT (*Flächenabsuchender* or surface-searching) torpedoes. The FAT could be set to a pre-determined course and distance to run, after which it would zigzag about rapidly changing direction until it found a target. It had proved particularly effective against convoys in the Atlantic, as it was almost certain to collide with one of the ships in the massed ranks at the end of its run. Against single ships it had yet to prove itself.

Unlike his predecessor, Lauzemis enjoyed the back-up of Dönitz's *Milchkuhs* (milk cows), as the U-tankers now operating widely in the Atlantic were known. They were big, 2,300-ton Type XIV boats, which carried 700 tons of fuel, provisions, spare torpedoes and shells, and were equipped with repair facilities. *U-68* topped up her tanks twice from *Milchkuhs* on her passage south, once off the Azores, and again off the Cape Verde Islands. She reached the Gulf of Guinea around 20 October with full bunkers and provisions on board.

After dark on the 21st, Lauzemis was on the surface sixty miles to the south-west of Monrovia, charging his batteries and heading in the general direction of Cape Palmas, where he knew from past experience he was very likely to find Allied ships proceeding unescorted. It was a dark, moonless night, the sea a flat calm, the visibility excellent, and the silence disturbed only by the beat of *U-68*'s diesels. Steadying his binoculars on the rim of the conning tower, Lauzemis constantly scanned the horizon ahead. The line where the sky met the sea was clearly visible, but nothing moved on it. Then, at around 20.00, three darker shadows appeared. Ships.

Lauzemis brought his boat to action stations, and increased speed. The three shadows became two, one large, one small; then they hardened into the silhouettes of a large tanker, probably under escort by a small patrol boat. Lauzemis submerged and began to stalk his prey.

Unwittingly steaming into Albert Lauzemis's sights were the Norwegian tanker *Litiopa* and the armed trawler HMS *Orfasy*. The 5,356-ton *Litiopa*, owned by Martin Mosvold of Farsund and under the command of Captain Trygve Olsen, was a veteran of the oil trade, having been built in Sunderland in 1917. Age and hard steaming had reduced her to a state where she should really have been long retired and scrapped, but such was the need for oil in this war, that she had been pressed into Admiralty service as a fleet auxiliary in 1940. On her current voyage she was sailing in ballast from Lagos to Freetown, her escort being the 545-ton *Orfasy,* an Isles-class trawler commanded by Skipper W.J. Connolly RNR and armed with a 4-inch, four machine guns and a handful of depth charges. She was only a token escort, little more than a morale booster for the tanker's crew. Since the *Leonardo da Vinci* sank the *Lulworth Hill* seven months earlier there had been no enemy submarines reported in West African waters, and it must be presumed that the Admiralty assumed the *Orfasy* was sufficient protection for an old tanker sailing in ballast. As it transpired, this assumption was very naïve.

Just before midnight on the 21st, the two ships were steaming in line, the *Orfasy* leading, but out of sight in the darkness. On the bridge of the *Litiopa,* Third Officer Karsten Johansen was handing over the watch to Second Officer Arnfinn Larsen, when they heard the sound of depth charging coming from somewhere ahead. Captain Olsen was called to the bridge, and as he entered the wheelhouse the *Litiopa* was shaken by a heavy explosion. Olsen and the two officers scanned the darkness ahead with their binoculars, but nothing could be seen. An attempt was made to contact the *Orfasy* by W/T and lamp, but there was no reply.

Olsen was aware that there might be danger ahead in the darkness, but he had no idea how imminent it was. *U-68,* in attempting to close in on the tanker, had been detected by *Orfasy's* Asdic operator and Skipper Connolly had immediately attacked with depth charges. Lauzemis retaliated by firing two torpedoes at the *Litiopa,* but both went wide. The heavy explosion following the depth charging heard on the bridge of the Norwegian ship was Albert Lauzemis's third torpedo, aimed at the *Orfasy.* This scored a direct hit, and its 600lb warhead literally blew the little trawler apart. Skipper Connolly and his crew of twenty-nine all perished with her.

At 00.40 on the 22nd, Lauzemis fired a FAT at the *Litiopa,* which passed harmlessly across the stern of the tanker, again going

171

unnoticed by those on board. Two hours later, Lauzemis tried again, this time using a standard T3 torpedo. To his great consternation and frustration, this executed a U-turn and narrowly missed sinking *U-68*, exploding only a few metres astern.

And all the time, blissfully unaware that her escort had been sunk, and that she herself was under determined attack, the *Litiopa* steamed on. Then, at 04.27, the war was brought home to her when the silence of the dark night was rent apart by the flash and thunder of guns. Lauzemis had opened fire with all guns, the 105-mm aiming at the tanker's engine room, the 37-mm anti-aircraft gun at her after gun platform, and the four 20-mm cannon at the bridge.

The effect was immediate. The *Litiopa*'s crew, taken completely by surprise, and with shells and bullets falling all around them, lowered their lifeboats and abandoned ship.

At 04.48, with his victim well afire, Lauzemis tried to deliver the *coup de grâce* with another torpedo. To his great consternation, again, this ran in a circle and sank without hitting anything. He once more resorted to gunfire, but a tanker in ballast is notoriously difficult to sink with shells. At 05.41, in desperation, Lauzemis used another torpedo, which also missed. Eleven minutes later, having moved in closer, he fired yet another torpedo, which surely should have been the *coup de grâce* for the *Litiopa* but, unbelievably, this also went wide.

Having now expended seven torpedoes on the tanker which stubbornly refused to sink, Lauzemis again resorted to his 105-mm gun. At 06.30, with fifty-eight rounds fired and fifty hits registered, the *Litiopa* was well alight, and appeared to be sinking. Dawn was breaking, and with it came the increasing risk of *U-68* being sighted and attacked from the air. Albert Lauzemis decided he must suffer his frustration and leave the flames to complete his night's work. He stood his gunners down, released an *Aphrodite* radar decoy balloon to baffle any ships or aircraft that might be hunting him, and motored away to the south-east.

The Norwegian tanker's thirty-five man crew had taken to the water in four lifeboats, which had become separated during the night. At daylight, two of the boats, the motorboat with twelve men and the starboard midships boat met up again, the motor boat taking the other in tow. They then returned to the ship, which was still afloat, but on fire and listing heavily to starboard, with her stern very deep in the water. Later, when they were debating whether to re-board the *Litiopa,* her ammunition began to explode, and they were forced to retire to a safe distance. At 12.45, they watched, powerless to intervene, as she gave up her struggle and capsized and sank in a cloud of steam and smoke.

The boats now headed for the land, all four eventually reaching Robert Port, a sheltered anchorage forty-five miles west of Monrovia. On the 24th, they were taken to Freetown by a British corvette, where they boarded the troopship *Orbita* to return to the UK. During the attack on their ship, only two of Captain Olsen's crew were slightly injured but, sadly, Chief Engineer Georg Stausland and the *Litiopa*'s cook, Reidar Haagensen, died on board the *Orbita,* both of heart failure, probably brought on by their ordeal.

As the *Litiopa*'s voyage came to a sudden and unexpected end, far to the south the Liverpool steamer *New Columbia* was only halfway through hers. Ninety-six miles up the Congo River, she lay alongside the wharf at Matadi loading ingots of copper, brought 400 miles by rail and river from the mines of Katanga.

Elder Dempster's *New Columbia,* commanded by Captain Frederick Kent, was a near contemporary of the *Litiopa,* in that she had begun life in the First World War as the replacement vessel *War Pageant.* She was a substantially-built, all riveted ship of 6,574 tons, broad in the beam and shallow draughted, ideally suited for the West African trade, which involved a great deal of river work. She carried a crew of fifty-five, plus ten DEMS gunners, who manned her wartime armament of one 4.7-inch gun, four 20-mm Oerlikons, two twin .5-inch Colt machine guns, and an assortment of anti-aircraft rockets. Unfortunately, her 4.7 could not be fired owing to a defective recoil, but in these waters so distant from the war, it seemed unlikely that the gun would ever be needed. Nobody on board lost any sleep over this, least of all the nineteen Kru labourers who had been employed in Freetown for the coastal voyage, and were looking forward to returning to their families.

Leaving Matadi on the 26th, the *New Columbia* followed the

coast north, calling at Libreville, in French Equatorial Africa, which was then under Free French control. Libreville, lying only a few miles north of the Equator, has an annual rainfall of eighty inches (2,000 mm) and, when the rain is not falling, swelters under a boiling sun, with a stifling humidity that hovers on the verge of 100 per cent. In 1943, it was no more than a trading post on the north shore of the Gabon River estuary, and for the *New Columbia*'s Europeans, living aboard a ship whose only air conditioning was an open porthole, not a place to linger an hour longer than necessary. When they thankfully hove up their anchor on the 30th, and headed out into the open sea, the *New Columbia* had on board, in addition to 1,500 tons of copper loaded in Matadi, 2,500 tons of cotton, 350 tons of copra, 100 tons of palm kernels and 350 tons of palm oil, all commodities desperately needed in wartime Britain, and 600 tons of beer destined to slake the thirsts of the white population of Lagos. As instructed in his sealed orders, Captain Kent took a wide sweep out to sea before heading north to Lagos, where he expected to arrive at around noon on the 1 November. Unwittingly, for he had been given no warning of any enemy submarine activity in the area, he was about to run into *U-68*.

Having left the *Litiopa* and her crew to their fate, Albert Lauzemis had moved south-eastwards into the languid waters of the Bight of Benin, where once the slave traders reigned supreme. It was his intention to try his luck off the busy harbour of Lagos and the various outports of the Niger delta, where many ships went to pick up cargoes of timber and palm kernels.

Captain Kent reported:

At 1725 on the 31st October an object was sighted one point on the port bow. As we had sighted a number of whales during the day, I thought this accounted for this object. It was only visible for a minute or two, then disappeared; it was in the exact position where we were to make an alteration of course and I realized later that it must have been a submarine. However, it was almost dark and I altered course three points to starboard, as ordered, and then made a further evasive alteration of two points to starboard three quarters of an hour later.

174

Hurrying north in fine, clear weather, with only a gentle breeze disturbing the surface of a calm sea, the *New Columbia* was consistently logging a speed of 11 knots. At sunset, Kent discontinued the daytime zigzag, and set course directly for Lagos, then only 200 miles to the north. The night was very dark, and no one saw the track of Albert Lauzemis's torpedo, which came streaking in on the port bow at 21.15.

As was standard practice, Lauzemis had aimed for the engine room, the largest watertight compartment of any ship, which once open to the sea would mean the end for the *New Columbia*. But he had overestimated the speed of this obviously elderly vessel, and the Elder Dempster ship was hit in her No.1 cargo hold.

The unfortunate sailor on lookout on the forecastle head, right in the bows, was the only one to experience the full blast of the explosion – and lucky to escape with his life. Those on the bridge, among them Captain Kent, heard only a dull thud, and it was only when the ship lifted bodily under them that they became aware of the disaster that had befallen them. Then, hatches, beams and derricks, bales of cotton and other items of cargo were thrown high in the air, some of the debris raining down on the bridge. Immediately following this, the ship began to settle rapidly by the head. There was no mistaking her distress.

When he had recovered from the shock of the blast, Kent called for a report on the damage to the ship. A quick survey showed that the torpedo had exploded in No.1 hold severely damaging the after watertight bulkhead, and both the forward holds were now flooding. There was little that could be done to save the ship. The engines were stopped, and when the way was off the ship, the four lifeboats, all of which were undamaged, were lowered to the water, and the life rafts were launched, all being in the water within three minutes. When the majority of his men had left the ship, Kent ordered No.1 boat, which was in the charge of the Chief Engineer, to remain alongside, while the other three boats pulled clear of the ship. Like all shipmasters down through the ages, Captain Frederick Kent was reluctant to desert his ship. He remained on board with Chief Radio Officer Hawkes and Fourth Engineer Clark. Hawkes was attempting to repair the main radio transmitter, which had been knocked out of action by the blast, while

175

Clark stayed below to keep the pumps operating. Kent was of the opinion that there might still be a chance of saving the *New Columbia*. But it soon became obvious that this was impossible. Fortunately, by this time Hawkes had succeeded in transmitting a series of SSS messages, although he had not received any replies. Reluctantly, Kent ordered Hawkes and Clark to leave the ship by the boat still remaining alongside.

When they had gone, Kent was left to consider his next move. Alone on a ship now so heavily by the head that her foredeck was awash, there seemed little he could do to save her, yet he was still loath to leave his command. The decision was made for him half an hour later, when Lauzemis's second torpedo struck. And this time his aim was true. The *New Columbia* was hit squarely in her engine room, which immediately began to flood. The lifeboat, which was standing by alongside to take off Kent and the others, was lifted by the blast and thrown against the ship's side, damaged and swamped; several of its occupants ending up in the water. This was the *coup de grâce* for the *New Columbia*. The battered ship plunged by head until her stern was high out of the water, and then slipped under the waves. Kent hurled himself over the side as she went, and swam to the boat, which was standing by to pick him up. As he was hauled aboard, Lauzemis brought *U-68* to the surface and motored close to the Second Officer's boat. He did not linger long, asking the basic questions regarding the ship's name, cargo and destination, before disappearing into the night. Those in the lifeboats who were able to get a close look at their attacker described her as a 740-ton boat with *U-739* painted on her conning tower, but it was very dark and their eyes must have been playing tricks. *U-739* was in Arctic waters in 1943.

When *U-68* was out of sight, Captain Kent brought the four lifeboats together and, at midnight, the little flotilla, with the motor boat towing the others, set course for Lagos, which Kent estimated to be around 150 miles away. The emergency lifeboat radio had been put in one of the boats before leaving the ship, and at daylight on 1 November an SOS was sent out, repeated two hours later. The sea remained flat calm, and with the motor boat's tanks containing thirty gallons of petrol, which Kent believed was ample to see them to Lagos and beyond, he was content to continue the tow. At an estimated speed of between 3.5 and 4 knots, he was confident of reaching the coast in less than two days.

The effort of a long tow was not required, for at 08.00, two hours after the SOS had been sent by the emergency transmitter, a search aircraft was sighted flying low about ten miles off. The survivors hurriedly set off a smoke float, which laid a cloud of thick orange smoke on the water around them. Captain Kent records that the reaction was as looked for:

> He immediately altered course towards us, circled the boats, and signalled 'Help is coming, will return later'. He diverted the *Conakrian,* and at 1015 smoke was sighted on the horizon. We altered course to intercept, and by 1120 we were alongside. All survivors were on board the *Conakrian* by noon on 1st November, three of the lifeboats being hoisted on board whilst the damaged boat was destroyed. Captain Imaz did all he could to make us comfortable, providing food and accommodation, and attending to the various slight injuries the men had sustained.

Frederick Kent and his men were extremely fortunate, in that the weather was calm when they were torpedoed and Albert Lauzemis had allowed them ample time to abandon their ship before he fired his second torpedo. On the other hand, it speaks volumes for Captain Kent and his crew that the evacuation of the ship was very professionally done, and that their lifeboats were all in first class condition, particularly the motor boat the engine of which ran so sweetly that they would have been able to reach Lagos without assistance.

U-68 may have quit the scene of the sinking in a hurry, but Lauzemis was by no means finished with the Gulf of Guinea. He moved westwards again to Cape Palmas, but by now the Admiralty was well aware of his presence in the Gulf. Air and sea patrols were stepped up, and any merchant ships that moved on the coast were well escorted. It was not until the Free French steamer *Fort de Vaux* attempted a dash from Takoradi to Freetown on her own that Lauzemis's luck changed.

The 5,186-ton *Fort de Vaux* was another First World War

survivor, completed in October 1918 by the Ropner shipyard at Stockton-on-Tees as the *War Gnat* for the British owners Miller & Richards. She was sold on to the French company Chargeurs Réunis in 1919 and renamed *Fort de Vaux*, her home port being Le Havre. She then spent a profitable life carrying cargoes between France and West Africa, until she met up with *U-68*.

On 30 November, continuously at sea for eighty-three days, and a month without sighting a suitable target, Albert Lauzemis reluctantly concluded that he would serve no useful purpose by continuing to cruise aimlessly in the region of Cape Palmas. He turned for home, and that night, when *U-68* was seventy-five miles to the south-west of Monrovia, the *Fort de Vaux*, plodding westwards at a steady 9 knots, conveniently steamed into her sights. Lauzemis fired a spread of two torpedoes, one of which passed harmlessly astern of the *Fort de Vaux*, but the other caught the French ship squarely amidships. She sank in just over half an hour, giving her sixty-one man crew ample time to take to the boats.

U-68 rounded Cape Finisterre on 20 December and entered the Bay of Biscay, which had become a very dangerous stretch of water for the U-boats. Air patrols by British and American long-range aircraft were at an unprecedented level, with radar-equipped Liberators, Catalinas and Sunderlands constantly criss-crossing overhead. Adding to the danger were the British hunter-killer groups; highly trained teams of destroyers and sloops, six or seven strong. Originally formed to combat Dönitz's wolf packs in the North Atlantic, they had now moved into the Bay of Biscay. Herbert Werner, commanding *U-230*, remarked in later years of his feelings after reaching Brest in November 1943: 'Two years before, our battle line had been far out at sea. Last spring, it had moved east to the Continental shelf. Now the front had settled at the very coast of France.'

Oberleutnant Lauzemis had been forewarned of the hazards he faced and, as advised, kept close in to the Spanish coast after Finisterre, remaining submerged, except to recharge batteries at night – and even that was a dangerous undertaking. On the 23rd, being then only a few hours from Lorient, he deemed it safe to surface in daylight, but was immediately pounced upon by an Allied aircraft. Lauzemis saved his boat by taking her down in

178

an emergency dive but, even so, the attacking plane inflicted considerable damage on *U-68*'s ballast tanks by machine-gun fire before she went down. The holed tanks sent the boat out of control, and it was only by the quick thinking of his engineer, *Oberleutnant (Ing)* Franz Volmari, who fought to control the trim, that she did not shoot to the surface again.

U-68 found sanctuary in her reinforced concrete pen in Lorient later in the day. Her patrol had lasted 106 days, during which she had covered some 10,000 miles, but sank only three ships and a trawler. She still had five torpedoes on board when she returned to port.

Chapter Fourteen

U-68 did not return to sea until 27 March 1944, and when she did, Albert Lauzemis and his crew sailed with the knowledge that their beloved homeland , which had aspired to such great glory, was now facing the humiliation of defeat. In the east, Field Marshal von Manstein's once invincible *Panzers*, after a bitter winter of retreat, were being pushed back to the borders of Poland by the overwhelming might of the Red Army, while at home the German cities lay in ruins under the hail of bombs that rained down day and night from Allied aircraft. Out at sea, the situation was every bit as bad, 237 U-boats having been lost in 1943 for a meagre 3.25 million tons of Allied merchant shipping, comparing very unfavourably with the previous year, when 7.75 million tons were sunk for the loss of only eighty-six boats. Furthermore, another fifty-five boats had failed to return since the beginning of the year. And over all this loomed the growing threat of the Second Front, the proposed Allied invasion of Western Europe. This was not a scenario likely to gladden the heart of any German submariner leaving port to challenge the dangers of the Atlantic.

Three months in Lorient had made good the damage inflicted on *U-68* on her last homeward passage, and when she sailed again her anti-aircraft armament had been substantially upgraded and she was equipped with the latest FuMO-61, or *Hohentwiel* radar. Given this new equipment, her chances of crossing Biscay safely were greatly improved. But beyond that, she also faced the prospect of falling in with one of the Royal Navy's hunter-killer groups, which were now making forays into the Bay. Deeper into the Atlantic, the US Navy was also deploying similar groups, or task forces, against the U-boats, consisting of a small escort, or 'Woolworth', aircraft carrier with a three or four destroyer screen. These American groups were proving highly successful, as evidenced by the performance of the carrier USS *Guadalcanal*, commanded by Captain Daniel V. Gallery, and her destroyers *Chatelain, Flaherty, Pilsbury* and *Pope*.

On 9 November 1943, *U-544*, a Type IX C, commanded by *Kovettenkapitän* Willy Mattke, left Kiel with orders to take up a position in mid-Atlantic, to the west of the Azores, where she would act as a *Milchkuh* and weather reporting station. On 16 January 1944, she made a refuelling rendezvous with two other U-cruisers, *U-129* and *U-516*. Unknown to Mattke, he had chosen a position only twenty miles from the area patrolled by the *Guadalcanal* task force.

Just before sunset on the 16th, two aircraft returning to the carrier from patrol spotted the three U-boats on the surface engaged in the refuelling operation. The aircraft immediately attacked with rockets and depth charges. The U-boats, lashed together by bunkering hoses and mooring lines were caught completely unawares. *U-516* was able to disentangle herself and submerge, but not before she was hit and badly damaged. *U-129* was also hit and managed to dive, but the *Milchkuh*, *U-544*, was sunk.

It was almost dark when the aircraft returned to the *Guadalcanal*, and both crashed on landing, but Captain Gallery's task force had the satisfaction of claiming at least two U-boats sunk. He was right about *U-544*, but the other two, *U-129* and *U-516*, both survived, and limped into Lorient, *U-129* on 31 January and *U-516* on 26 February.

U-68, escorted by a destroyer as far as Cape Finisterre, reached the open Atlantic unmolested on 29 March. *Oberleutnant* Lauzemis's orders were to return to the Gulf of Guinea and attempt to repeat his success of the previous patrol. Course was set to the west of Madeira, Lauzemis electing to remain on the surface for much of the time, relying on his new radar to give early warning of the approach of enemy ships or planes. The weather was boisterous, dominated by spring gales, and progress was slow.

Approaching Madeira early on 9 April, Lauzemis received a signal from BdU warning that an American task force was in his immediate vicinity. From then on, he proceeded with extreme caution, keeping a good watch on the skies for patrolling aircraft. As the day wore on, he decided to run submerged. That afternoon, his hydrophone operator reported hearing the sound of depth charges exploding some distance ahead. Another U-boat was under attack.

The recipient of the depth charges was Werner Henke's *U-515*, back at sea again after a long lay-up in port. She had been caught on the surface by aircraft flying patrols from the carrier *Guadalcanal,* and had dived to escape. Henke hoped to slip away to the south, but the American pilots called in *Guadalcanal*'s destroyers, which soon located the fleeing U-cruiser by sonar. The four destroyers, USS *Chatelain, Flaherty, Pilsbury* and *Pope,* made a coordinated attack, with the inevitable result that *U-515* was sunk after a very short time. Henke and forty-three of his men survived, and were made prisoner aboard the *Guaducanal,* but sixteen others lost their lives. So ended the remarkable partnership of Werner Henke and *U-515,* who together had sunk twenty-seven ships, totalling 165,018 tons in just fifteen months.

The warning from BdU and the crash of the depth charges brought Albert Lauzemis to the correct conclusion that the reported American task force was in his immediate vicinity. He decided he would be safer on the surface. With extra lookouts posted, all guns permanently manned, and ready to dive at the first sign of the enemy, *U-68* proceeded with extreme caution. That night was fine and clear, with a brilliant moon giving excellent visibility and the U-cruiser ran to the south-west, her exhausts belching black smoke and her powerful diesels beating out a steady tattoo. With dawn approaching on the 10th and still no sight of the enemy, Lauzemis had begun to congratulate himself on a lucky escape, when the Americans found them.

When his lookouts reported the aircraft approaching – three fighter-bombers from the carrier *Guadalcanal* – Lauzemis had only two choices, to crash-dive or stay on the surface and fight back. He chose the latter, ordering his gunners to open fire as soon as the enemy planes were in range.

Ignoring the curtain of fire thrown skywards by *U-68*'s battery of 37-mm and 20-mm cannon, the leading aircraft, an Avenger, opened the attack with a salvo of eight rockets. She was followed in by another Avenger and then a Wildcat, which bracketed the U-boat with rockets, machine-gun fire and Mark 47 depth charges.

Despite her heavy anti-aircraft barrage, *U-68* was helpless in the face of this savage onslaught. She was hit several times before Lauzemis realized his mistake by staying on the surface. He ordered his men below, hit the klaxon, and took her down in a steep dive. She left a trail of oil from her punctured tanks as she plunged.

In the confusion Lauzemis failed to ensure that everyone was below before slamming the conning tower hatch shut. *Matrosengefreiter* Hans Kastrupp, who had been manning the 37-mm quick-firer on the *Wintergarten* deck, heard the klaxon, but stopped to secure the gun before making a dash for the conning tower. On his way there, he came across one of the other gunners lying badly wounded on the deck. Unable to bring himself to abandon the injured man, Karstrupp dragged him towards the conning tower, but when he reached there with his burden he was horrified to see that the hatch was firmly closed.

The boat began to sink under them, and within seconds Kastrupp found himself struggling in the water and fighting to avoid being pulled under by the suction. He continued to support his wounded companion, who soon lapsed into unconsciousness. The two men drifted away from the widening patch of oil left by *U-68*.

The oil patch was clearly visible from the air, and one of the Avengers swooped down to drop a pattern of depth charges. This proved to be the end for *U-68*. Her pressure hull, already weakened by the first attack, split apart, and she carried on down into the depths of the Atlantic, never to rise again. Albert Lauzemis and fifty-five of his crew went down with her.

To Hans Karstrupp, alone and still supporting the unconscious man, it seemed that he was facing a slow death from exposure, and he would have done so, had it not been for an act of compassion by one of the Avenger pilots, who dropped a small inflatable dinghy close to the two men. Karstrupp swam to the dinghy, dragged the other man aboard, and then lost consciousness himself. Three hours later, they were picked up by one of *Guadalcanal*'s destroyers. Karstrupp survived, but the other gunner was already dead when taken aboard the American ship. Transferred to the carrier, Karstrupp joined Werner Henke and the other *U-515* survivors, accompanying them to a prisoner of war camp when the *Guadalcanal* reached Norfolk, Virginia eight days later.

Admiral Dönitz's U-boats were now on the run, and there was little rest for Daniel Gallery's men. The *Guadalcanal* sailed again on 15 May, and with her went the five destroyers *Chatelain, Flaherty, Jenks, Pillsbury* and *Pope*. Gallery's orders were to scout off the West African coast in the region of Cape Verde, where intelligence from British and American sources indicated that a number of U-boats were currently operating. His confidence, boosted by the sinking of *U-544* and *U-68* – and perhaps others – Gallery now intended to go a step further and capture a U-boat intact. He communicated his plans to all the commanders in his group, and instructed them to train up boarding parties ready for the day, should it come. He did not however, and for good reasons, let his superiors know of his intentions.

One of the U-boats cruising off Cape Verde was *U-505*, returning to West African waters after a year in which she had suffered an incredible run of bad luck. After sinking the Dutch ship *Alphacca* south of Cape Palmas in April 1942, Axel Loewe had moved west into the Caribbean. There *U-505*'s voyage was brought to a premature end when Loewe fell ill with an inflamed appendix. In great pain, he took the U-cruiser back to Lorient, where he was hospitalized.

Loewe was still unfit for sea by the time *U-505* was ready sail on her next patrol, and his command passed to twenty-four year old *Oberleutnant* Peter Zschech. The voyage began well with the sinking of the 7,191-ton US steamer *Thomas McKean* in the Caribbean on 29 June, but then misfortune struck again. *U-505* was caught on the surface by a Hudson of 53 Squadron RAF and suffered major damage to her superstructure and conning tower, her second watch officer and one of the lookouts being seriously wounded. The damage to the U-cruiser was so bad that she was unable to dive, and Zschech had no alternative but to make for home. He made a rendezvous with the supply boat *U-462* in mid-Atlantic, and sufficient repairs were made to allow limited diving

184

capacity. And so, running on the surface, submerging to a shallow depth only when absolutely necessary, *U-505* crawled back to Lorient.

Seven months passed before *U-505* was fit and ready to resume her role in the war at sea, and when she did finally sail outward from Lorient again she had not gone many miles into the Bay of Biscay before defects were revealed that forced Peter Zschech to return to port. The same pattern was repeated no less than four times before it was discovered that French dockyard workers in Lorient were sabotaging the boat. Swift retribution for these men followed, and when Zschech took *U-505* to sea on 9 October 1943, it seemed that all her technical problems had been solved. But the Jonah riding on her back was still there.

Two weeks out from Lorient, *U-505* was detected by an Allied hunter-killer group and subjected to a heavy and prolonged attack by depth charges. This proved to be the final straw for Peter Zschech, who ever since taking command had been under the most severe stress. He retired to his tiny curtained cabin and shot himself. First Watch Officer Paul Meyer now took command, but was unwilling to take the responsibility of carrying on with the patrol. Once again *U-505*'s voyage was aborted, and she set course for Lorient.

U-505's third commanding officer since she was commissioned in August 1941, *Oberleutnant* Harald Lange, took over in November. Lange, at forty-one was, in the U-boat world, old for the job and he had very little experience as a submariner, having spent most of his service with the *Kriegsmarine* in patrol boats. Nevertheless, he was a first-class seaman, calm in the face of adversity, and well liked by his men.

U-505 put out from Lorient on her sixth attempt to rejoin the war on Christmas Day 1943, hardly an auspicious day on which to leave port. But then Lorient, by this time being subjected almost daily to heavy Allied bomber raids, was no longer a place for U-boats to linger, even though they were protected by sixteen feet of reinforced concrete in their pens. To return to the open sea, to their own natural element, even with all the risks involved, was almost a relief to the hard-pressed U-boat men.

But this proved to be yet another of *U-505*'s war patrols

destined to be brought to an abrupt end. She was still in the Bay of Biscay when, on 26 December her radio operator intercepted a signal from BdU asking any U-boats in the vicinity to render assistance to the survivors of the blockade runner *Alsterufer*. The homeward bound *Alsterufer* had been crossing the Bay when she was sighted by a Sunderland of RAF Coastal Command. A Liberator was called in, which attacked and sank the ship with rockets. German destroyers and motor torpedo boats on their way to escort the *Alsterufer* in, had at the same time run into a British cruiser force. A fight ensued, in which two MTBs and one destroyer were sunk, with the result that a large number of German survivors, from the *Alsterufer* and her intended escort, were either in the water or adrift in lifeboats. Canadian corvettes picked up seventy-four of the *Alsterufer*'s crew from four lifeboats, while *U-505*, searching for more survivors from the ship, found thirty-four men from the MTB *T 25*. Another boat, *U-618*, which had answered BdU's call despite being severely damaged, rescued twenty-five survivors from the destroyer *Z-27*.

With thirty-four survivors on board, some of whom were wounded, Harald Lange had no alternative but to cut short his first war patrol in command of *U-505*, and make for the nearest German controlled port, which was Brest. As she was nearing that port, disaster struck again. One of her main electric motors caught fire and was completely burned out. Replacing this involved dry docking and cutting a large hole in the pressure hull through which to lift out the damaged motor. As result, *U-505* languished in Brest for more than two months under repair.

It was mid-March 1944 before Lange took *U-505* to sea again and when he did he took the huge risk of crossing the Bay of Biscay at full speed on the surface. Although the Bay was at the time heavily patrolled by Allied ships and aircraft, Lange's gamble proved worthwhile. Within twenty-eight hours, *U-505* was clear of Cape Finisterre, and out in the open Atlantic. Lange's orders were to take her south to the approaches to Freetown.

Bad weather dogged *U-505* for much of the passage south and when she finally reached the vicinity of Freetown, Lange found that there had been a considerable change of policy since the

U-cruiser was last in these waters. Now nothing moved in the Gulf of Guinea unless it was heavily escorted.

There followed six weeks of sheer frustration during which Lange searched far and wide for accessible targets for his torpedoes, but without success. Enemy aircraft seemed to be constantly overhead, and patrolling destroyers and corvettes were everywhere. He was forced to spend much of the time, day and night, skulking beneath the waves. In order to escape the attentions of the searchers, he moved further in towards the African shore but, in doing so, on 4 June, when Allied landing craft were massing in the Channel ports for the invasion of Normandy, he sailed into the arms of Captain Daniel Gallery's hunter-killer group.

Just after 11.00 on the 4th, when 150 miles off the coast of Spanish Sahara, *U-505*'s hydrophone operator reported faint propeller noises. The sounds became louder, and were identified as the fast-revving beat of a warship's engines. It also became clear that there was more than one ship bearing down on the U-cruiser. At this point it might have been wise for *U-505* to go deeper and remain silent. Instead, Lange decided to go to periscope depth to investigate. What he saw there gave him no comfort at all. In view were three destroyers, and behind them something much larger. When a single-engined aircraft appeared flying low, it confirmed Lange's suspicions. This was an enemy carrier group.

Hastily lowering the periscope, Lange gave the order to dive deep, but he was too late. The rattle of bullets striking the hull told him the aircraft had spotted the boat below the surface, and was machine-gunning them. A few minutes later came the unnerving ping of a sonar beam striking the hull. They had been detected by the destroyers.

Had *U-505* been a Type VII, she might have stood a chance of diving quickly and shaking off her attackers, but inevitably her larger bulk slowed her down. Lange released a Bold decoy, a canister containing a compound of calcium and zinc, which created a mass of bubbles designed to confuse sonar operators. At the same time he fired a T5 acoustic torpedo, which he hoped would find a target amongst the enemy ships.

Gallery's task group had been at sea for three weeks, during which time it had steamed extensively in search of U-boats off the African coast without success. On the morning of 4 June, with all his ships running low on fuel, Captain Gallery decided he must go north to Casablanca to refuel. Ten minutes after Gallery signalled the destroyers to alter course, at 11.09 USS *Chatelain,* commanded by Lieutenant Commander Dudley S. Knox, USNR, reported a sonar contact 800 yards on her starboard bow. The *Guadalcanal* immediately steamed clear to allow the destroyers to attack.

Chatelain confirmed the sonar contact as a submarine, and raced in to attack, firing depth charges from her 'hedgehog' ahead of her. She lost contact as she passed over the U-boat, but two Wildcat fighters from *Guadalcanal* were overhead and able to see the outline of *U-505* in the clear Atlantic water. They dived and marked out her position for *Chatelain* with machine-gun fire. Knox swung the destroyer round, regained sonar contact, and ran back dropping a pattern of depth charges set to shallow.

The resulting scene inside *U-505*'s pressure hull was chaotic. *Chatelain*'s 300lb Torpex charges exploded with devastating effect all around the diving boat. Gauge glasses shattered, all the lights went out and, in those few terrifying moments until the emergency lighting cut in, men screamed as they were thrown about in the darkness by the blast. When the explosions at last stopped and their deadened eardrums slowly returned to normal, they heard the sound of water rushing into the boat. It was the sound of approaching doom.

Lange called for damage reports and what he heard was not good. The stern torpedo compartment was breached and flooding rapidly. Ordering the compartment to be evacuated, Lange then sealed off the after part of the boat but it was too late and when the ballast pumps were switched on, they failed to function. With nothing to check the inflow of water *U-505* was going down by the stern, and circling to starboard under the influence of her jammed rudders and one of her electric motors which was still running.

In order to prevent his boat sinking deeper and deeper, Lange took the only action left open to him, using all his precious supply of compressed air to blow the main ballast tanks. This was a last desperate measure, for once the air was used up there would be no second chance; *U-505* would keep on sinking until the pressure of the water crushed her and everyone in her.

Fortunately, the compressed air flooding into the tanks was sufficient to halt the U-cruiser's downward spiral. She hung motionless for an anxious moment, and then began to shoot to the surface. Lange had warned his men to be ready to abandon ship, for they had no other alternative left, and he was crouching below the conning tower hatch, ready to lead them out. When he felt the boat rocking in the swell, and judged them to be on the surface, Lange threw open the hatch.

U-505 erupted from the sea only 700 yards from USS *Chatelain*, and the destroyer immediately opened fire with her machine guns. *Pilsbury* and *Jenks* joined in with their light weapons, using anti-personnel shells, and the two Wildcats circling overhead also entered the fray. When Lange and his men tumbled out of the conning tower hatch, they were met by a hail of bullets. Lange, first out of the hatch, was hit by shrapnel from an exploding shell and lost consciousness. First Watch Officer Paul Meyer, made an attempt to man one of the submarine's guns, and was also wounded. As the rest of the U-boat's crew poured out onto the casings, Wireless Operator Gottfried Fischer fell dead, and many others were wounded by the enemy fire.

U-505 was still under way, and running in circles out of control at about 7 knots. Seeing the U-cruiser turn towards *Chatelain*, Lieutenant Commander Knox assumed his ship was being threatened and retaliated with a torpedo. Fortunately for Knox, his torpedo missed, as Gallery had decided to put into action his plan to capture a U-boat intact. He ordered a general ceasefire and signalled *Pillsbury* to send away a boarding party.

Harald Lange had anticipated that an attempt might be made to capture his boat and, before bringing *U-505* to the surface, he had given orders for her to be scuttled before she was completely abandoned. However, in the face of the murderous fire opened up by the American ships, the need to save their own lives was uppermost in the minds of the men struggling to extricate themselves from the doomed boat, not least that of *Leutnant* Josef Hauser, who had been entrusted with setting the demolition charges. The charges were forgotten. This was discovered only at the last minute by one of the engine room petty officers, who organized a party to go below again to open the valves of the main diving tanks. To their consternation they found the valves jammed tight shut, and no amount of brute force could move them. As a last resort before abandoning ship the men removed the cover of the main cooling water pump. The sea surged into the motor room, which was quickly awash.

The rest of U-505's crew had already left her in the rubber dinghies stowed in containers on the casing. Lange's wounds, caused mostly by shell splinters, were severe and he had lain unconscious for some time, apparently unnoticed in the chaos that reigned. But when he came to, he managed to climb down from the bridge onto the casing to supervise the launching of the dinghies. While this was being done, he was washed off the casing, but seen by two of his crew, who pulled him into one of the rafts.

While Chatelain and Jenks were busy picking up survivors from the water, USS Pillsbury sent away its motor boat with a boarding party of eight men, led by Lieutenant (Junior Grade) Albert L. David. Although they were quite aware that the abandoned submarine might blow up at any moment, David and his men boarded her and scrambled below. Fortunately, it took them only a few moments to find and replace the cover of the cooling water pump and disconnect the scuttling charges. U-505 was now secure, and although lying heavily by the stern, was afloat. Daniel Gallery's dream of capturing a U-boat intact had been realized.

U-505's batteries had now run flat, which left her without means of pumping out the water flooding a large part of her hull. Characteristically, the US Navy came up with an ingenious solution to the problem. A salvage crew put on board disconnected her diesel engines from her electric motors, she was then taken in tow by the Guadalcanal, and towed at high speed. The forward movement of the boat set her propellers spinning which, still connected to the electric motors, turned these motors, thus recharging the batteries. With her ballast pumps once more in action, the salvage crew was able to pump U-505 dry.

After three days under tow by Guadalcanal, U-505 was taken

over by the fleet tug *Abnaki* which, escorted by Captain Gallery's victorious task group, brought her into Port Royal Bay, Bermuda on 19 June 1944. Her capture had been a landmark in American naval history; the first enemy ship boarded and captured on the high seas by US ships since the War of 1812. The treasure she yielded included a complete four-rotor Enigma machine, code books, signal books, charts and a wealth of technical information regarding the U-boats.

Although the capture of *U-505* by Gallery and his task group was a considerable achievement, the news was not well received in Washington. Admiral King, Chief of Naval Operations, is said to have been furious, and on the point of court-martialling Gallery. It transpired that Allied cipher experts had then only just succeeded in cracking the U-boat codes and, unknown to Admiral Dönitz, were reading his messages within minutes of them being transmitted. King knew that if Dönitz found out that one of his U-boats had been captured intact, he would immediately change the codes, leaving the Allied code breakers powerless – and with the invasion of Normandy only hours away.

Admiral King ordered Gallery to maintain the strictest secrecy regarding his capture; a very ambitious undertaking, considering that the task group comprised 3,000 men. Furthermore, no attempt had been made to hide the capture of their boat from Harald Lange and his surviving crew of fifty-three. Held prisoner aboard *Guadalcanal*, they could clearly see *U-505* corkscrewing on the end of a towline astern of the carrier. However, Gallery swore his men to secrecy, and to their great credit, they held their silence until after the war. As for Lange and his men, when they were landed they were kept in a camp apart from all other prisoners of war, and denied access to the Red Cross, for fear that they would pass the news of their boat's capture back to Germany through that source.

The Type IXC U-boats, the U-cruisers, were originally designed mainly for reconnaissance work and minelaying. As attack boats, they were seriously disadvantaged by their sluggish manoeuvring and when on the surface, running at high speed or in bad weather, the conning tower was usually awash, which made life very uncomfortable for those on watch above decks. It is not surprising that Admiral Dönitz decided they were not suitable for the cut and thrust of convoy work. They did, however, subsequently prove their worth as long range raiders preying on unescorted ships. As such, they required commanders of a certain calibre; mature, experienced and level-headed, of which Axel-Olaf Loewe and Karl-Friedrich Merten were two good examples. Under their command, over a period of twenty-one months, *U-68* and *U-505* were responsible for severely disrupting the vital Cape-Freetown route, on which so much of the Allied war effort depended in 1942 – 1943. Inevitably in this bitter war of attrition, both boats were lost and, coincidentally, both to the ships and aircraft of Captain Daniel Gallery's hard-hitting hunter-killer group, but the men who commanded them in their glory days survived the war.

Karl-Friedrich Merten who, in his short and brilliant sea-going career, sank twenty-seven ships totalling 170,171 tons, ended the war with the rank of *Kapitän-zur-See* with a post ashore in the *Marine Oberkommando West*. When Germany fell in 1945, he was unfortunate enough to be taken prisoner by the French, who put him on trial for the so-called illegal sinking of the Vichy French tanker *Frimaire* in the Caribbean in June 1942. Although these allegations were proved to be unfounded, he was not released from French custody until March 1949. Merten then found work on the River Rhine salvaging sunken ships, and later moved into the ship-building industry. He died, aged eighty-eight, on 2 May 1993.

Axel-Olaf Loewe had a less distinguished career. Although he played a major role in the attack on the Cape-Freetown route, he sank only seven ships of 37,789 tons. It was pure bad luck that his promising career in command was cut short when he fell ill in July 1942. He did not return to sea again, becoming a consultant with the Operations Department of the U-boat Arm. He died on 18 December 1984, aged seventy-five.

Today, sixty years on from the era of the U-cruisers, the waters of the Gulf of Guinea are once more in turmoil. Merchant ships of all nations, many as slow and vulnerable as their predecessors of the 1940s, are under attack by pirates using high-speed launches, and armed with automatic weapons and grenades. There are now no Sunderlands overhead to watch over them, and no ships of the Royal Navy to come to their rescue. Ships are being hijacked, their cargoes sold off on the international black market, and merchant seamen, who are denied arms to defend themselves, are dying in disturbing numbers.

Bibliography

Barker, Ralph, *Goodnight, Sorry for Sinking You*, Collins, 1984

Beaver, Paul, *U-boats in the Atlantic*, Patrick Stephens, 1979

Blair, Clay, *Silent Victory*, Bantam Books, 1975

Churchill, Winston, *The Second World War Vols. 3–5*, Cassell, 1950

Cowden, James.E., *The Elder Dempster History 1852–1986*, Mallett & Bell Publications,1986

Fletcher, C.R.L., *The Great War*, John Murray, 1921

Hoyt, Edwin P., *U-boats-A Pictorial History*, Magraw-Hill Book Co., 1987

Hydrographic Dept., *Africa Pilot Vol. I*, Hydrographer of the Navy, 1967

— *Bay of Biscay Pilot*, Hydrographer of the Navy, 1956

Jackson, Robert, *The Sky Their Frontier*, Airlife Publishing, 1983

Janes Publishing Co., *Jane's Fighting Ships of World War II*, Random House, 2001

Jones, Geoffrey, *Defeat of the Wolf Packs*, William Kimber, 1986

Knight, Stanley Macbean, *The History of the Great European War*, Caxton Publishing Co., 1914

Mallmann-Showell J.P., *Enigma U-boats-Breaking the Code*, Ian Allan, 2000

— *U-boats Under the Swastika*, Ian Allan, 1973

Martienssen, Anthony, *Hitler and His Admirals*, Secker & Warburg, 1948

Mason, David, *U-boat-The Secret Menace*, Macdonald, 1968

Ministry of Defence (Navy), *German Naval History, The U-boat War in the Atlantic*, HMSO, 1989

Padfield, Peter, *Dönitz-The Last Führer*, Cassell, 1993

— *War Beneath the Sea*, John Murray, 1995

Parker, Mike, *Running the Gauntlet*, Nimbus Publishing, 1994

Paterson, Lawrence, *Second U-boat Flotilla*, Leo Cooper, 2003

Poolman, Kenneth, *Persicope Depth*, William Kimber, 1981

Rohwer, Jürgen, *Axis Submarine Successes 1939-1945* , Patrick
    Stephens, 1983

Savas, Theodore P., *Silent Hunters-German U-boat Commanders
    of World War II*, Naval Institute Press, 1997

Slader, John, *The Red Duster at War*, William Kimber, 1988

Tennant, Alan J., *British & Commonwealth Merchant Ship
    Losses*, Sutton Publishing, 2001

Terraine, John, *Business in Great Waters*, Leo Cooper, 1989

US Navy Dept., *Sailing Directions for the West Coasts of Spain,
    Portugal, and NorthWest Africa and Off-Lying Islands*,
    Hydrographic Office, US Navy, 1942

Wheeler, Harold, *The People's History of the Second World War*,
    Odhams Press, 1940

Whitehouse, Arch, *Subs and Submariners*, Doubleday & Co.,
    1961

Wiggins, Melanie, *U-boat Adventures-Firsthand Accounts from
    World War II*, Naval Institute Press, 1999

Williamson, Gordon, *Aces of the Reich*, Arms & Armour, 1989

Young, George, *Farewell to the Tramps*, Dr J.F. Midgley, 1982

Index

8th Army, 106, 148, 149
8th Submarine Flotilla, 47
26th Training Flotilla, 168
53 Squadron, RAF, 184
95 Squadron, RAF, 34
204 Squadron, US Navy, 169
307 (Polish) Squadron, RAF, 169

Aberdeen Hill, 132
Achilles, *Kapitänleutnant* Albrecht, 41
Afrika Korps, 148
Alfred Holt & Company, 12
American West Africa Line, 94
Anderson, Captain David, 25, 27–34
Andrew Weir & Company, 58
Armitage, Able Seaman Colin, 162–4
Ayrshire Dockyard Company, 52

Bank Line, 58, 65
Barkleyville Methodist Mission, 57
Baron Line, 52
Bay of Bengal, 46
Bay of Biscay, 9, 11, 35, 78, 95, 134,
    139, 169, 178, 180, 185, 186
Befehlshaber der Unterseebooten (BdU),
    53, 77, 78, 89, 90, 93, 168, 181,
    182, 186
Begg, Commander, 153
Ben Line, 25
Bight of Benin, 174
Blue Funnel Line, 12
Blyenburgh, Chief Steward, 128
British & African Steam Navigation
    Company, 6
Britt, Chief Officer Sydney, 145–7
Bock, Field Marshal von, 106

Bom, Captain N.E., 121, 122
British Imperial Airways, 27
Bromfield, Cadet, 82
Bullock, Fifth Officer, 153, 158
Burmeister & Wain, 121

Canadian Pacific Railway Company,
    148
Cape Finisterre, 12, 165, 178, 181, 186
Cape of Good Hope, 12–14, 19, 25, 27,
    34, 45–7, 66, 69, 76, 77, 89, 91,
    99, 121, 135, 137, 165, 167, 192
Cape Hatteras, 87
Cape Henry, 3
Cape Mesurado, 2
Cape Mount, 69
Cape Palmas, 17–19, 28, 48, 50, 51, 53,
    54, 56–8, 62–6, 68, 69, 70, 76, 77,
    89, 91, 95, 96, 98, 101, 103, 104,
    150, 167, 170, 177, 178, 184, 187
Cape Sierra Leone, 132
Cape St. Ann, 120
Cape St. Vincent, 7
Cape Three Points, 54
Cape Verde, 95, 132, 184
Charles Connell & Company, 25
Chesapeake Bay, 3, 87
Christie, Boatswain, 31, 32
Churchill, Winston, 36
Clark, Fourth Engineer, 175, 176
Clark, Joe, 154
Clark, Chief Officer J.S., 152, 158
Clausen, *Korvettenkapitän* Nicolai, 41
Coastal Command, 11, 12, 186
Connolly, Skipper W.J., 171
Convoy GAT 49, 169

196

Convoy SL 78, 15
Convoy SL 119, 135
Convoy TS 37, 167, 168
Conway, Father, 57
Cooke, Carpenter Kenneth, 160, 162, 164
Counties Ship Management Company, 159
Cowper, Chief Engineer, 152, 158
Cussack, Charles, 155

David, Lieutenant (Junior Grade) Albert L., 190
De Gaulle, General, 35, 37, 74
De Laan, Captain Reindert van, 99, 101
De Neumann, Second Officer Bernard, 110
De Vries, Chief Engineer Jacob, 99
Dik, Captain Kornelis, 125–8, 132, 133
Dobeson, Captain Gerald, 15–17, 110, 111, 113, 115
Dönitz, Admiral Karl, 9, 10, 40, 41, 54, 78, 86–8, 90, 119, 135, 166, 168, 170, 178, 184, 191, 192
Dover Strait, 11
Dutch West India Company, 53

Earles Shipyard, 136
East Asiatic Company, 121
Eckart, Captain Thure, 46
Edmead, Third Steward/Writer Jack, 140, 145, 146
Eisbär Pack, 135
Elder Dempster Line, 166, 173, 175
Ellerman Line, 136
English Channel, 11, 12, 35
Ewing, Captain William, 53–7, 63

Farrar, Captain Thomas, 45–51
Faulds, Chief Engineer Robert, 137
F.C. Strick & Company, 46
Fey, Mr, 57
Firestone Tyre Company, 62, 68
Fischer, Wireless Operator Gottfried, 189
Förster, Fritz, 104
French Foreign Legion, 106
Furness Withy Line, 65

Gallery, Captain Daniel V., 181, 184, 187–92
Gazzana-Priaroggia, *Capitano di Corvetta* Gianfranco, 149, 151, 158–60, 165
Gercke, *Korvettenkapitän* Hermann, 1, 2, 6–9
Gerrard, Carpenter, 31
Gnodde, Chief Officer Pieter, 128
Goebeler, Hans, 89
Goodwin, Captain James, 52
Graham, Able Seaman John, 114, 118
Greger, *Oberleutnant* Eberhard, 87
Goold, Captain George, 148, 150, 151, 156, 157
Grosse, Enzo, 166
Guinea Current, 50, 51, 61
Gulf of Guinea, 1, 8, 9, 11, 30, 34, 38, 43, 53, 54, 57, 69, 89, 91, 98, 107, 109, 120, 130, 134, 149, 169, 170, 177, 181, 192
Gulf of Mexico, 76

Haagensen, Reidar, 173
Harper, Captain Harold, 76, 77, 79–86
Hartenstein, *Korvettenkapitän* Werner, 41, 135
Hauser, *Leutnant* Josef, 189
Hawkes, Chief Radio Officer, 175, 176
Haynes, Bill, 72
Helgesen, Captain Nils, 40, 42, 44
Henke, *Oberleutnant* Werner, 166–8, 182, 184
Hill, Captain William, 65, 66, 68
Hitler, Adolf, 26, 78, 119, 136
Hogarth, Hugh, 52
Hull, Gunner, 160, 161
Hunter, Petty Officer, 153, 158

Imaz, Captain, 177

Jackson, Second Officer T.R., 86
Jansen, Third Officer Aloysuis, 99, 101
Johansen, Third Officer Karsten, 171
John Readhead's yard, 48
Jorgensen, Captain This, 17
Jorgensen, Third Officer, 122, 124

Kastrupp, *Matrosengefreiter* Hans, 183, 184
Kent, Captain Frederick, 173–7
Kinashi, Takaichi, 47
King, Admiral, 191
Knox, Lieutenant Commander Dudley, 188, 189
König, *Kapitän* Paul, 3
Kooy, Second Engineer Pieter, 99

Lancashire Shipping Company, 76
Langanesi-Cattani, *Capitano di Corvetta* Luigi, 120, 121, 124, 126
Lange, *Oberleutnant* Harald, 185–91
Larsen, Second Officer Arnfinn, 171
Lauzemis, *Oberleutnant* Albert, 168–72, 174–83
Lever Brothers, 74
Loewe, *Kapitänleutnant* Alex-Olaf, 10–14, 25, 29–31, 42–5, 47, 54, 57, 89–93, 95
Lemaire, Lieutenant Commander, 17
Lykes Brothers, 57

MacCall, Captain, 142, 145
MacDonald, Quartermaster Angus, 143–6
Manstein, Field Marshal von, 180
Marine Oberkommando West, 192
Martin Mosvold Company, 170
Matson Navigation, 41
Mattke, *Korvettenkapitän* Willy, 181
McEwan, Captain William, 159, 160
Merten, *Korvettenkapitän* Karl-Friedrich, 10–14, 18–21, 24, 47–9, 53, 54–61, 65–8, 70–2, 76, 77, 80, 82, 86, 87, 134–6, 139–41, 168, 169, 192
Meusel, *Fregattenkapitän*, 5
Meyer, First Watch Officer Paul, 185, 189
Millar & Richards Ltd., 178
Miller, Doctor, 158
Ministry of War Transport, 46, 58, 125
Montgomery, General Bernard, 148
Moody, Third Officer, 80, 86
Mooney, Mr, 61, 62
Moreau, Commandant, 112, 114, 115

Morel & Company, 68, 69
Mussolini, Benito, 119, 149, 166

Netherland Shipping Committee, 99
North Channel, 26
Norwegian Shipping & Trade Mission, 39
Nostitz und Janckendorff, *Korvettenkapitän* von, 5

O'Brien, Lieutenant, 152, 158
Office of Chief of Naval Operations, 96
Ogawa, Tsunayashi, 47
Olsen, Captain Trygve, 170, 171, 173
Operation Barbarossa, 26
Operation Menace, 37

Persian Gulf, 46, 125, 167
Pétain, Marshal, 35
Prince Line, 65, 68
Prize Regulations, 4

Radeboldt, Captain Paul F., 120, 121
Raeder, Admiral, 35, 36
Ramus, Mr, 62, 63
Rees, Radio Officer W.H., 127
Richard, General, 115
Roaring Forties, 149
Roberts, Charles, 150, 154, 156
Robson, Bombardier Ted, 125, 128, 130–2
Rogerson, Captain William, 137–9
Rommel, General, 53, 106, 148
Ropner Shipyard, 178
Rosenstiel, *Kapitänleutnant* Jürgen von, 41
Rotterdam South America Line, 124

Ryder, Commander R.E.D., 78
Rylance, Chief Officer, 79, 86

Savery, Captain Philip, 12, 13, 18–23, 34
Schau, Thorstein, 43, 44
Scown, Chief Officer Basil, 162
Selness, Captain Torleif, 94, 95
Shepard Company, 120

Ships
Abnaki, USS, 191; Active, HMS, 165; Afghanistan, 121; Aikoku Maru, 47; Air France IV, 17; Alioth, 124, 126, 127, 130, 132, 133, 149; Allende, 68–72, 74, 76, 105–9, 113–15; Alphacca, 98–101, 103, 105, 184; Alsterufer, 186; Ann Strathatos, 85; Archer, HMS, 132, 133; Arkansas, 41; Arran, HMS, 168; Atlantis, 67; Aubretia, HMS, 85

Baluchistan, 45–50, 58, 62, 69, 70; Bandar Shahpour, 167; Barbarigo, 166; Barham, HMS, 37; Baron Newlands, 52–5, 57, 58, 63, 70; Batory, 34; Beaconsfield, 21–3; Belgian Fighter, 135; Bendoran, 145; Benmohr, 25–32, 34, 42, 89; Birdlip, HMS, 167, 168; Bombala, HMS, 7; Boreas, HMS, 157; Breedyk, 135; British Confidence, 43; British Consul, 41; Bremen, 4; Burutu, 6–8

Campbelltown, HMS, 78, 79; Ceres, 169; Chatelain, USS, 181, 182, 184, 188–90; Chile, 121, 122, 124; Christian Knudsen, 87; Cilicia, HMS, 15; Cities Service Missouri, 169; City of Cairo, 136–41, 145, 147; City of Singapore, 168; Clan Alpine, 146; Clan Macwirter, 135; Clan Macpherson, 168; Clan Macquarrie, 149; Conakrian, 177; Copinsay, HMS, 94–8; Corabella, 167; Corinthian, HMS, 157; Cornwall, HMS, 47; C.O. Stillman, 134; Criton, 15–17, 110–13, 115, 117; Crocus, HMS, 157; Cumberland, HMS, 37

Deutschland, 3–5; Devonshire, HMS, 47; Doryssa, 165

Empress of Canada, 148–51, 154, 155, 158, 159; Esperance Bay, HMS, 15; Examelia, 135

Flaherty, USS, 181, 182, 184; Florence Luckenback, 46;

Foresight, HMS, 37; Fort de Vaux, 177, 178

Frimaire, 134, 192

Gambian, 35; Gassterkerk, 135; Gneisenau, 11; Guadalcanal, USS, 181–4, 188, 190, 191

Helenus, 12, 13, 17–24, 27, 34; Highland Monarch, 115; Hokoku Maru, 47

Ile de Batz, 57–63, 65, 68, 70; Inglefield, HMS, 37

Jenks, USS, 184, 189, 190; John Drayton, 165

Kate, 52; Kongsgaard, 41; Kota Tjandi, 167; Koumoundouros, 135

La Surprise, 75, 105; Le Glorieux, 17; Le Heros, 17; Lennox, 41; Leonardo da Vinci, 119, 121, 127, 149, 151, 159, 165, 171; Litopia, 170–3, 174; L.J. Drake, 134; Lulworth Hill, 159, 160, 165, 171

Malmanger, 116; Manaar, 165; Max Albrecht, 134; Meliskerk, 103; Milwaukee, USS, 166; Mokambo, 168; Mokihana, 41; MTB T25, 186; Muncaster Castle, 76, 77, 79–83, 85, 86

Nagina, 167; Ness, HMS, 165; New Columbia, 173–6; Norness, 40

Orangestad, 41; Orbita, 173; Orfasy, HMS, 170, 171

Pedernalis, 41; Petunia, HMS, 157, 158, 166; Pilsbury, USS, 181, 182, 184, 189, 190; Pope, HMS, 181, 182, 184; Prinz Eugen, 11; Pungue, 91; Python, 67

Quanza, 91

Rapid, HMS, 164; Reine Marie Stewart, 120; Resolution, HMS, 37; Rhakotis, 143–6; Richelieu, 15, 37; Roper, USS, 87, 88

Sangara, 166; Sarthe, 135; Scharnhorst, 11; Scottish Prince, 62, 65–8, 70; Scylla, HMS, 146; Sembilan, 165; Spaniard, HMT, 124; Swiftsure, 135; Sydhav, 39, 42–4, 47, 89

199

Ships *(continued)*
  Takoradian, 35; *Thode Fagelund*, 17; *Thomas McKean*, 184; *Tirpitz*, 78; *Titanic*, 81; *Trevilley*, 135
  Ulster Monarch, HMS, 45–7, 51, 54, 64, 68
  War Gnat, 178; *War Pageant*, 173; *West Hobomac*, 57; *West Irmo*, 94, 98; *West Zeda*, 41; *Wyvern*, HMS, 51, 64, 68
  Z-27, 186
Skinner & Eddy Corporation, 57
Souter, Chief Engineer William, 114, 118
South African Air Force, 136
South Wales Argus, 72
Stausland, Chief Engineer Georg, 173
Subbubo Point, 51
Suez Canal, 13, 14, 148

Taylor, Lieutenant, 86
Thorne, Roy, 116
Thornton, Chief Steward Herbert, 162, 163
Thomson, Alexander, 25
Thomson, William, 25
Tirpitz, Admiral von, 4, 5
Trygve Lodding, 39

U-boats
  Enrico Tazzoli (Italian), 165, 166
  E-35 (British), 7, 8
  I-162 (Japanese), 47; *I-164* (Japanese), 47
  U-66, 40; *U-68*, 10, 11, 14, 19, 21, 25, 47, 53–5, 65, 68–71, 76, 78, 80, 82, 86, 91, 95, 105, 116, 134–6, 139, 140, 147, 168–72, 174, 176, 178–84, 192; *U-69*, 166; *U-85*, 87; *U-90*, 12; *U-109*, 40; *U-123*, 40; *U-125*, 40; *U-129*, 41, 181; *U-130*, 40; *U-151*, 5; *U-153*, 7, 8, 11; *U-154*, 1, 2, 6–9, 11; *U-155*, 5, 169; *U-156*, 41, 135; *U-157*, 5; *U-161*, 41; *U-172*, 135; *U-257*, 169; *U-410*, 146; *U-459*, 135; *U-462*, 184; *U-502*, 41; *U-504*, 135; *U-505*, 10, 12, 14, 24, 25, 29–31, 42–5, 47, 54, 57, 89–93, 95, 97–9, 104, 184–92; *U-515*, 166, 167, 182, 184; *U-516*, 181; *U-544*, 181, 184; *U-600*, 169; *U-615*, 169; *U-618*, 186; *U-739*, 176
Union Castle Line, 99
United Africa Company, 35

Van Nievelt Goudriaan & Company, 99
Volmari, *Oberleutnant* (Ing) Franz, 179

Watts, Captain A.S., 58–64
Werner, *Kapitänleutnant* Herbert, 178
Wilhelm Wilhelmsen, 17
Williamson, Captain Thomas, 69–72, 74, 105, 107, 108, 111, 113, 114
William Thomson & Company, 25
Wijngaarden, Third Engineer Arie van, 99

Yardley, Captain, 6, 7

Zschech, *Oberleutnant* Peter, 184, 185